RECLAIMING COMMUNITY IN CONTEMPORARY AFRICAN AMERICAN FICTION

Reclaiming Community in Contemporary African American Fiction

— Philip Page —

University Press of Mississippi—Jackson

http://www.upress.state.ms.us
Copyright © 1999 by University Press of Mississippi
All rights reserved
Manufactured in the United States of America
02 01 00 99   4 3 2 1
The paper in this book meets the guidelines for permanence and durability
of the Committee on Production Guidelines for Book Longevity of the Council
on Library Resources.

Library of Congress Cataloging-in-Publication Data

Page, Philip.
    Reclaiming community in contemporary African American fiction /
Philip Page.
        p.   cm.
    Includes bibliographical references and index.
    ISBN 1-57806-122-9 (alk. paper). — ISBN 1-57806-123-7 (pbk. :
alk. paper)
    1. American fiction—Afro-American authors—History and criticism.
    2. American fiction—20th century—History and criticism.   3. Afro-
Americans in literature.   4. Community in literature.   I. Title.
PS374.N4P34   1999
813'.5409896073—dc21   98-39517
                                                         CIP
            British Library Cataloging-in-Publication Data available

For my mother

CONTENTS

Acknowledgments

This study was initially funded in 1994 by a summer reading grant from the National Endowment for the Humanities. In 1995 and 1997 I received grants from California State University, San Bernardino, to continue the work, and in the 1996–97 academic year I was awarded a sabbatical leave during which most of the book was drafted. By reading and discussing some of the novels considered here, the students in my courses on contemporary African-American fiction stimulated my own thinking. In particular, I want to thank Kasmira Finch for her helpful suggestions and her research and editorial assistance. Two former students, Yvonne Atkinson and Sally-Anne Josephson, have continued to be valuable sounding boards and unflinching critics. Another former student, Tracy Viselli, helped clarify my thoughts about Gloria Naylor's fiction. My colleagues in the English department and the School of Humanities at California State University, San Bernardino, have consistently supported the project. Michelle Pagni-Stewart offered many useful suggestions and queries on the chapter on Ernest Gaines, and Rong Chen and Wendy Smith provided research assistance on questions relating to linguistics. As I prepared a chapter for an edition of essays on Gloria Naylor, Margot Anne Kelley helped me rethink my ideas about Naylor's fiction. I also thank the editors of the *College Language Association Journal* and Greenwood Press for permission to include the parts of the chapter on Naylor that they previously published, and I thank the editors of *African American Review* for permission to use material from a previously published review of *The Cattle Killing*. I received courteous and professional support from Seetha A-Srinivasan, Anne Stascavage, and many others at the University Press of Mississippi and from Ellen D. Goldlust-Gingrich, who copyedited the manuscript. Last, but certainly not least, I thank my wife, Reba, who, again, as always, has been invaluable.

Reclaiming Community in Contemporary African American Fiction

1

AT THE CROSSROADS

After cautioning her readers about the dangers of oversimplification, Margaret Atwood asserts that every country and culture has a "unifying and informing symbol": for England, it is the island; for Canada, survival; for the United States, the frontier (31). At the heart of the American dream, the concept of the frontier embodies the freedom to leave behind a personally unfulfilling or unsatisfactory place in the expectation of a better one. Moving on to a better place also creates a new time, substituting a projected new future for a no-longer-desired past. For the dream of the frontier to function, movement must be free, readily available, and perceived as advantageous. As Lawrence Levine notes, "spatial mobility" has been important "throughout American history for all segments of the population" (262), for physical mobility in American culture is the key to upward social mobility, economic success, and political expression. The frontier is the creative edge of the ideal "democratic social space" by which, according to Philip Fisher, the United States invented its national identity (72).[1]

Among the many realities that render this concept an unrealized American myth, slavery is "clearly the most radical contradiction possible" (Fisher 87). Beginning with the Middle Passage, movement for Africans and then African Americans was not free but forced, was not pursuit of a dream but exile from a desired space to an horrific new one, and constituted not progressive renewal in a new time but displacement from immersion in holistic African time to alienation in linear Euro-American time. Emigration was not an optimistic quest for a new home but the almost unendurable loss of home, community, family, and identity: "Whereas Columbus conquered 'new' lands for Europeans, thus increasing their mobility and freedom and providing them with new perspectives, the African diaspora stands for the end of freedom, for the loss of perspective; . . . it meant [the slaves'] expulsion from history [and it] threatened them with social and physical annihilation" (Sollors and Diedrich 5). For slaves, America meant not the chosen rejection of an undesired past but the imposed eradication of a desired one. In America, there was no desired place either where one was or anywhere else; there was no desired frontier. The antithesis of the American dream, movement for most slaves was not a chosen quest but a coerced passage.

African-American culture was formed in the context of involuntary passages. Carl Pederson posits that "the Middle Passage is arguably the defining moment of the African-American experience" (225). Examining slave narratives, Melvin Dixon concludes, "In their long search for freedom, as in their religion and literature, slaves defined life as a pilgrimage" ("Singing" 313). Eleanor Traylor defines "the Afro-American paradigm of creation" as "a journey into experience conducted by a people who wrenched from a coherent past [and] cast refugee upon a sea of circumstance confront incoherence and give it form" (68). From the diaspora and the Middle Passage, to being sold down the river, to northward journeys to freedom, to westward and urban migrations, African Americans have been forever on the move, forced or pressured into one passage after another in the attempt to find a tolerable place in American society, to reinvent a past and a future, and to forge a cultural identity. The unifying symbol for African-American culture is therefore not the frontier but passage itself.[2]

Partly because the forced passages to America and within America were so scarring, willed movement became particularly valued in African-American culture. Myths abound of heroic returns to Africa, such as the flying African(s) or Africans walking back across the ocean to Africa. Escaping slavery to the North or to Canada became a reality for some and a legend for others, and slave narratives, documenting and embellishing such passages, became the first widespread form of written expression by African Americans. After the Civil War, the desire to move away from the sites of slavery reinvigorated this emphasis on movement, and "significant movement of Negroes began as soon as freedom made it possible" (Levine 262–63). Newly freed African Americans moved for the sake of moving, often wandering aimlessly or taking railway excursions (Levine 263). Subsequent migrations to western states, such as Oklahoma and Kansas, and the Great Migration to northern cities, like European migrations to America, were characterized by the attempt to forget the past in the hope of a better future in a more desirable place. For Lawrence Rodgers, "the history of African American life is a history of migration" (10), and for Cornel West, "the fundamental theme of New World African modernity is neither integration nor separation but rather migration and emigration" (qtd. as an epigraph in F. Griffin).[3]

The idea of passage as the informing symbol of African-American literature has many implications. It suggests African Americans' continued search for place, both literal and figurative, in American society. As Houston A. Baker, Jr., contends, African Americans were consigned first to holds on slave ships, then to rural cabins, and later to urban kitchenettes and have historically not been allowed their own places but been relegated to places imposed on them (*Workings* 108). Parallel to that quest for place is the quest for an acceptable African-American past, the quest to fill in the "cultureless past" of African-American history (Early 11). The temporal devastation for African Americans was twofold: first, slaves were denied their African past, and then ex-slaves had to repress their slave pasts to become psychically whole. Because of these unresolved issues of place and time, African-American identities have historically been unsettled, constantly placed, replaced, and displaced in figurative passages from one attempted identity to another. As Ralph Ellison puts it, "Negro Americans are in desperate search for identity" (*Shadow* 297), and West identifies African Americans' "triple crisis of self-recognition," in which they are simultaneously African in appearance and mores, in America without American status, and, like all Americans, alienated from Europe (31).

One response to these displacements was an emphasis on creating and maintaining a cohesive African-American culture. In three contemporary novels, these communal and cultural ties are figured by an infinite system of invisible threads connecting individuals and collectively forming the community. As Velma Henry recovers her sanity in Toni Cade Bambara's *The Salt Eaters*, she senses the connections between herself and others in her community: "She tried to look around, to take in the healer, the people circling her, the onlookers behind. But there were so many other things to look at closer at hand. The silvery tendrils that fluttered between her fingers, extending out like tiny webs of invisible thread. The strands that flowed from her to Minnie Ransom to faintly outlined witnesses by the windows" (267). Similarly, in Paule Marshall's *Praisesong for the Widow*, as Avey Johnson begins to rediscover her racial identity, she remembers people gathering for boat rides on the Hudson River: "As more people arrived to throng the area beside the river and the cool morning air warmed to the greetings and talk, she would feel what seemed to be hundreds of slender threads streaming out from her navel and from the place where her heart was to enter those around her" (190). Doot, John Edgar Wideman's alter ego in *Sent for You Yesterday*, recalls his grandmother's intricate connections to everything in the family house on Cassina Way: "I'm trying to remember the inside of her house, its shape, the furniture, the way things in it would trap the silence and spin a dusty, beaded web around her so if you peeked in from Cassina you'd see a young woman draped by layers of transparent gauze, a young woman standing up asleep, her eyes open, threads stretched from the top of her head to all the walls, the things in the room" (29–30). These images of weblike strands connecting each of these women to the people and objects around them are metaphors not only for the women's ties to their communities but also for the communities themselves. The strands are made up of people's relationships to each other, the words they exchange, the activities they share, and their thoughts about each other. Collectively, the tangled threads of these infinitely connecting strands create an unusually powerful intersubjective web that characterizes African-American culture.[4]

In novels written between 1978 and 1996, Toni Cade Bambara, Ernest Gaines, Charles Johnson, Gloria Naylor, and John Edgar Wideman create texts that explore such issues as the consequences of endless passage, quests for meaningful places, temporal discontinuities, the vagaries of identity formation, and the necessity and the difficulties of maintaining African-American cultural cohesion.[5] In their content these novels document the spiritual and psychic disintegration that accompanies the loss of community and cultural heritage as well as the redemptive possibilities of reaffirming such ties. At the same time, through their polyvocal narrations and intricate interweavings of multiple stories, perspectives, and times, these novels enact the tangled web of African-American culture.

In *The Location of Culture,* Homi Bhabha argues that contemporary culture is intertwined in the complexities of space, time, and identity. As opposed to the reliance on the fixity and stereotypes of colonial discourse, postcolonial discourse for Bhabha creates access to time and space outside the linear and the ordinary: "We find ourselves in the moment of transit where space and time cross to produce complex figures of difference and identity, past and present, inside and outside, inclusion and exclusion" (1). Contemporary culture is in a "middle passage" (5) of displacement and disjunction that transcends fixed identifications and "opens up the possibility of a cultural hybridity that entertains difference without an assumed or imposed hierarchy" (4). This "interstitial perspective" (3) allows us "to be part of a revisionary time" in which we can simultaneously "return to the present," "renew the past," and "touch the future on its hither side" (7). In more down-to-earth terms, Albert Murray argues that the blues creates just such a discourse because it relies on improvisation, "the ultimate human (i.e., heroic) endowment," which best enables human beings to learn how "to be at home with [their] sometimes tolerable but never quite certain condition of *not* being at home in the world" (*Hero* 107).

For African Americans, one layer of such complexities is the surrounding contradictions of American culture. A sense of this complexity is conveyed by Jacques Derrida's whimsical yet serious remark that "America *is* deconstruction" (*Memories* 18). The remark is whimsical because he "risk[s]" the "hypothesis" "with a smile," yet it is serious because, as Derrida elaborates, America "is that historical space which today . . . reveals itself as being undeniably the most sensitive, receptive, or responsive space of all to the themes and effects of deconstruction." In a subsequent volume of essays titled *Deconstruction Is/in America*, Anselm Haverkamp speculates that America is deconstruction, is in deconstruction, and/or is "an exemplary place for deconstruction" because of "a *sense of difference* in America that is different from Europe" (3) and because after that original difference "America had to take on, and has taken on, differences of another dimension that are completely incommensurable with the older, European one" (5). From its motto—*e pluribus unum*—to its political principle of a balance of powers, to its myths of the melting pot and multiculturalism, America is defined by differences, by the ongoing interplay among different groups, by, in Sacvan Bercovitch's terms, "dissensus," "heterogeneity and pluralism" (22, 372). Among Haverkamp's "differences of another dimension," distinct from European-Americans' original differences from Europe and African-Americans' original differences from Africa, the two differences that most defined this country are those between blacks and whites and those between South and North. African-American writers, inheritors of a placeless culture in continuous passage within American society, are ironically well placed to analyze such differences.

Denied a legitimate social, economic, and political place in American society, African Americans' figurative place is the Other, the outsider, the historically and principally unassimilated minority. Slavery depended on the enforcement of an absolute opposition between privileged European Americans and excluded African Americans, so that American culture is built on "the complex dialectic between 'white' and 'black' cultures" (Sundquist, *To Wake* 2). Even 135 years after the abolition of slavery, that rigid binary opposition continues to define American society, as several provocative events of the 1990s remind Americans (for example, the Rodney King beating, the Clarence Thomas/Anita Hill hearing, the Million Man March, and the O. J. Simpson case). Henry Louis Gates's comment on the Simpson case applies to all four events: the differences between whites' and blacks' reactions showed whites "that this race thing was knottier than they'd ever supposed" (144).

Just as African Americans are the Other in America's racial opposition, so the South is the Other in the nation's geographical opposition. The South is the nation's most clearly recognized and recognizable region; as Peter Applebome puts it, the South is "as close to [a separate country] as this nation has ever known within its borders" (10). For most of the nineteenth and twentieth centuries, the South—associated with the "peculiar institution" of slavery, with its attempt at secession, and with a less modern economy—has been not only the most separate American region but also the least privileged one and therefore the Other.

For African Americans who migrated to the urban North, the South becomes a special kind of Other, two edged and bittersweet, emotionally burdened both positively and negatively. It is depicted nostalgically as "an idyllic, rural paradise" (Allen 115) and "a spiritual homeland" (Allen 116) that cannot be forgotten, yet it is a reminder of guilt and servitude that had to be abandoned. While the North is present and tangible, the South is absent and memory. It remains in the mind because it is the site of the birth of African-American culture, the locale of one's ancestors, and therefore the source of one's collective and individual identity. It is like a ghost, haunting the consciousnesses of northern African Americans, always already both present and absent, undying yet inaccessible. As Lawrence Rodgers asserts, the key to the migrants' success was to learn what to retain from their southern, African-American heritage and what to discard: the South "represents a usable set of experiences, cultural artifacts, and values that exemplifies an ideal and a kind of salvation—even if only momentary—from the pressures of the North" (38).

In contemporary African-American fiction, the South is sometimes reproduced metaphorically in a northern African-American community. The settings of Toni Morrison's novels usually cohere around such reconstructions of the South: for example, in *Sula,* the Bottom "was once a neighborhood" (3), a place that retains the character of rural, southern, African-American culture. Like the Bottom, the cafe and its mystical neighborhood in Naylor's *Bailey's Cafe* evoke the South; in David Bradley's *The Chaneysville Incident,* the Hill is the southern-like neighborhood to which John Washington returns; and in much of Wideman's fiction and nonfiction, the Homewood neighborhood of Pittsburgh, particularly Bruston Hill, where Wideman's ancestors first settled, functions as a trace of the absent South. Typically, these echoes of the South reflect the positive values of rural African-American culture, such as the strong family ties among Pilate, Reba, and Hagar in Morrison's *Song of Solomon* and among the members of the French family in Wideman's *Sent for You Yesterday.* At the same time, these transplanted echos of the South are far from utopian, instead reflecting realistically the harsh conditions of life in the racialized North.[6]

When the South is a literal setting, its effect is usually double edged. Nel Wright's trip to New Orleans is a defining moment in her quest for selfhood during which she discovers that "I'm me. I'm not their daughter. I'm not Nel. I'm me. Me" (Morrison, *Sula* 29). But her newly discovered identity is as short lived as the trip, and she succumbs to her mother's more enduring efforts to efface Nel's personality. In Morrison's *Tar Baby,* Son attempts to go home again, but his visit to Eloe, the site both of his upbringing and of his accidental murder of his wife, leads to his separation from Jadine and his permanent exile. In Johnson's *Oxherding Tale,* Andrew Hawkins loves his parents and Minty, but to survive he must abandon them and leave the South. In Sherley Anne Williams's *Dessa Rose*, the South provides opportunities for Dessa, but those opportunities are severely restricted by the dominant slaveholding culture. In Naylor's *Mama Day*, Cocoa and George pass from the North to Willow Springs off the coast of Georgia and South Carolina, but in that rural southern setting George must die to save Cocoa.

When the South is not rural but urban, it is also double edged. In Johnson's *Middle Passage*, Rutherford Calhoun reverses the migration pattern by fleeing his and his brother's idyllic farm in Illinois for the hedonism of New Orleans. For him, the South means a life of corruption, thievery, and sensuality, but it is also where he meets his true love, Isadora. In Bambara's *The Salt Eaters*, the southern city of Claybourne is the site of breakdown at all levels—personal, familial, communal, environmental, global—but at the same time the novel chronicles the eclectic forces of recovery that foreshadow a new era of potential wholeness and meaningfulness.

Southern locales, whether literal or metaphorical, are highly charged spaces in contemporary African-American novels. Metaphoric southern spaces in the North often function, in Farah Jasmine Griffin's terms, as "safe spaces" (8), havens where southern immigrants can find respite from the onslaught of northern urban life. Such havens can allow time and resources for creating a new personality, but they can also allow the immigrant to remain complacent and provincial (F. Griffin 8–9). In either case, evocation of the scenes, language, and customs of the rural South is a nostalgic attempt by the novelists, and often by their characters, to retain in the contemporary northern city crucial elements of African-American culture, formed in that rural southern past. On the one hand, this aim is impossible—one cannot go home again. But on the other hand, it is essential: only by connecting with and thereby redeeming the past can the immigrants envision a viable present and future; only by combining African-American culture and Euro-American culture can they survive. The effort to bridge the apparently unbridgeable, to be both southern and northern, rural and urban, reenacts the dual perspective of insider/outsider that epitomizes African-American culture.[7]

Just as a secure place in American culture has been problematic for African Americans, they have also been excluded from time: first, their African history was repudiated, then their slave past could not be acknowledged, and throughout American history they have been denied full participation in the American dream of a utopian democracy. As Bonnie Barthold puts it, African Americans have been "cut off and dispossessed from both the mythic cycle of Africa and the linear flow of Western time" (16) and therefore are vulnerable to the "possibility of temporal dispossession" (17) and the "chaos of time" (31). Andrew Hawkins, the protagonist of *Oxherding Tale,* expresses this sense of dispossession: "the past is threatening [for African Americans] because there *is* no history worth mentioning" (132). There is no history—or rather no acknowledged history and no felt sense of meaningful history—because the African diaspora meant not only "the end of freedom" and "the loss of perspective" but "for the slaves it meant their expulsion from history" and "the threat of social and physical annihilation" (Sollors and Diedrich 5).[8]

Given this historical exclusion, part of the cultural work of African-American literature is to bridge such temporal gaps. Kimberly Bentson contends that "all of Afro-American literature may be seen as one vast genealogical poem that attempts to restore continuity to the ruptures or discontinuities imposed by the history of black presence in America" (152). Accordingly, characters in contemporary African-American novels often look for ways to rediscover their cultural past, to reconnect with history. These quests may involve a physical return to Africa, as in Alice Walker's *The Color Purple* and *Possessing the Secret of Joy;* a depiction of the Middle Passage as in Johnson's *Middle Passage;* an account of slave life and escape to freedom, as in Morrison's *Beloved,* Williams' *Dessa Rose,* and Johnson's *Oxherding Tale;* a representation of a mythical, free African-American community as in *Mama Day;* or a historical search into the records of the slave past, as in David Bradley's *The Chaneysville Incident.* Most often, the quest entails characters' memories of the past, retold through passed-down family and communal stories, shared between two or more characters or envisioned inwardly by single characters. For example, Morrison's *Beloved* and *Jazz* are built around the characters' painful but necessary reworkings of the traumas of the past, and much of Wideman's fiction focuses on re-creations of his personal, familial, and communal past in Homewood or on evocations of eighteenth-century Philadelphia.

Since the South conflates the spatial and temporal origins of African-American culture, it is often evoked through memory. Sweet Home in *Beloved* and Vesper County in *Jazz* are presented only as the characters' remembered pasts. In both cases, the South is particularly double edged and most noticeably Other. Sethe, Paul D, Joe, and Violet must remember the southern past or its repression will kill them, but the remembering may kill them as well, so they must remember it carefully, must retell and rehear it gradually, must circle back to it gingerly. In *The Chaneysville Incident,* John Washington, a "modern subject who needs a temporary unification between the past and the future in the present" (Hogue 449), can only resolve his present conflicts by immersing himself—through meticulous historical research and his own imagination—in his ancestors' past. In *Bailey's Cafe* the series of stories documenting the characters' pasts must be remembered and articulated before the community can unite in the ritual celebration of George's birth. Presence is only meaningful when absence is acknowledged; presence and absence must not be considered mutually exclusive but complementary, interrelated, inseparable. To survive, the characters must work through the paradoxical process of remembering to forget. The South—Sweet Home, Vesper County, the graveyard in *The Chaneysville Incident,* the delta dust that Eve can never wash off in *Bailey's Cafe*—is what they must never forget yet must forget, what is absent yet present, what is past yet never past. It is the elusive trace of a previous self that cannot be erased but must be transcended in ongoing re-creations of the self.

Ernest Gaines's *A Gathering of Old Men* combines a physical southern setting—a former plantation in Louisiana—and memories of the southern past. The present African-American community is spiritually bankrupt, reduced to children and spiritually weakened old people, overgrown with weeds, and under the economic and social domination of Cajun and Anglo whites. But, prior to making their stand against legal and illegal white power, the old men assemble at the African-American graveyard and regain their vitality through memories of their ancestors. This implicit absorption of the southern past becomes explicit when the men—and women—chronicle their deeper reasons for finally standing up to the white-controlled system. In the novel's most profound scene, a series of characters testifies to past racial injustices and to their failures and/or inabilities to oppose such injustices. Now, at last, with nothing more to lose, the old people stand up to reclaim the past and thereby regain their dignity and their identities. Whereas in *Beloved* and *Jazz* the past must be remembered so that the characters can move beyond it, here the past must be remembered so that the characters can redeem it. That past is horrifying and shameful in terms of racial injustice yet simultaneously rich in terms of natural beauty, communal bonds, and meaningful employment.[9]

The South symbolizes that past life—its brutality but also its meaningfulness—in contemporary African-American fiction. The South is the cultural memory and identity that is no longer physically present but is indelibly marked within. As Johnny Paul, one of Gaines's old men, avers to Sheriff Mapes, "You don't see what we don't see" (89). The white man, Mapes, cannot see in his mind's eye—cannot remember—the beauty, the communal brotherhood, and the individual integrity that the black people can and always will envision. By seeing what the whites cannot see, the blacks do not allow their southern past to be plowed under, they communally repossess their cultural heritage, they bridge the apparent gap between present and past, they refuse to be marginalized as Other, and thereby they revalidate their identities. Like all African Americans, they are, in Cornel West's terms, the Americans who cannot forget, "who could not not know" (qtd. in O'Meally and Fabre 3). As they insist on the relevance of the past, the men enact their redemption of it. Through their actions and words, they attempt to atone for their past failures, and, by rewriting the past, they create a new present on which to build a newly envisioned future.

The South as site of the origins of African-American culture is often symbolized by ancestor characters. As Morrison claims, ancestors are "sort of timeless people whose relationships to the characters are benevolent, instructive, and protective," and "the presence or absence of that figure determine[s] the success or the happiness of the character" ("Rootedness" 343). Karla F. C. Holloway sees the idea of ancestry as fundamental in African-American women's fiction, for the ancestor is "a metaphorical construction intersecting these texts" (*Moorings* 115). Farah Griffin places the northern migrant character between the influences of the benevolent ancestor and the confounding stranger, showing, for example, that Ellison's invisible man does not adapt well to the northern city as long as he is seduced by strangers (130–31) but that Morrison's Milkman Dead does succeed because of his tutelage by such ancestors as Pilate, Reverend Cooper, and Circe (172–73).

Contemporary African-American fiction abounds with ancestor figures: some are flesh-and- blood older relatives or friends who guide protagonists toward remembering and revaluing their cultural heritage, such as Thérèse in *Tar Baby*, Aunt Cuney in *Praisesong for the Widow*, Miss Emma and Tante Lou in Gaines's *A Lesson before Dying*, and Mama Day and Abigail in *Mama Day;* some are legendary figures in the distant past, like Jake Solomon, who flew back to Africa, or the Ibos, who walked back, in *Praisesong;* and some are the ur-ancestors who established families and communities, such as Sapphira Wade in *Mama Day* and Sybela Owens in Wideman's Homewood trilogy.

Johnson's *Middle Passage* introduces the most ancient of ancestors. Aboard a slave ship, the freedman Rutherford Calhoun encounters the fictional Allmuseri tribe, who are alleged to be an "old people . . . who existed when the planet—the galaxy, even—

was a ball of fire and steam" (43) and who seem like "the Ur-tribe of humanity itself" (61). Also on board the slaver is the Allmuseris' god, which, in Rutherford's presence, takes on the form of Rutherford's father and "the *complete* content of the antecedent universe to which my father . . . belonged" (169). Both this novel and *Oxherding Tale* are bildungsromans, charting their young protagonists' development from irresponsible flight to reimmersion in family and community. The Allmuseris are the protagonists' ancestor figures—their griots—guiding them through this moral growth and linking them with their fathers and, in turn, with all their ancestors, all humanity.

In *The Salt Eaters*, a cluster of healing ancestors presides over the herculean effort of reversing the negative flow of energy at all levels of existence in Claybourne: Minnie Ransom, the hands-on healer trying to bring Velma Henry back from a nervous breakdown; the Master's Mind, twelve "disciples" who telepathically assist Minnie; Sophie Heywood, one of the twelve and a mystic and healer in her own right; Doc Serge, the administrator of the health clinic and a trickster who resembles a con man and a mafia boss; and the shadowy Cleotus Brown, who never appears in the novel but is consulted by the other healers. One of the healers—Minnie—even has her own healer, the ghost of Karen Wilder, now called Old Wife, explicitly an ancestor figure, who taught Minnie to be a healer and now converses with her protégé about how to help Velma, herself, and the current generation.

These ancestor figures have many functions. They embody and articulate beliefs common in traditional West African religions, such as the idea of the living dead—that physically dead people are still present, still in a sense living, as long as anyone remembers them (Mbiti 25). Thus, the living dead metaphorically revive the African roots of African-American culture as they literally bring the African and the African-American pasts into the present lives of the novels' protagonists. Since those pasts have been so problematic throughout American and African-American history, part of the cultural work—and appeal—of contemporary African-American novels is to address these vulnerabilities. Ancestor figures, with their ties to the African and southern origins of African-American culture, help northern protagonists learn how to use that heritage as they attempt to survive and succeed in the modern world. Aunt Bessie guides Tommy in Wideman's *Hiding Place*, Pilate guides Milkman in *Song of Solomon*, Aunt Cuney guides Avey Johnson in *Praisesong for the Widow*, and Mama Day guides Cocoa in *Mama Day* so that these novels can demonstrate how northern migrants and all African Americans can value their heritage and use it effectively in contemporary America.

Despite the prevalence and significance of ancestor figures, many characters, not merely older ones or those associated with protagonists' ancestors, perform the similar function of connecting characters to their African-American heritage, the South, and the past. *Culture bearers* is a more encompassing term. Shadrack in Morrison's *Sula* retains an Afrocentric harmony with nature especially in his affinity with the river, and he takes on the role of community leader with his National Suicide Day ritual. Milkman is guided not only by ancestor figures but also by Calvin, Small Boy, Luther, and Omar, who initiate him during the hunt and offer him the bobcat's heart, thereby inducting him into his past and his racial identity and midwifing his rebirth in harmony with himself, his family, his community, and nature. In *A Gathering of Old Men*, the hero who emerges as the unifier of past and present and of human and cosmic is not one of the old men, the ancestor figures, but Charlie, the only middle-aged man in the community. In *A Lesson before Dying*, Grant Wiggins reluctantly becomes a culture bearer as he convinces himself and the condemned young man, Jefferson, of their responsibilities to family and community. In *Bailey's Cafe*, all four proprietors plus Miss Maple are culture bearers, creating an oasis of traditional African-American culture for racially and sexually abused refugees. In *The Salt Eaters*, not only the four principal healers—all ancestor figures—but nearly every character in the novel becomes a culture bearer, aiding the forces of recovery that promise to heal the community and the earth. In *Praisesong for the Widow*, Avey Johnson is guided toward her spiritual rebirth and return to her cultural heritage not only by her literal ancestor, Aunt Cuney, and by her symbolic ancestor, Lebert Joseph, but also by her daughter, Marion, by the Carriacou women on the boat, by Lebert's daughter, and by everyone at the Beg Pardon celebration. In Wideman's *Reuben*, the ancestor or griot figure is also one of the struggling protagonists. Reuben, who guides community members through the legal and procedural difficulties of the city and specifically returns Kwansa's child to her, is haunted by his own problematic past and his doubts about the legitimacy of his role.

In Wideman's *Sent for You Yesterday*, several clusters of characters transmit the culture to the young protagonist, Doot. Some are ancestors, such as Doot's grandparents, John and Freeda French, former anchors of the Homewood community who maintained their cultural integrity while learning to survive in the North. Doot's Uncle Carl and Carl's lifelong friend, Lucy, inculcate community values and history on Doot by retelling the stories of Homewood. Another culture bearer, Albert Wilkes, becomes Homewood's mythical champion for his unforgettable piano playing and his defiance of white power in openly sleeping with a white woman. Even in death he remains mythical: his body is disseminated like the collective memory of his prowess as he personifies the community's sense of itself. Brother Tate, Lucy's brother, incorporates Wilkes's artistic, communal, and mythical powers. With no apparent training, he suddenly plays the piano as beautifully as Wilkes had, draws hauntingly powerful pictures of Homewood residents, and like Wilkes seems to personify the community. Even the infant Junebug is a culture bearer, for, at least in Brother's imagination, he absorbs the rhythms of African-American culture. Despite the deaths of Albert, Brother, and Junebug, the multiple culture bearers succeed in initiating Doot and thereby passing on the culture.

Denied a past, or at least a respectable past, and often living in a nearly unbearable present, African-American culture often accentuates the future. This emphasis resembles Euro-American faith in progress and the eventual fruition of the American dream, and it has affinities with white Christianity's orientation to a future life after death. Because life under slavery and segregation was so horrific and so incompatible with the American dream, however, the idea of a radically better future gained special prominence in African-American culture. Since slave life was so intolerable, many slaves identified with the children of Israel, convinced that deliverance would eventually come (Dixon, "Singing" 300). As African-American culture evolved, the continuing sense of betrayal by the dominant American society and the continuing precariousness of African Americans' position in America led to greater concern for a future in which justice would finally be done (Fabre 72). Because the American dream so obviously failed to materialize for blacks, "the image of the promised land . . . became and has remained for over three hundred years the central theme in the lives of African Americans" (Hubbard 2).

The tradition of black theology illuminates this theme of a longed-for future. Faced with the inhuman conditions of slavery, African-American theology emphasized release from the present and faith in an idealized, nonworldly future. African-American spirituals stressed "hope, heaven, faith, and redemption" (Lincoln 147–48), and the sermon became a "cathartic release from the tyranny of the everyday" (Hubbard 24). According to Sterling Stuckey, African-American religion in the middle of the nineteenth century was a version of Christianity that emphasized the championing of oppressed people, the immanence of God, and faith in God's return to deliver the oppressed (33). Liberation and emancipation were such dominant themes that "Black theology is the theology of black liberation" (J. Johnson 129).

This supreme faith in ultimate salvation rested on belief in a just God. "The ethos of black religion is that there is a God somewhere" (Hubbard 17) and that God is "waiting in the wings of history to secure the safe passage of those who loved Him and did His will" (Spillers 88). Just as the spirit of the blues assures that the agonies of life can be transcended (Cooper-Lewter and Mitchell 18; Hubbard 22), black theology tries to address "the yearnings of a stolen people to be free and whole under God" (Cooper-Lewter and Mitchell 11): "Slaves survived their shackles with a magnificent affirmation of the justice of God, contemplating the final judgment with celebration" (Cooper-Lewter and Mitchell 35). This transformation cannot happen in the foreseeable, worldly future but only in the "by and by," a vague, otherworldly time beyond time, a time free of the conditions of the present and free of the difficulties of remembering the African or the slave past. Transcending time, "the converted black had been to Heaven and *knew* God and *knew* Jesus and *knew* himself saved. African time had become Afro-Christian time; past had become future!" (Sobel 245). Black theology thus delineates a myth by which African Americans can sidestep the temporal chaos that Barthold describes and by which the circular Great Time of West African religion and myth is translated into the timelessness of the Christian belief in life everlasting.[10]

Parallel to this faith in heavenly salvation, black theology also describes faith in a worldly utopia in which the American dream would be actualized and blacks would be redeemed. According to Lawrence Jones, most nineteenth-century African-American Christians hoped that the ideals of the United States would be realized "and that there would arise an earthly city, a beloved community," in which they would be full citizens" (8). Martin Luther King, Jr., combines these themes of a heavenly vision and an earthly utopia. In the tradition of black preachers, King asserts that he has "been to the mountaintop" and "seen the promised land" (286) and therefore knows God's justice (314) and knows that eventually "in luminous splendor, the Christian era will truly begin" (328). But his dream is for a better future in *this* life. Despite centuries of prejudice and discrimination, he "still ha[s] a dream. It is a dream deeply rooted in the American dream that one day this nation will rise up and live out the true meaning of its creed" (219). This dream will "redeem the soul of America" (318), will require "new methods of escape" from the ghetto (317), and will require "restructuring the whole of American society" (250).

In both visions—of a just afterlife and of an earthly utopia—emphasis is placed on a future that will redress the tribulations of the past and the injustices of the present. Envisioning an alternative future creates a meaningful space and time for African Americans and has the potential of revitalizing American culture. It can do so only if the projected future remains ongoing and open, for overly precise definitions would restrict the necessarily full participation in the process of (re)imagining that future, the African-American community, and America itself.

Several commentators analyze depictions of the future in recent African-American fiction. Maxine Lavon Montgomery delineates the apocalyptic tradition in African-American literature as "a mode of expression revealing a concern with the end of an oppressive sociopolitical system and the establishment of a new world order where racial justice prevails" (*Apocalypse* 1). Reflecting the always doubled position of African Americans, this tradition is characterized by "a peculiar dualism" between nostalgia for an idealized nineteenth-century American past and radical dissent from the failed promises of white America (4). Also in apocalyptic terms, Melvin Dixon asserts that the hoped-for future is depicted in African-American literature as the mountaintop, an "alternative landscape where black culture and identity can flourish" (*Ride* 2) and where "protagonists transcend identity through self-mastery" (4). After centuries of slavery and the breakdown of traditional African value systems, "passage into the alternative space is but one step toward the recovery of wholeness" (5). In Michael Awkward's reading of African-American women's fiction, that imagined future is "comm(unity)," the goal of "a common Afro-American woman's quest for (psychic and narrative) unity and community" (14).[11] For Charles Scruggs this idealized African-American future is the visionary city as opposed to the city as "ash heap" (7), and the idea of an imagined urban refuge, akin to Josiah Royce's Beloved Community (3), becomes "anywhere people gather together" (216), any time people "recognize the need for the invisible bonds of community to resist that breakdown [into dystopia] and create a *where*, a home that overcomes placelessness" (223).

Another cultural mechanism for projecting an alternative future is the carnivalesque. In the decades preceding the Civil War, black governors were annually elected in some northern states, with no legal power but often with much control over the black population (Stuckey 77). Free blacks in the North often celebrated such elections as well as holidays with special meaning for African Americans, such as the first of January in commemoration of the abolition of the foreign slave trade, the fifth of July as a counter to Independence Day, and the dates—for example, the fourteenth of July in Massachusetts—when individual states abolished slavery (Fabre 73–82). As Genevieve Fabre contends, these public celebrations were motivated by northern blacks' desire to invent an alternative future, a different America in which they were not betrayed or vulnerable (72–73). The public festivities, featuring speeches, music, dancing, and parades, focused on "major aspects of black life: African identity, freedom, leadership, solidarity between free blacks and bondsmen, between African-born and American-born blacks" (79).

These festivals are akin to carnival celebrations throughout the Americas. The Pinkster festivals in the Pinkster Hill district of Albany, New York, were known as "the carnival of the African race" (Stuckey 80). Like these festivals, carnival throughout the Americas was associated with liberation: Errol Hill posits that carnival in Trinidad was "a symbol of freedom for the broad mass of the population, . . . rooted in the experience of slavery and in celebration of freedom from slavery" (qtd. in Reyes 187). Carnival is ideally suited to become such a vehicle. As Mikhail Bakhtin defines it, carnival is a temporary suspension of ordinary authority, represents the normal world turned inside out, and conveys a utopian vision of participatory community, equality, liberation, and abundance (*Problems* 100–105, 133–39; *Rabelais* 9–12). The carnivalesque spirit is the inversion of the normal system—it is "life turned inside out," "life the wrong way 'round" (*Problems* 101); it "celebrated temporary liberation from the prevailing truth and from the established order; it marked the suspension of all hierarchical rank, privileges, norms, and prohibitions" (*Rabelais* 10). For Victor Turner, carnival is "play" (124), "antistructure" (130), and "the denizen of a place which is no place, and a time which is no time" (123).

As such, carnival offers at least a temporary solution to African-American placelessness and timelessness. It provides an imaginary space and a brief time in which the ordinary system is inverted. Just as black theology is the theology of black liberation, carnival affords periodic relief from an unjust system that African Americans could neither overthrow nor escape. By providing a comic but nonetheless mythic sense of the overthrow of the system, carnival modifies the harshness of that system, allowing the subjugated a psychological haven. It allows African Americans to participate, albeit indirectly, in the American dream by providing a myth and a ritual of an idealized, just, and inclusive society. As opposed to the implacable fixity of slavery and segregation, carnival offers absolute flexibility and open-endedness.

Carnival is also compelling because it jibes with African-American cultural beliefs. Since its time is outside European linear time, more like cyclic time or Great Time, it provides solace to African Americans for whom time and space are problematic. Like West African philosophies, "carnival brings together, unites, weds, and combines the sacred with the profane" (Bakhtin, *Problems* 101).[12] Carnival enacts the West African belief in the necessary harmony among all levels of being, the holistic unity of individual, community, nature, and cosmos: "all were considered equal during carnival" (Bakhtin, *Rabelais* 10), and "carnival . . . brings the world close to man and man close to his fellow man" (Bakhtin, *Problems* 133). Carnival also enacts the blues modality, in which hardship and uncertainty are accepted without eliminating hope for a better future. Like the blues, carnival is deeply ambivalent, both accepting the inevitability of change, including death, and celebrating the creativity of change and renewal (Bakhtin, *Problems* 102; Bakhtin, *Rabelais* 11).

By converting the carnival mechanism into a modern myth,

contemporary African-American novels help to reclaim the problematic African-American past. At the same time, since the carnivalesque reopens the possibilities of a just society, a society of full and equal participation by all its members, invoking it also works to revalue the African-American and American future. Marshall's Avey Johnson, Johnson's Rutherford Calhoun and Andrew Hawkins, Gaines's old men, everyone in Bambara's city of Claybourne, and some of Naylor's pilgrims pass into the carnivalesque to be released from the ever-present restrictions and displacements of a racialized society and to gain or regain their full identities and their cosmic balance.[13] As the authors guide such characters through this often perilous but necessarily revitalizing process, the novels acquire much of their power and their appeal because the characters' carnivalesque redemption models the potential redemptive future for all African Americans.

In contemporary African-American novels, the envisioned future is usually problematic. Johnson's Allmuseris, despite their roles as griots for his African-American protagonists, are culturally isolated, with "nowhere to *go*" (*Middle* 125). Wideman is especially ambivalent, wanting to believe in an earthly paradise to come but absorbed with prophecies of a more deadly, apocalyptic future, particularly in *Philadelphia Fire*. In his 1996 novel, *The Cattle Killing*, he projects a mixed view of a future balanced between the need for a purging apocalypse and the possibility of a better day to come. *The Salt Eaters* presents the most explicit and most developed vision of the future in contemporary African-American fiction, a future that is clearly apocalyptic, not fully known, better than the present, but nevertheless ambivalent. The onset of this portentous future is repeatedly announced by a booming, mysterious sound resembling everything from thunder to African drumming to a nuclear explosion. A new future is clearly being ushered in, but its details are fuzzy and include many predictions and projections, ranging from recovery from radiation exposure to harder work than people have ever known but foreshadowing the radical regeneration of individuals, families, community, the city, and by extension all human beings.

The endings of Naylor's four novels envision passages to a better future as they simultaneously place that future under suspicion. The women of Brewster Place achieve community wholeness in their brick-throwing demonstration, but the solidarity is short lived and the community dissolves. Willie is poised to pursue his artistic and empathetic endeavors at the end of *Linden Hills,* and in *Mama Day* Cocoa has her baby and shares her and the baby's life with George despite George's death, but in both cases these futures are only possible because of the sacrificial deaths of principal characters—Mrs. Nedeed and George. The community of *Bailey's Cafe* comes together in its multifaith and multicultural celebration of the birth of Mariam's baby, but the joy of that celebration is tempered by the fact that this baby is the same George who dies in *Mama Day.*

Because it does not yet exist in the material world, the envisioned future exists primarily in the mind. It is an idea, a dream, a vision, the often momentary product of an individual imagination or a community. Morrison projects such visions of the future in Nel's epiphany at the end of *Sula,* in the newly possible future implied by the end of *Beloved,* and in the similar restoration of family and community at the end of *Jazz.* Marshall envisions an idealized future for Avey Johnson, who, reunited with her heritage and reconciled with Aunt Cuney, will continue her aunt's work in passing on knowledge of the Ibo past. Johnson's *Oxherding Tale* and *Middle Passage* similarly project rosy futures, in which Andrew and Rutherford, having survived dangerous passages through the violent present and now having reconnected themselves with their ancestral pasts, are positioned to live happily ever after. In a more realistic vein, Gaines's novels also chronicle the characters' working through of psychological and social problems. Although the future is far from clear for Phillip Martin in *In My Father's House,* Gaines's novels usually end with the characters' success at resolving at least a portion of their problems and with a blues-like acceptance of life's hardships. Their futures may not be materially better than their pasts, but most—such as all the African Americans in *A Gathering of Old*

Men and Grant and Jefferson in *A Lesson before Dying*—gain a stronger sense of inner worth and a belief in themselves that at least allow them to face the future more confidently.

Although contemporary African-American novels tend to project a reimagined future, like black theology and carnival rituals they typically do not spell out the details of that future. Sethe and Paul D, like Violet and Joe, are finally ready to look toward a future, but Morrison does not attempt to delineate their new lives. The residents of Claybourne also rediscover their own internal resources so that they can imagine a future, but again that future is not foretold. Similarly, Grant Wiggins and Gaines's old men have been catalysts for a paradigm shift the details of which are yet to unfold. The future cannot be spelled out in detail because, the novels imply, it remains in the imaginations of individuals—characters and readers—and they, not the authors, must continue to envision a future radically different from the problematic past and the intolerable present.

This open-endedness about the imagined future of the African-American community and American society is related to a more pervasive quality of openness that characterizes contemporary African-American novels. Speaking only of women's novels, Holloway stresses the openness of the texts, their "fluidity" (*Moorings* 68) and their dissolution of distinctions (*Moorings* 72). Openness is highly privileged: in *Bailey's Cafe,* the proprietors in the neighborhood welcome all visitors and tolerate everything except intolerance; in *The Salt Eaters,* one of the principal lessons is that everyone always has choices about the future; and in Johnson's two novels, the Allmuseris are so open to the influences of the Other that they try to efface the self entirely. Openness is also achieved in the recurrence of unanswered questions, particularly those that ask the equivalent of "what's going on here?" or "what's going to happen?" When such questions are repeatedly left open, the gaps created by the lack of answers force characters, like their authors and their readers, to wrestle with the issues raised and to recognize the validity not only of what is said but also of what is not said, what is not seen, what is absent.

Typically, the movement is from the relative fixity of binary oppositions to the openness of an all-embracing position in the *différance*.[14] In Johnson's two novels, both protagonists begin in worlds dominated by binaries, especially the oppositions of race and gender. Each young man is initially loosened from the binary system, and the progress of each is to take advantage of his relative freedom to discover a more relativistic and enlightened position. In this "education," each hero must learn that people and events are not single valenced but likely to be multiple and unresolvable. Correspondingly, unresolved paradoxes are encountered throughout contemporary African-American fiction; for example, George's birth at the end of *Bailey's Cafe* is both a miracle that momentarily restores a sense of cosmic harmony to the novel's characters and a bittersweet event since in *Mama Day* the same George sacrifices himself to save Cocoa, and Wideman's entire oeuvre is dominated by the endlessly open tensions between such polarities as community and isolation and internal and external realities.

Just as the South becomes a paradoxical place in contemporary African-American fiction and a place whose oppositional values must be constantly renegotiated, the narrow strictures of linear time must also be transcended. As Holloway puts it, black women's texts "reconstruct a logic of repetitive, circular complexity rather than a binary and linear polarity" (*Moorings* 108). This shift occurs in *The Chaneysville Incident* when John Washington suspends his linear-based research mode to plunge imaginatively into the wholesale retelling of his ancestors' collective suicide. In all his novels and stories, Wideman explores the paradoxes of time, increasingly preferring the organic, biological, circular time of nature and myth to the linear time of clocks and calendars. In *Praisesong for the Widow*, Avey Johnson's physical journey to Carriacou is also her temporal journey outside the established time of her original cruise and into the circular time of the islanders' annual pilgrimage to celebrate their ancestors. The inexplicable events of the immediate past and the unknown events of the near future place the characters of *A Gathering of Old Men* in a curious temporal limbo. But the old men transform that potential discomfort into redemption by moving beyond linear time into a deeper past that they make present and that becomes the basis for their newly discovered future. Similarly, in *The Salt Eaters* the mysterious thunderlike sound propels the characters beyond linear time into a transcendent time and place when "everything that is now has been before and will be again in a new way, in a changed form, in a timeless time" (249).

The envisioning of alternative futures, the open-endedness, the unresolved ambivalence, and the renegotiation of the past in contemporary African-American novels are related to the emphasis in African-American culture on the collective creation of an intersubjective web of shared assumptions, mutual values, and participatory relationships. That emphasis is suggested when Baker refers to the "spirit work" of African Americans (*Afro-American* 8) or to the "nonmaterial transactions," "the work of *consciousness*," that was essential to the slaves' survival (*Workings* 38) and when Holloway articulates the "innervision of the word" (*Moorings* 25) or the emphasis on consciousness (*Moorings* 37) in black women's novels.

The emphasis on the intersubjective web in African-American culture stems in part from the belief in West African cultures that individual fulfillment only occurs through harmony with the community and the cosmos. As Geneva Smitherman puts it, "the community of men and women . . . is based on [the] assumption" that the "cosmos is an interacting, interdependent, balanced force field" (108). The individual could not thrive, indeed, could not exist, in isolation from the infinitely interwoven relationships with other members of the community and with the community as a whole. This emphasis also derives in part from the exclusion of African Americans from the material pursuits of Euro-American culture. Since material opportunity, even the possession of material objects, was extremely limited, African-American culture developed along nonmaterial lines, lines that further deepened the importance of the intersubjective links between individuals and community.

In contemporary African-American novels, the infinite interconnections of African-American culture are continuously recreated by the characters' projections of their consciousnesses into the future, the past, and each other. In *A Gathering of Old Men*, the old people's collective ability to reenvision the past leads to a realignment of values for each individual, both within the African-American community and in the multiracial society. In *Mama Day*, Miranda's mental ability to relive her dead father's trauma enables her to save Cocoa and Cocoa's child and thus to salvage a future. In the face of the isolating pressures of their lives, Wideman's characters and personae struggle to bridge the gaps between themselves and others and between their imaginations and objective reality. Heavily influenced by Maurice Merleau-Ponty and other phenomenologists, Johnson charts the progress toward enlightenment that accompanies his protagonists' developing powers of projecting their identities into the souls of others. For Bambara, the recovery of individual, community, and global health depends on countless acts of mental power—including recall and revalidation of the past, mental telepathy, and reenvisionings of alternative futures—all of which can potentially repair the damaged cultural web.

One of the most pervasive of these techniques for demonstrating and deepening cultural connections is storytelling. For countless African-American characters, recalling and (re)telling familial and communal stories are the primary means of linking themselves to the past, their families, their community, and their culture and therefore are a principal means of (re)establishing viable identities. The old men's testimonials in *A Gathering of Old Men* literally express and thereby revalue the lost, past community. For Johnson's protagonists, inventing stories—including lying—is one way of trying on and thereby absorbing new identities. In *The Salt Eaters*, the future will be characterized by the remembering and the telling of all the stories of the communal and cultural past. Stories are especially crucial in Wideman's novels because the tangled, interwoven stories and their multiple versions and interpretations are equated with the community and the culture. One of Wideman's volumes of short stories is titled *All Stories Are True* because he sees African-American culture as made up of "the countless individual stories constituting the grand fabric of history" (*Fatheralong* xi) and because stories create the fabric not only of a community and of African-American culture but also of the interconnected subjectivities of all human beings.

This idea of culture as an intersubjective web and the sense that African-American culture is based on an unusually strong emphasis on such a web have significant parallels with the novel as a genre. In J. Hillis Miller's classic formulations, "a novel is a structure of interpenetrating minds" and "interpersonal relations are the fundamental theme of fiction" (2, 29). Those minds include not only the novel's characters but also its narrators, its author, and its readers. The medium is written, but, as in African-American culture, the reader (listener) is as fundamental as the writer and narrator (speaker). Furthermore, just as African-American culture was and is primarily a creation of the collective minds of the community, so a novel exists only in the minds of its participants. Both fiction and African-American culture rely on the nonmaterial, the imagined, the transcendent, and both require that all the participants join the collective enterprise.

To take advantage of this parallel and thereby to perform their cultural functions as effectively as possible, African-American novelists balance traditional and nontraditional narrative techniques. The novels retain enough traditional features, such as realistic protagonists who undergo significant development, so that the novels can depict the quest for wholeness and the need for individual fulfillment hitherto denied, displaced, or called into question for African Americans. At the same time, the novels transcend the traditional conventions of Euro-American fiction to subvert them and the subjugation they embody. They are thus prime examples of what Alan Wilde terms "midfiction," fiction that is neither naively realistic nor experimentally antimimetic

(24). Through such open forms as flamboyant storytellers, nonlinear narrations, radical jump-cuts, magic realism, dreams, and ritual, African-American novelists, like jazz artists, undermine Euro-American narrative traditions while using them. Baker characterizes African Americans as "deconstructionists par excellence" who have "continuously shaken (or solicited) Western discourse with spirit work" (*Afro-American* 8), Holloway sees black women's texts as revising traditional contexts "in an intentional effort to destabilize them" (*Moorings* 73), and Amritjit Singh, Joseph T. Skerrett, Jr., and Robert E. Hogan argue that ethnic writers use subversive strategies, such as "deny[ing] the validity of the linear progression of the traditional narrative," to "valorize the subjectivity of narratives and undermine the very nature of hegemonic constructions of history and culture" (19). In the fiction of the five writers in this book, physical movement becomes symbolic passage as external space and physical places become metaphors for internal states of being; time becomes fluid, not linear or chronological, but like Great Time, in which past, present, and future are simultaneously available; and, through the openings of memory, the past is revalued, while the future is constantly reenvisioned.

The novels discussed here also undermine traditional Euro-American narratives by pushing beyond conventional boundaries, by exploring the liminal zone. Both *Mama Day* and *Bailey's Cafe* are set in locales that are not on any map, not even fixed in any state, and Rutherford's voyage on the *Republic* takes him into "a rogue sea" (*Middle* 158) in which Western navigational techniques are worthless. Paralleling such transcendence of spatial limits, linear time is often replaced by nonlinear time in which the usual distinctions between past, present, and future are blurred if not eliminated. Such boundaries seem to disappear when Gaines's old men mentally re-create the past, when the numerous narrators of Wideman's novels conflate past stories and present events, when the linear, picaresque narrations of Andrew and Rutherford are repeatedly interpolated with embedded flashbacks, and most notably in the last sections of *The Salt Eat-*

ers when the future collides with the present and the past and the characters are propelled headlong across undefinable "borders" to new, equally undefinable "frontiers" (280).

These novels also stretch conventional narrative form by using multiple narrators. Twentieth-century fiction is rife with such polyvocalism, and postmodern theories have accustomed readers to think of texts as plural. Bakhtin argues that all texts are polyphonic, that any telling is in essence a retelling, and that one's own words are to a certain extent a "double-voiced narration of another's words" (*Dialogic* 341). Roland Barthes shifts the focus from the closed, completed work to the "methodological field" of the irreducibly plural text, which is "woven" into a multivoiced "network" (76–78). For Brian McHale, postmodernism itself is plural, polyvocal, dialogic, and indeterminate; language is a web of constant interchange and circulation; and a text is the endless play of its signifiers (99–109).

The potential meanings of such multiplicity are enhanced in African-American culture because of the dualities—indeed, multiplicities—inherent within that culture. Given their forced position both inside and outside American society, African Americans developed both a double consciousness and a double language—an oral Black English and a white English that is both oral and written.[15] In the African-American oral tradition, listeners are as important as speakers, for example, in the performance of such modes as signifying and toasting. Witnessing, the assurance of shared experience, is inseparable from testifying, the oral recounting of individual experience. Black English allowed slaves a medium for in-group communication and a degree of expressive freedom from their white oppressors, and it further strengthened nonmaterial connections within the African-American community. As a result, a doubleness and hence a multiplicity of voices and languages is explicit in African-American culture. Lawrence Levine argues that "the socialization process" for African Americans "increasingly became a dual one: an attempt to learn to live both within and outside the group" (153).

Expressing this cultural and linguistic pluralism, African-

American novels have traditionally been "hybrid narratives" (Bell xii), combining African and African-American folklore and Western written genres. Part of that hybridity is the spreading of the narrative consciousness among a multitude of character- and noncharacter-narrators.[16] The varying perspectives of the many narrating voices and the relationships among those consciousnesses become the primary focus of contemporary African-American novels. Multiple voices are needed: all the old men, not just Bailey but each proprietor and each visitor, a communal mixture of the voices of Homewood, a constantly shifting focalization among the people of Claybourne. Given a history of having one's story told by others, contemporary African-American fiction asserts the necessity for multivoiced communal telling and retelling.

Reflecting the oral tradition, contemporary African-American novels call attention to the roles of listeners as well as narrators. Beloved, as Denver's listener, becomes cocreator of the story of Denver's birth; through mutually listening to each other's life stories, Violet and Alice Manfred regain their identities; "Bailey" is aware that Nadine is listening to his narration; to become integrated with his family and community, Doot must hear all the stories and all the versions of all the stories; the old men's stories must not only be told but heard and heard not only by their fellow African Americans but by white authority figures. The presence of multiple narrating voices in most of these novels suggests that the characters listen to each other.

The existence of multiple narrators and multiple listeners focuses attention on the reader's role, for the reader is the ultimate listener. The novels' openness and their tendency to stretch conventional boundaries require readers to participate actively. When texts by Gaines, Bambara, and Wideman ask but do not answer question after question, readers, like the characters, are asked to wrestle with the unanswered questions, to wonder what is happening and what will happen. Johnson forces both Andrew and Rutherford to abandon their traditional perspectives on the world, and simultaneously, because of the slipperiness of the novels' texts, readers become aware of their role and are implicitly urged to reevaluate their positions. Wideman's fiction constantly prods the reader to join in the author's and the characters' processes of mentally (re)imagining reality, requiring his external readers to be as active as his internal readers and listeners. Like Morrison's idiosyncratic narrator of *Jazz*, who ends her discourse by asking readers to "make me, remake me" (229), Wideman asks readers to create him: "Imagine yourself making me up, being me, freeing yourself as I start to take on the weight and independence of a personality as lifelike as the one you possess, as real as the one you've dreamed" (*Fatheralong* 145).

Since readers are asked to become not merely passive recipients but participating cocreators, they take on the roles of witnesses and testifiers in the African-American oral tradition. Geneva Smitherman defines *testifyin* as a "concept referring to a ritualized form of black communication in which the speaker gives verbal witness to the efficacy, truth, and power of some experience in which all blacks have shared" (58). As her definition implies, witnessing is not a passive act but is inseparable from testifying or "giv[ing] verbal witness." Witnessing is based on experience and therefore to a degree on watching, but it is not valuable until it is voiced, shared with the community to corroborate another individual's testimony. By requiring readers to be active, contemporary African-American novelists urge them to become not merely passive witnesses but vocal ones who will testify by returning their experience to the community. As Albert Murray puts it, "the emotional response of the reader to his experience of a book of fiction is also a reenactment (of a reenactment!)" (*Hero* 23).[17]

The narrative form I have been describing is ideally suited to help contemporary African-American novels perform their requisite cultural work. The narrations enhance the interplay among multiple speaking and listening minds, including characters, narrators, readers, and authors. As they do so, they reproduce and further create the invisible threads of African-American culture. The two are inseparable: the narrative and temporal multiplicity formally re-creates the intersubjective web that characterizes both African-American culture and the novel as a genre. Since the community consists of its network of interrelated minds, the novels should include as many such minds as possible and should allow those minds to function in the most complex relations to each other. To accomplish such representations, the primary focus of the novels becomes the many forms of thoughts of the many narrating voices and the relationships among those consciousnesses, as opposed to the events of their plots.

This form has many implications. Since the point of view can flow back and forth among the characters, the multiple and shifting connections among the novels' participants, and by extension, among all human beings, are reinforced. Closed endings are less effective than in traditional Euro-American novels, since an overly decisive conclusion might suggest an end to the ongoing flux of the web of subjectivities. As the novels depict and enact the cultural web, they address cultural dislocations of space, time, community, and identity by mirroring the doubleness associated with those dislocations. They thus transform the doubleness into a positive vehicle for expressing temporal and psychological alienation and thereby move beyond such alienation to new harmonies. As Awkward claims for African-American women's novels, fiction by the five men and women examined in this book uses "double-voiced strategies of narration" in an attempt "to end debilitating psychological disjunction . . . and isolation from the larger black community" (14). Similarly, by calling into question conventional Euro-American notions about the linearity of time, these novels open alternative, visionary, and even apocalyptic futures. Such futures offer the possibilities not just of a viable place for African Americans but also of a just American society, a society of full and equal participation by all its members.

The novels' collective significance is suggested by their multiplicity of influential characters. Just as many culture-bearers are invoked, many protagonists' development is usually charted: not just Velma Henry but everyone in Claybourne; not just Cudjoe but also Wideman's persona, JB, and even Richard Corey in *Phil-adelphia Fire;* not just one old man but the whole group; not just "Bailey" but all the proprietors and many visitors. The novels tend to depict not an individual *bildung* but a collective *bildung.* A set of characters moves toward a clearer understanding of their locations in time and space, specifically the significance of their pasts, their places within the African-American community, and their uncharted futures.

This collective bildungsroman, with its multiple protagonists and multiple griots, is couched in terms of a complex negotiation between traditional binary oppositions. One ever-present opposition polarizes African-American and Euro-American characters, leading to the displacement of the former. Protagonists also move between the two poles of the North-South dialectic, sometimes physically in journeys from one to the other, almost always meta-phorically through stories and memories. As they do so, the direction is toward attempted renegotiation and possible recon-ciliation of the two. At first, characters tend to overprivilege the present, overvaluing their present consciousness and devaluing their personal and cultural pasts. Gradually, through memory, storytelling, the conveyed experience of ancestor figures, and the intuitive wisdom of culture-bearers, they learn to balance past and present and then to conceive of a viable future. Relegated to Otherness by the dominant white society, characters struggle to believe in themselves and in those they want to love. Rather than the typical Euro-American privileging of the self to the exclusion of the Other, these characters need to revalidate the Self to in-clude and love the Other.

The psychological and communal work of the novels is to re-place the seemingly unbridgeable gaps between these and other oppositions with more fluid, more balanced, and more open-ended interplay between and among them. That is to say, the characters need to deconstruct the oppositions, to enter the *différ-ance.* Those who are able to do so—such as Doot, the residents of Claybourne, Rutherford Calhoun, Andrew Hawkins, Miranda Day, the proprietors in *Bailey's Cafe,* Grant Wiggins, and

Gaines's old men—emerge with a traditional West African sense of harmony among self, community, nature, and cosmos that accompanies their return to a meaningful reconciliation of past, present, and future, their discovery of their meaningful place in the African-American community, and therefore their reconstruction of their own identities and their rediscovery of their ability to love.

As a group, the novels in this book eloquently depict such themes. Their characters grapple with the issues of reconnecting with a hitherto neglected past, of seeking individual fulfillment in harmony with their community rather than in isolation, and of redeeming a future for themselves and their communities. What matters to them is not so much what they do as what they think, not their actions but their intersubjective links to other community members past and present. At the same time, the novels' open-ended, nonlinear temporality suggests the ongoing and unlimited process of individual development and community formation, and the novels' overlapping narrations embody the emphasis on community. In their content and their form, therefore, these novels express African-American cultural concerns as they enact new variations of that culture and of American culture.

If America is indeed founded on differences, then one of the greatest challenges for Americans is to find creative ways of responding to such differences, of working with them, not merely against them, in the continuous creation of the American community. The five novelists examined here take up that challenge. Their creative talents plus their problematic position in American time and space give them unusual opportunities to perform this cultural work. The double consciousness imposed by a racialized society provides, as for W. E. B. Du Bois, the gift of "second sight" (5) and, as for Ralph Ellison, a "special perspective" (*Shadow* 131). With such strategic insights, these novelists are not merely writing for African Americans, not merely working out how African Americans can survive in the North or the South, not merely rediscovering and revalidating African-American identities by redeeming the past and by reassessing African

Americans' symbolic place in American society. They are doing all those things, and they are redefining America itself. By assuming an "inclusive audience" (Callahan 29) and by creating "a narrative discourse of democratic possibility" (Callahan 257), they are attempting to create a more cohesive nation. Like Legba, the West African deity who links the human and the divine, they are poised at the crossroads where postmodern ideas intersect issues of race, the repressed American past, and contemporary Americans' awakened consciousnesses about themselves. Voicing such intersections, they are enacting deconstruction as America. Their fiction gains its special power because it gives voice to these national concerns, because it risks opening the nation's stubborn oppositions, and because it dares to leave them creatively open.

2

"ALWAYS YES AND ALWAYS NO"

Affirmation and Doubt in John Edgar Wideman's Fiction

Of the five authors considered in this book, John Edgar Wideman's fiction most explicitly displays the characteristics of contemporary African-American fiction described in chapter 1. In his thirteen published volumes (eight novels, two memoirs, and three volumes of short stories), his characters and narrators are caught in the passage between isolation and community. Around them are the invisible threads that bind individuals to each other, to family, to neighborhood, and to African-American culture, but social and psychological pressures make it difficult for them to enter into or to remain in the intersubjective web. This tension between community and isolation is reflected in corresponding tensions between the exigencies of external reality and the powers of the imagination to create its own realities, between linear time and circular time, and between the influences on Wideman of his mother and her family as opposed to those of his father and his. As Wideman's fiction and memoirs depict and enact these tensions, they document numerous strategies for dealing with them—principally, communications with other people, imaginative projections, memory, storytelling, retrieval of the past, insistence on open-endedness, and participation in the volumes themselves. The processes of explaining, enacting, and working through the tensions and the intricate strategies for dealing with them are complex and difficult, so that no sudden breakthroughs occur, yet over the course of Wideman's oeuvre there is progress

on the arduous passage toward understanding, and even reconciliation, of the abiding tensions.

In Wideman's fiction and memoirs, the desire for community
is always balanced by the risks of isolation, and the protagonists
feel this tug between connection and separation. *Hiding Place*
charts the movement from Bess's and Tommy's chosen isolation
to their chosen reintegration; *Brothers and Keepers* focuses on
the potential spiritual isolation of both Robby and John and their
attempts to overcome it; in *Philadelphia Fire* the social breakdown that led to the MOVE massacre is reflected in the near
alienation of every male character; in *Fatheralong* "Wideman"
worries about his father's and his sons' separations from the family in the context of racial oppression that deprives fathers and
sons of their company and their stories; and the young preacher
in *The Cattle Killing* wanders a social landscape dominated by
breakdown and isolation yet manages to retain his own sense of
community and his abiding love for Kathryn.

Some characters move from community to isolation, such as
Orion in "Damballah," the blacks and Jews who are blamed for
the plague in "Fever," Richard Corey in *Philadelphia Fire*, and
Wideman's son, Jake, after his incarceration. Sometimes this
movement takes the form of the collapse of characters' efforts to
form intimate minicommunities, as in the case of the four men in
The Lynchers or of Robby's gang in *Brothers and Keepers*. In
more optimistic works, the dominant movement is from isolation
toward community, as for Cecil Braithwaite in *Hurry Home*,
Tommy and Bess in *Hiding Place*, and Robby and John in *Brothers and Keepers*. Sometimes the isolation is initially chosen, and
then reintegration represents the character's realization that his
or her period of isolation must end so that continued growth can
occur within community and self, as in *Philadelphia Fire* when
Cudjoe ends his self-imposed exile. Still other characters remain
in an uncertain state between integration and isolation. This
limbo often takes the form of an attempt to form a minicommunity whose permanence is left open-ended. In *A Glance Away*
Eddie, Bob, and Brother may provide lasting help for each other,

but the outcome is far from certain. In *Reuben* Reuben and Wally, as well as Kwansa and Toodles, temporarily help each other, but again the long-term efficacy of their mutual help is unknown. Similarly, in the memoirs and fictions, Wideman's personae struggle inconclusively to prevent the isolation of his brother, his father, his son, and himself.

The ubiquity of this tension between isolation and community in Wideman's works, as well as its presentation from so many angles, implies its dominant significance. Not surprisingly, for most of the figures, the tensions are unresolved, presumably unresolvable, because for Wideman this is the central issue of life. It is traceable to the differences he represents in his two parents—his father's reserved distance versus his mother's nurturing love. It is evident in his own life—his successful career in the largely white academic world versus his early upbringing in Homewood, his efforts to hold the family together, and his psychological return to his extended family.

Wideman's principal image for the intersubjective web of human relationships is twisted or interwoven strands of fiber, the "tangled skein." His fullest articulation of this image asserts that everything in life is inextricably linked: "You never know exactly when something begins. The more you delve and backtrack and think, the more clear it becomes that nothing has a discrete, independent history; people and events take shape not in orderly, chronological sequence but in relation to other forces and events, tangled skeins of necessity and interdependence and chance that after all could have produced only one result: what is" (*Brothers* 19). Characters' lives are bound up in the complex threads of events and time; for example, the narrator's ninety-three-year-old grandmother in *Philadelphia Fire* "could encompass a skein of time close to the age of this country" (118). The image of the skein or the web depicts the infinite ties that bind some of Wideman's characters to the objects around them: Doot remembers Freeda French, a fictional representation of Wideman's grandmother, surrounded by "a dusty, beaded web . . . threads stretched from the top of her head to all the walls, the things in the room" (*Sent* 29–30). More importantly, the threads often tie characters to each other; for example, to describe his mother's all-encompassing love, Wideman asks readers to "think of thread spun finer than silk but steel-strong, stronger, much stronger as it stretches, loops, weaves, webs" (*Fatheralong* 52). Conversation between a mother and daughter "weaves back and forth" to the extent that the daughter sometimes "wouldn't know who was doing the talking and who the listening" (*All* 130–31).

Besides figuring the social connections among characters and events, the image of the tangled skein also represents the stories people tell. Stories, which are better when "twice-told, thrice-told" (*Fatheralong* 13), not only help us break out of our rigid habits of separation and selfishness but also lead us to the higher realities of the imagination, "where boundaries are breached" and where all the voices are heard (*Fatheralong* 71). Stories constitute and create the collective life of humans, "the infinite history of our lives intersecting" (*All* 32). Since each story is "a sport of time" (*Philadelphia* 133), it can carry teller and listener beyond ordinary time into the timelessness of Dreamtime and Great Time. In a transcendent looping or doubling—"double-talk" (*Reuben* 64)—the stories become us, reflect back to us our own imaginations: "imagine our fictions imagining us" (*Philadelphia* 98). Stories are the ultimate human reality, the joint creations of our collective mind, "as real as we are" (*Fatheralong* 192), "saving us" (*Cattle* 208), able to "free us" (*Cattle* 207), and able "to create the world" (*Fatheralong* 21). Each of Wideman's own fictions is such a story—a complex, tangled web of interrelated events and consciousnesses that "is twisting and hissing and crackling like a churning rope" (*Philadelphia* 138).

That Wideman repeatedly uses the image of the tangled skein to describe interpersonal relations, individual consciousnesses, characters' stories, his own fictions, and life itself underscores his dominant theme: for any human activity, the complex interweavings of weblike strands of interconnections are valued, and the contrasting loss of interpersonal ties that constitutes isolation is dreaded. At all social levels—from African-American culture, to a neighborhood, to an extended family, to the nuclear family, and to any pair or small group—Wideman portrays successes at creating and maintaining such webs of interconnection as well as failures to do so. Similarly, he reveals the weblike consciousnesses of individual characters in their complex thoughts, feelings, and dreams. At the same time, the stories that his characters and narrators tell further exemplify the values and necessity of interwoven connections, and Wideman's formal and stylistic techniques re-create the same complex webs in his own volumes.

The sense of tension surrounding Wideman's treatments of such connective webs and the contrasting harshness of isolation are suggested by the image of passing through the needle's eye. As for the narrator of "All Stories Are True," the "skein of life" must inevitably be "dragged bead by bead through a soft needle's eye" (*All* 3). But the needle's eye—that is to say, the unyielding and often bitter realities of life—is not always "soft." Just as cars getting on a ferry must pass "one car at a time through the needle's eye" (*Philadelphia* 59), individuals, despite their intersubjective webs, must pass individually through the meat grinder of life: "the people an unbroken chain of sausages fed in one end and pulled out the other" (*Cattle* 149). Similarly, "When Junebug died, Brother [Tate] had to crawl through the needle's eye" (*Sent* 176); that is, his mourning became an alienating passage, a harrowing regression from within the human web of community to the alienation of insanity and death. Wideman's fiction can be characterized as open-ended explorations of the tensions between the highly valued complexities of human interaction and verbal representation on the one hand and, on the other, the confining strictures of life that reduce such complexities to frightening and debilitating isolation.

Although Wideman focuses on the local and familial levels, he also suggests broader applications of the web of intersubjectivity. At its broadest, it incorporates all human minds—"one gigantic brain" whose collective wisdom would be "lots smarter than the sum of each of our smarts," an ideal sensed momentarily by the baby in "Newborn Thrown in Trash and Dies" as she hurtles to her death (*All* 121). The young preacher who narrates most of *The Cattle Killing* achieves unity with all other minds as his consciousness emerges from his epileptic fits: "He was all the others. They were thinking with his thoughts. Their thoughts were his. He lived uncountable lives. Breathed for all of them, dying and being born so quickly life never started or ended. It flowed. One continuous sweet breath, just as his vision never alighted on one object, one place, but danced to them, through them, so he missed nothing but nothing halted his gaze either and the world was one sight, one luminous presence inventing his eyes" (69). Just beyond ordinary human awareness, then, Wideman posits a mystical unity of all minds and all things, a cosmic oneness. But it can only be glimpsed, for the newborn baby is about to die and, as the young preacher returns to normal consciousness, his mystical vision gives way to reality as "the universe kneels, retreats through the needle's eye" (*Cattle* 69).

In *Fatheralong: A Meditation on Fathers and Sons, Race, and Society,* Wideman characterizes the less mystical intersubjective web that connects all African Americans. "Linked" (*x*) by "common ground" (*ix*)—in particular "a continent, a gene pool, a history" (*xi*)—any two African Americans have a "shared sense of identity" (*ix*) that is instantaneously transmitted with a glance. This cultural fabric is continually rewoven through the collective process of "sharing the work of giving meaning to difference" (*x*), of coping with being "situated . . . first as *different*, then *other*, then *inferior*" (80). For Wideman, African-American culture and history are not external events but "the activity over time of all the minds comprising it" (101), the "collective enterprise of mind" (102); that is, history *is* the intersubjective web. Heroically, "the historical mind of African people captive in the American South learned how to 'get over'" (102), to survive by "fashion[ing] visions, dreams, an immaterial, spiritual realm with the density, the hard and fast integrity of rungs on an iron ladder" (102). Wideman sees the greatest achievement of African-American cultural survival as the collective creation of a nonmaterial, mental intersubjectivity that is as tough and real as the iron chains that bound African Americans. In the collective African-American "chorus of achievement," the individual can achieve fulfillment inside the community "when self merges with something greater than self" (*xxi*). In such formulations, the intersubjective web must be complex and varied, must allow for the merger of individual and community, and must help achieve the traditional West African harmony among self, society, nature, and cosmos.

Throughout Wideman's works, one underlying cause for isolation and the breakdown of community is racial oppression. The evidence is everywhere: in the economic conditions of Homewood, in the dead babies of "Daddy Garbage" and "Newborn Thrown in Trash and Dies," in the exaggeration of both Robby's and Jake's crimes. As early as *The Lynchers*, Wideman reminds readers of the history of lynching of black people in America in the twenty pages of evidence included in the Matter Prefatory, and as recently as *The Cattle Killing* he writes of "This New World" as "a graveyard for African people" (127). Whites kill blacks—for example, Orion in "Damballah" and Albert Wilkes in *Sent for You Yesterday*—and persecute them. Tommy riffs at length on the "plenty" of blacks who have been killed or ruined by racial oppression (*Hiding* 149), and Wideman's persona reflects that "a law lodged in the heart of the country" is that blacks "have no rights which the white man was bound to respect" (*Brothers* 187).

Reinforcing this historical sense of racial oppression, Wideman often alludes to slavery and the Middle Passage. Visiting Robby in prison reminds the author's persona of "auction blocks" (*Brothers* 186), the insidious isolating power of fever began "when one of us decided to sell one of us to another" (*Fever* 133), and Reuben reflects on the "mind chains and body chains" (*Reuben* 19) that confine us all. The phrase "The dark ships move" (*Reuben* 9) haunts Kwansa because she has heard a poem about the Middle Passage and the "sharks eating the poor Africans they throwed overboard," sharks about which Cudjoe has read (*Philadelphia* 60). In "Fever," the text jumps unexpectedly to the point of view of an African in the hold of a slave ship: "curled in the dark hold of the ship he wonders why his life on solid green earth had to end, why the gods had chosen this new habitation for him, floating, chained to other captives" (*Fever* 130). In *Fatheralong*, Wideman asserts that "we are in the midst of a second Middle Passage" (xxii) because the present degree of violence and dislocation is comparable to the earlier event. He describes both in terms of the breakdown of community and the subsequent isolation of individuals: the first one "separated [enslaved Africans] from traditional cultures, deprived [them] of the love, nurturing, sense of value and identity those cultures provided," while the second one is "a configuration of devastatingly traumatic forces" that make "young people feel rootless, deserted, adrift" with "a void behind, a void ahead" (xxiii).

The effects of this cultural breakdown appear regularly throughout Wideman's writing. Homewood itself is disintegrating, "coming apart" (*Sent* 67), "stripped . . . bare" (*Brothers* 40). Characters have no positive futures; as Carl, a talented artist, is reminded when his art teacher asks him "What do you think you're doing?" and he realizes the impossibility of a career in art (*Sent* 150); similarly, Kwansa notices how the young men of Homewood become disillusioned with their menial jobs (*Reuben* 145). In *Fatheralong*, Wideman laments the breakdown in communication and fellowship between African-American fathers and their sons, a breakdown that results from racial oppression. When fathers' stories are not passed on to their sons, sons become "semi-orphans" and fathers exist "in exile" (65). Father-son relations become dominated by "the walls between them" (65), and fathers and sons become more like prisoners than loved ones. Feeling abandoned, the children respond with "frustration, anger, rebellion" (66), and the country becomes "a vast orphanage" (82). Insistence on racial difference leads to racial discrimination, which deprives black men of their rightful place in the society and consequently of their proper role in their families: "The paradigm of race works to create distance between sons and fathers" (71).

In many of Wideman's books, the abstract sense of the larger African-American community is made concrete and individual in the Homewood neighborhood of Pittsburgh where he grew up. In "the old Homewood," "relations with people in that close-knit, homogeneous community were based on trust, mutual respect, common spiritual and material concerns. Face-to-face contact, shared language and values, a large fund of communal experience rendered individual lives extremely visible in Homewood" (*Brothers* 73). The shared language is rendered in "voices [that] are a river you step in once and again never the same" (*All* 64), a stream of anonymous voices that jointly narrates "Everybody Knew Bubba Riff." The communal web is so tight that everybody in the neighborhood did know Bubba, just as anyone in Homewood would know that "a French girl was somebody who lived in Cassina Way, somebody you didn't fool with or talk nasty to" (*Brothers* 73). In the old Homewood such communal knowledge also afforded protection, so that Freeda French is comforted knowing that "people look out for Lizabeth. They know she's my girl" (*Sent* 85).

Part of the closeness of the community derives from the story of its founding by the runaway slave Sybela Owens and Charlie Bell, the white man who helped her escape from slavery. As Wideman's Aunt May tells the story, it becomes a myth, replete with Sybela's mystical power over people and comparisons between her escape and that of the Israelites from Egypt (*Damballah* 201, 202). In "The Beginning of Homewood" the narrator interweaves multiple strands of the web by incorporating the story of the founding of Homewood into a "letter" to his imprisoned brother, Robby. He sees links between Sybela and Robby— both committed a crime, both had the "urge for freedom" (*Damballah* 195), and both were prisoners. He asserts that the complex connections that constitute Homewood will keep both stories, as well as Robby's life story, from ending: "So the struggle doesn't ever end. Her story, your story, the connections. But now the story, or pieces of story are inside this letter and it's addressed to you and I'll send it and that seems better than the way it was before. For now. Hold on" (205). Sybela, Robby, Aunt May, and Wideman are linked because they are part of the Homewood community, and the linkage, like the stories, can never end—only "for now" it is temporarily marked off in a convenient strand—for the intersubjective web is always in process, always being further created by the participants.

Sent for You Yesterday, Wideman's fifth novel and the third in his Homewood trilogy (the others are *Hiding Place* and *Damballah*), clearly illustrates his themes. At the end of the novel, Doot, a fictional representation of the author, dances in the presence of Uncle Carl; Carl's lifelong friend and lover, Lucy; and the ghosts of Lucy's adopted brother, Brother Tate, and the mythical Homewood hero, Albert Wilkes: "Everybody joining in now. All the voices. I'm reaching for them and letting them go. Lucy waves. I'm on my own feet. Learning to stand, to walk, learning to dance" (208). The novel is about the process that leads to this magical moment of communal harmony that unites the whole community ("*all* the voices") and that completes the absorption of Doot/Wideman into the community as it marks his individual integration. But the novel is also about the forces that work against such communal unity and about the anxieties that such forces will prevail. Albert Wilkes expresses such fears: "They got us on a rack, John French. They gon keep turning till ain't nothing connected where it's supposed to be. Ain't even gon recognize our ownselves in the mirror" (62). The novel is about the tensions between these two passages, between connection and disconnection, with a tilt toward the need for the former. As John Bennion puts it, "existence is a dance between life and death . . . set firmly in tradition, in an interlinked net of remembered people" (148). It is such a "balance" (Bennion 150), but its insistence on that interlinked net, on what Ashraf H. Rushdy terms its "intersubjectivity" (321), is Wideman's affirmation—in this novel—of the dominant force of community.

In the novel, Wideman returns to his Homewood roots. With his fictional representative, Doot, he re-creates the Homewood community, especially through the layered memories of its past.

As the collective minds of Doot and the Homewood residents remember the old days, Doot, and through him Wideman, hears the voices, joins the collective dance, and (re)enters the community. At the same time as he asserts this celebration of community, however, Wideman doubts its efficacy. Like its stories, the community itself is "fragile" (117). Characters can easily slip into fatal isolation, and even the seemingly well-integrated characters are wracked with fears. This ambivalence is manifested in a series of paradoxes: for example, the city surrounding Homewood both "trapped and saved" the community's residents (21); Albert Wilkes is both "here" and "gone" (70); and Carl feels that Lucy loves him and does not love him, that "he could be in both places at once, lovemelovenot one ripple of sound, always yes and always no" (115).

Reality in Homewood is relentlessly harsh. Life is a constant economic struggle in which even skilled craftsmen like John French have to beg for work, and it is a constant psychological battle that drives able people to the solace of drugs. Life is like a giant fist constantly pounding the characters, like John French's perpetual backache: "Nasty-colored drops that harden and ball up so it's like somebody rams in a fist back there and knuckle grinds his spine every time he moves" (62). Life is like the power of a train, overpowering the characters, as in Brother's train dream and Albert Wilkes's dreams "about a piano. Big and black and greasy as a train hurtling down the track" (60).[1] Fist and train coalesce in two images of one of the "scare games" (18), versions of "chicken," in which Brother and Carl test each other to see who can come closest to being hit by a train: in the split second before the train passes, "nothing inside you works because the train has rammed its fist up your hynie" (18); and the train leaves Carl "shaken like a rag doll in a giant, black fist" (23).

As Bennion also asserts (150), the novel's prologue, "In Heaven with Brother Tate," epitomizes this harshness. In heaven, Brother shares dream stories with another member of that community. They thus model the human characters' swapping of dreams, stories, and memories in the humans' attempts to retain a sense of community. But, just as their consciousnesses are permeated by their fears of the ultimate breakdown of community, even in the ideal community of heaven the characters' dreams are nightmares of their worst fears. In Brother's train dream, other people become shattered pieces of bodies in a boxcar; community has become isolated individuals banging into each other; instead of enjoying heaven, Brother fears a holocaust. Similarly, for Brother's interlocutor, his former community has become the site of his paranoid fears about "freaks," "spiders," "a whole army of cops," "the police and marines and FBI," and a particularly frightening "big greasy-assed elephant" (11).

Even as fear controls the heavenly dreams of Brother and his companion, it dominates the earthly psyches of most of the characters. Freeda is afraid that Albert Wilkes's return will threaten the life of her husband and her son. Those concrete fears expand to her more pervasive fear that nothing is secure or reliable: "whenever she looked away from something, she was never sure it would be there when she looked back" (32). Carl French absorbs both his mother's specific fear for her husband's safety (27) and her fearful orientation to life. Like Freeda, he worries about the permanence of the external world, fantasizing that Homewood would disappear if he were not there to observe it: "What would happen to Homewood if he ran away? What would happen to his mother and father if one morning, a bright, lazy spring summer morning, he didn't wake up and start the dream of Homewood? Carl is suddenly afraid" (28). Dominated by fear and by the compulsion to overcome his fears, Brother invents scare games to confront and therefore defuse his fears, but his fears cannot be overcome, for he is haunted by his "train dream" (159) both in heaven and on earth. Similarly, Lucy is scared when she hears the news about Pearl Harbor (202), and she is "always scared" when she visits Mayview, the sanatorium where Samantha is committed (145). Her fears emanate from her anxiety that her own sanity is precarious, that "one of the guards would grab her and sling her in a straitjacket and lock her in a room."

The characters' fears for the loss of external reality and their own identities subconsciously express their anxiety over the gradual disappearance of their community. Brother's dreams about fragmenting bodies are echoed by John French's worries that Homewood is breaking up: "All Homewood coming apart" (67). For Lucy the decline began with World War II, as she intuited that the war would bring irreversible changes to Homewood: "the walls of the house on Cassina started tumbling down" (200–201).

Evidence of the community's decline piles up in the accounts of characters who become isolated from it. Despite his role as community fixture, Brother becomes increasingly alienated, especially after the death of Junebug. He declines from occasionally speaking to never speaking, becoming a witness who will not or cannot testify (171). Formerly an essential listener for Carl— "Carl talking and needing me to listen so I put everything out my mind awhile" (168)—in his isolation he condemns Carl's talk as mere lies, "Carl always lying" (180). Like Brother, Samantha is also cut off from the community after Junebug's death. Her utopian vision of founding an ideal community of beautiful, strong children is shattered by the radical dismembering of her minicommunity when the other children kill Junebug. As a result, Samantha loses faith in her myth, her connections to the larger community, and her mind.

Surrounding the isolation of these major characters is a pervasive fear of isolation throughout Homewood. When Carl returns from World War II, he feels like "a stranger in a strange land" (148), and the ensuing period of drug addiction for him, Lucy, and Brother separates them from each other and the community. Despite her strong communal ties, even Freeda French fears isolation, worrying that she will disappear or that there "won't be nobody there to scare" (38). Miss Pollard plays the communal role of witnessing everything that happens—she "has the job of watching Cassina" (21)—but her later death verifies the dangers of isolation: "Miss Pollard will die in a fire . . . because nobody remembered she was up there on the third floor" (22). Growing old for Carl means the fear of dying like Miss Pollard: "plenty old people still out in the street ain't even got social security. You look in the paper you read about one every day. Starved or frozen. Or burnt up in some tinderbox" (197).

Despite the multiple and intense pressures against it, there is a strong sense of community in Homewood, and Wideman's insistence on the dangers of isolation and on the fears that the community will disintegrate intensifies the power of the novel's community-building theme. The sense of community is expressed in the characters' extensive community knowledge: John French accurately predicts that Albert Wilkes will be at the Tates' house (52), and Albert in turn knows that John will wait for him in the Bums' Forest (76). When Albert returns after seven years, everything and everyone are in their predictable places at McKinley's bar: "Albert Wilkes gone seven years but if he walks through the door this afternoon he'll know who to speak to, what to say, where to stand and nobody'd hardly notice" (70).

Critics agree that the novel charts the passing down of community traditions from Albert Wilkes through Brother to Doot/ Wideman and that this linkage reconfirms the circular permanence of the community.[2] The cohesive strength of the community is also suggested by the bonds among small groups of characters, such as Albert Wilkes and John French, the French family, "the three musketeers" (Carl, Lucy, and Brother), and the new group of Carl, Lucy, and Doot. In addition to her husband and her children, extended family is essential for Freeda, who is "as familiar" with Uncle Bill and Aunt Aida's house "as her own house" (48). Family is even more important for Lucy, who, displaced from her biological one, creates a family at the Tates' and maintains a family-like relationship with "her men"—Carl, Wilkes, Brother, and now Doot (190).

An extreme sense of community is suggested when characters are able to empathize so fully with other characters as to become them. Such "conflations of personalities" (Rushdy 319) include parallels between Brother and Wilkes (89, 160), Doot and Brother (199), and Freeda and her daughter, Lizabeth, who become "two Freedas" in John's mind (82). Similarly, Carl is "just like John French" (109), Carl is also "like his sister, Elizabeth" (151), and "June[bug] was like" Brother (182).

Even more powerfully, characters can merge their consciousnesses with other characters in acts of complete empathy. To tell Junebug's story, even to herself, Lucy knows that "you had to be Samantha to understand" (127). Into her story of her visit to Samantha, Lucy interpolates Samantha's perspective on her life and on Junebug's death. In the midst of Lucy's story, the merging is doubled when Samantha in turn becomes Junebug: "Cause in the dream I'm him. I'm little Junebug. . . . Like he's telling me his side of the story so I have to listen and I'm inside. I get caught and I'm him while he sings it" (141). Lucy is Samantha is Junebug. Lucy's and Samantha's empathetic powers echo Doot's ability to merge his consciousness with each of the novel's characters as he orchestrates their voices and memories, as "he loses himself in narrating the lives of the Others who help make him the multiply defined self he is" (Rushdy 322).

The sense of an enduring community and of individuals' connections to that community is implied by the novel's title and the full title of the song from which it comes: "Sent for You Yesterday, and here you come today" (202).[3] Someone, perhaps even a whole community, asks someone (or someones) to join him or her, and, in a mininarrative of completion, that someone does so. The previously incomplete group is completed, individual and group complement each other, and the individual is fulfilled within the community. Since the song is the same one to which Doot danced as a toddler with Lucy's encouragement, it evokes the characters' common past and suggests the enduring significance of family and communal stories. The song is a paradigm for the characters' memories—they "sent for" their remembered stories, and those memories return.

Wideman's use of a song title for his title calls attention to the presence of music everywhere in the novel, a presence that symbolizes communal ties.[4] The almost magical piano playing of Albert Wilkes and then of Brother captures the souls of Homewood residents and seems to represent the entire community.

Just as "all the voices" join in Doot's celebratory dance, so the music contains all the voices for Lucy: "Albert Wilkes's song so familiar because everything she's ever heard is in it, all the songs and voices she's ever heard" (189). Because it contains all, it links all: "but everything is new and fresh because his music joined things, blended them so you follow one note and then it splits and shimmers and spills the thousand things it took to make the note whole, the silences within the note, the voices and songs" (189).

Even more than music, shared stories of the communal past bind the community together. To become a member of the community, Doot must hear and rehear these stories, and by writing the novel Wideman re-creates his own reimmersion into his community and his rediscovery of his communal and familial self. Many stories are fond recollections of past events, such as the story of Freeda breaking the window with her hand, the caterpillar story, or the story of how Bill Campbell won the numbers with 725. The stories repeatedly demonstrate the links between people and generations, as Doot feels connected to Junebug because of "the stories I've heard" (16) and Carl feels connected to many past generations by his aunts' stories about the past (26).

Since people in this community love to tell endless versions of stories, there is a never-empty reservoir of stories waiting to be told, regardless of actual events. Because of this propensity, no single version or telling of any story is adequate. An issue such as who told the police that Albert Wilkes had returned generates as many versions as residents: "gather all the stories, listen to every tale and all of Homewood guilty" (80). Doot, who has "heard the stories of Cassina Way a hundred times" (116), learns to adopt this perspective, wishing that he had "paid attention before. When May and the rest were telling stories" (146) and urging Lucy to tell the story of his first dancing because, although he knows the story, he has never heard it from her (203).

Because of such multiplicity, the stories incorporated in the novel are decidedly nonlinear. Carl's stories are especially known for their tendency to ramble, Lucy accusing him of "talking in circles" and of "begin[ning] a sentence then get[ting] way off" (118). Lucy tells her stories in the nonlinear way she rethinks them: the story of Junebug "unfold[s] like a fan" (124), beginning "for some reason" with Albert bathing her and Brother and requiring her to become Samantha (126). Part of the nonlinearity is the intermingling of the various stories; as Carl tells Doot, "I know I'm supposed to be telling you his story. But how Ima tell his without telling mine. And Lucy's" (154). Rather than single strands with clear beginnings and endings, the stories are like the "storytelling quilt" under which Brother sleeps, all part of "the weave of stories" (93) that constitutes and represents the community.

Stories and storytelling also require listeners, and Doot's role as avid listener to all the stories brings him into the family and the community and represents at least a temporary triumph over isolation. It is not easy to be a good listener, for it requires hearing what is not said as well as what is said, as when Doot misses what Carl implies about Brother's unusual means of communicating (121): "You listening but you ain't hearing, Doot" (121). Carl's memories of his life story cannot be adequately told until he has a witness, a role that Doot learns: "he's waiting for a witness. A voice to say amen. Waiting for one of the long gone old folks to catch his eye and nod at him and say *Yes. Yes. You got that right, boy*" (149). Having heard the stories, having "got it right," Doot, as Wideman's alter ego, can then in turn become the storyteller, the story writer.

Sent for You Yesterday is a tour de force, enacting in its narrative form what it asserts in its content. It argues that community exists in the complex overlapping of multiple versions of the communal stories and memories of its members, and it presents its story in the same way, as a mixture of related stories and memories in the minds of many characters. It thereby tries to be the complex community that Wideman asserts. To do so, its form must be tangled, like the "circles and circles and circles inside circles" (118) with which Carl describes the world.[5] Both African-American culture and this novel rely on the nonmaterial, the imagined, the transcendent, and both depend on the participants' willingness to join in creating the collective enterprise.

One characteristic of this complexity is the necessity for multiple perspectives. Since for Wideman the community is comprised of the intersubjective web of the minds of its members, to represent that community he must reveal many of those minds in operation. He cannot literally transcribe "all the voices," but he can assert that they are all heard (208), and he can depict so many of them that the novel seems to include all. The thoughts of minor characters, such as Miss Pollard (21, 61), Aunt Aida (47), and Bill Campbell (45) are woven into the "shifting" mix of "voice and perspective" (Marcus 322). Wideman further emphasizes his all-inclusiveness by including the thoughts not only of major and minor characters but also of characters when they are dead (Brother Tate in heaven), infantile (Junebug), and not present (Freeda's italicized words in Carl's head [20, 24, 95]).

To suggest a comprehensive communal mixture of voices, Wideman often records medleys of anonymous residents commenting on a situation, such as the men in McKinley's bar arguing about which of them first saw Albert Wilkes return (56–57), various opinions on who informed on Albert (80–81), comments by several customers at the Velvet Slipper (103), and people's exclamations about the revival meeting (175). It does not matter if these voices are actually spoken or only imagined, for the community exists in each member's mind, as the totality of possible voices, thoughts, and dreams of all the community's members. Therefore, community is present when Albert imagines what the crap players would be saying (76), what people would say to Freeda if Carl were killed (36), and what a witness for Carl's inner story would say (149).

A second characteristic of the tangled narration of the novel is its lack of chronology. For Matthew Wilson, time in the novel is "nonlinear" (240), for Bennion it is both "nonlinear" (143) and "convoluted" (145), and for Rushdy one of the novel's subjects is "the collapsing of temporal differences" (319). Since the retelling of communal and familial stories is crucial to the novel's themes, memory and its evocation of the past are paramount. What is unusual, though, is that Wideman not only uses Doot's memory but also relies on the interwoven memories of all the major characters. Their voices and perspectives are needed to re-create the multivocal communal mind, and their memories are necessary to invoke the multivocal past. Just as John French counts forward and backward (70–71), so the narration can flash forward into the future, foreshadowing events that it will later describe, such as the deaths of Junebug (17), Brother (23), and Albert (51, 65, 79). Occasionally, it breaks into the distant future to describe events that are not enclosed within the narration: "A hophead friend of my brother's will kill Indovina" (22), and "Carl will travel around the world" (115).

The blending of past, present, and future in a nonlinear sense of the simultaneity of all times and all events is captured in the image of Brother looking as far as he can down the railroad tracks: "In his song like a window Brother could see way down the tracks. To now when he is dreaming. To the time when he will speak to a son. To the time he wouldn't speak to anyone anymore. To the lives he would live and the lives he would be inside. Albert Wilkes's song like a hand over the troubled waters, and then the water was still and he could see everything. Everything gone and everything coming not mixed up together anymore but still and calm" (163). Like the intersubjective communal web, past, present, and future are all equally present, stretched out forever along the tracks.

The blurring of temporal distinctions is significant because it enables the characters, Wideman, and the reader to enter the past and thereby reclaim it. The familial, communal, and cultural pasts are in jeopardy, since the heros of the past—John and Freeda French, Albert Wilkes, Brother Tate, Samantha, and Junebug—are dead. When the new generation, represented by Doot, moves outside the present to rehear the stories of the past, that past is retained, and the community and the culture are therefore sustained. By circling forward and backward in time, the narration creates a sense of the inseparability of past, present, and future—in other words, a sense of cyclic Great Time in which all times are equally "present." In general, Wideman prefers this synchronous time, finding that "the usual notion of time, of one thing happening first and opening the way for another and another, becomes useless pretty quickly" (*Brothers* 19).

As Wideman's narrative form imitates the collective communal consciousness, that form becomes highly elastic and richly layered. Any voice can erupt into the text at any time, as when Carl "hears" Freeda's italicized remonstrances (20, 24, 95), remembers his father singing "Sunshine, you are my sunshine" (24), or imagines the men in the Bums' Forest demanding "What you want, boy?" (26). The most complicated layering of the narration involves Lucy. When Carl starts to tell Doot the story of Junebug's death (122), the narration follows Lucy's thoughts as she imagines how Carl will tell it. Because of the music in the bar, she "couldn't hear if she wanted to" (124), but she has no need to hear, for, knowing the story and the teller and the listener, she can follow the telling by simply watching Doot: "She sees enough on Doot's face. Reads the words plain as day" (124). The narration then proceeds with Lucy's internal rendition of the story— "She's telling it to herself. Her way" (124)—rather than with Carl's spoken rendition to Doot. The layers of narration become delightfully thick: Wideman is writing the story for the reader; Doot, Wideman's persona, is recounting his reception of the story; Carl is purportedly telling the story to Doot; Lucy is partially following that rendition but at the same time imagining the story to herself in her own words; and within this multilayered narration, Samantha narrates to Brother the "facts" and her "dream" of Junebug's death (140). As Bennion puts it, the novel is narrated "as if [the narrating Doot], the reader, and the characters were all sitting inside each other's head" (149). Indeed, they are, for the novel's evocation of community requires exactly that kind of untrammeled passage from one mind to another, that perpetual reweaving of the intersubjective web.

Whereas *Sent for You Yesterday* is based on the premise of Doot's integration into the community, *Reuben* leaves unresolved the balance between integration and isolation. Reuben locates Kwansa's lost son, thereby healing the rift caused by his loss, but Reuben's role is ambivalent as he both stabilizes the community and is isolated from it. Reuben's course from integration to isolation and back to a tentative integration is set against Wally's struggle to avoid complete alienation.

Reuben himself personifies the community. His power derives from his ability to see into the heart of things and then to use that power to hold the neighborhood together: as he puts it to Wally, "You see through things. You try to take your pleasure from what's behind things, inside things, propping all this mess up" (37). Like the community itself, he is everywhere and nowhere, everything and nothing, "messenger, factotum, busybody, moron, spy, gossip, hustler, old dog tray, cuckold, cocksman, nothing, everyman, flunky, fool, mountebank, wizard, storyteller, mute" (132). His methods are communal, depending on his knowledge of a complex web of individuals and practices—"it's a word here, a promise there, a favor asked or returned, *quid pro quo* barter or bargain, a draft choice for future considerations, that's how things usually work" (197). Despite his role as communal helper and representative, Reuben becomes a scapegoat, symbolically giving up his life for the good of the community by bearing the psychological scars of the racial degradation and fire at Flora's, surrealistically becoming the murdered victim of "the recruiter"/Wally, and then being jailed as a fraud.

In this novel, the effects of separation from the community threaten the integrating effects of community. Reuben's quasi-legal work for the community takes him into the inner recesses of the broader social web, yet he works and lives alone, and his odd physique sets him apart as only marginally human, people thinking of him as a "dog," a "fox," and even a "rat" (3). Community is threatened to the extent that Reuben worries about its total collapse. He frets that he may be the last person who remembers things, and he worries about what will be lost if no one remembers: "If all the witnesses disappeared, who would remember? Nothing caused Reuben to feel more lonely than the thought that he was the only one left who remembered" (125–26).

Wally is even more alienated, enmeshed in the insane world of athletic recruiting and boiling over with anger. He has lost his sense of a true self, slipping instead into false appearances, distancing himself from himself and reality: "Wally treats his life like a memory so he won't have to worry about what's happening to him" (102). Knowing that his identity is lost and that he has become merely "a fly" or "a spider" (102), he dreams of bashing anonymous faces (24), imagining (and perhaps actually) murdering an anonymous white man, and living by "abstract hate" of white people (116, 163). Unable to locate his own identity in his world of appearances, Wally wonders if all the other businessmen he sees, like him, "were flying from life to life, a merry-go-round circus of identities and nobody else knew their names" (33). He is out of step with himself and reality, "his life long gone or sometimes just a half step away," so that everything goes wrong, even in his fantasies as "the pass buzzes through his sure fingers" (98).

Given the novel's emphasis on isolation and community breakdown, the characters' strategies for maintaining sanity and a cohesive self are almost desperate. One such strategy is the creation of a double. Even though their personalities are opposite, Toodles seems to double Kwansa (96), and Reuben finds a sympathethic Other in the early photographer, Eadweard Muybridge. Reuben and Wally, though quite different in most respects, merge into each other in their actual and imagined dialogues, finally switching places when Reuben, the helper, needs Wally's help to get out of jail. The ontological status of most of the doubles is uncertain: Reuben imagines that there are two Floras, one "real" and one "invisible" (83); Kwansa fictionalizes a "better self" (140, 142) and later "sees . . . a woman moving in slow-motion" (209) who seems to be Kwansa's second self; and Wally fantasizes that his friend Bimbo is not one but "twin Bimbos" (172). Wally himself dissolves into multiple imagined and possibly real personages—"two Wallys," one self "battling his own self" (163). He is confused about his possible doubles and disguises and often writes letters to himself, projecting not one double but "a million other Wallys" (1970). One such alter ego is "the recruiter" who may or may not be the real Wally, both of whom may or may not have killed the white man in a public restroom.

The most fully developed double is Reuben's lost twin brother, whom he calls "Reuben II" or "Two" for short (65). Reuben has a vision, which seems like a memory but whose status cannot be confirmed, of this loss: "He thought his heart had been broken in two when his brother was stolen from his side" (64). In the attempt to retain physical connections to his brother, Reuben wears a charm of "a man, severely stylized, African style" (65), as well as a gold chain, "the comfortable presence of that other lost one, his brother, next to his heart" (131). He suspects that his brother is in prison: "In a dream or vision or during one of the extra lives he grew more certain he had lived, the longer he lived, Reuben had learned his brother was in prison" (66). Through Reuben, Wideman grieves over the imprisonment of his own brother and expresses his fear that Robby also will be lost. Like Wideman's persona in *Brothers and Keepers,* Reuben needs his brother to complete himself: "Perhaps he'd lost a precious part of himself forever. A loss Reuben needed his brother to heal" (68). For Reuben and Wideman, *brother*—whether abstract concept or actual sibling—is part of what one grieves for, part of the past that one cannot directly recover, in Reuben's terms part of the "Philadelphia" that "all black men have," a past disaster that "even if you escape . . . you leave something behind. Part of you. A brother trapped there forever" (93). The loss or potential loss of a brother is symptomatic of the ever-present threat of community breakdown.

Another strategy for attempting to maintain wholeness is characters' creations of imaginary conversations or of conversations whose reality is ambiguous. One example is when Reuben "talks" with his imaginary interlocutor, Eadweard Muybridge (61–64), but the motif is most fully developed in several exchanges between Reuben and Wally. Often, it is not clear whether they are having an actual or an imagined conversation, as when their alleged talk is presented like stage dialogue (36–38) or when Wally seems to be hearing Reuben but slips into his own thoughts (104). The question of Wally's possible killing of the white man is the most elaborate example. Wally seems to confess the murder to Reuben (40–44), and Reuben asks if the story is true (44), but later Wally says that the murderer was merely "the recruiter" whom Wally met on a plane (117–24). Throughout this rendition, Wally addresses Reuben, and Reuben seems to be listening, but later Reuben denies ever hearing the story:

> I told you about the dude on the
> plane. The one told me the crazy
> story.
> No. You didn't tell me that story.
> Well, I meant to tell you. (199)

Wally then wonders if "maybe it's all in my mind" (199). The conversations as well as the murder may exist only in Wally's or Reuben's head, for imagined conversations have as much reality as actual ones.

Another coping strategy is to modify reality or its perception to maintain community and one's connections to it. Reuben succeeds in helping his clients because he is adept at "creating a counterillusion" within the law and the legal system, "forestalling an inevitable conclusion by the logic of another conclusion" (17). Skillfully manipulating appearances within the legal system, he becomes a magician able to reenvision legal consequences and to convince others that his envisioning is valid: "A sort of sleight of hand. This paper, this plea—now you see it, now you don't. Presto chango—the bear goes over the mountain, the mountain comes to Reuben—whatever it takes" (197).

The ending of *Reuben* reinforces the idea that such strategies are tenuous at best. In the bar scene when Toodles and Kwansa attack Waddell and in the final scene when Reuben finds Cudjoe, the narrative perspective is withdrawn almost to the point of non-existence. For the bar scene, "we," both narrator and reader, are placed at an extreme spatial and temporal distance from the action: "From a great distance, longer than the time it's taken all the voices that have ever told stories to tell their stories, in the welcome silence after so much lying, so much wasted breath, the women's voices reach us. Where we sit. Imagining ourselves imagining them" (207–8). This distance separates readers and narrator from the characters but also allows "us" to encompass the entire scope of all narrations of all the stories ever told. All those narratives have little or no value, being reduced to lies and "wasted breath." "Our" activity—narrator's and readers'—is complex: not merely the narrator (and the author) but also readers engage in their act of imagining the characters; and the narrator, author, and readers are also conscious of their act of doing so—they imagine the characters, they imagine themselves, and they imagine themselves imagining the characters. A tangled skein indeed.

The near-disappearance of the narrator, as well as the reader, continues in the short concluding chapter. "Our" vision is extremely limited—"as far as we can see" there are no other people in the entire building, and our hearing is suspect, as "we think we hear the ticking" of Reuben's watch (214). "We" are not even told that the man is Reuben, but instead we must "imagine a short, gimpy, immaculately dressed, bearded, brown man" (214). When the man and the boy see each other, our sight degenerates further, as "we are momentarily blinded." We then mysteriously break apart, "The sides and backs of our skulls have dropped away" (215), but since we are not corporeal beings in the first place, this loss does not matter—"It's scary, but seemly, doesn't hurt." We then disappear into the glory of the rescue, ignoring anyone else who might be present: "If others are in the room, they shouldn't be. So we lose them and lose ourselves and ride the wave of light long enough to hear the old man say, Hello" (215). Even though at the end of all narratives, narrator and readers cease to exist, Wideman's deliberate calling attention to these impending disappearances reinforces the sense of precarious connections and fragile communities in this novel.

In *Philadelphia Fire,* Wideman's most pessimistic novel, the balance shifts even farther toward alienation and the absence of community. Published in 1990 following the imprisonment of Wideman's son, Jake, in 1985, the novel is set in Philadelphia after the government bombing of a row house where the revolutionary group called MOVE was located. The bombing suggests for Wideman that there is no more community, that "we are all trapped in the terrible jaws of something shaking the life out of us" (22). And in his anger, Wideman is tempted to call for the complete annihilation of the city: "Best to let it burn. All of it burn. Flame at the inmost heart" (159).

The psychological loss of Wideman's son is portrayed in the novel through Cudjoe's search for the boy, Simba, who allegedly escaped from the bombed building. The loss or potential loss of a child prompts one of Wideman's most poignant passages: "My wife said her mother told her it doesn't matter how old you are when your last parent dies. What you feel, however old, is orphaned. You are an orphan in the world. But what is the word for a parent who's lost a child. I have no word, no place to begin. Nothing to start you thinking, no word like my wife's mother's word to tell you how I feel" (119). The lack of a word expresses the absence not only of one's child but also of self, place, community, and time. In the next paragraph, Wideman searches for metaphors to express this greatest of losses: "If you've lost a child it's like undoing that picture of four generations, or the one yet to be taken of five. Having it but then watching it burn, or be erased, or unwinding, or waking up one morning to the news it was all a mistake. Never happened. Forget it. A child lost cancels the natural order, the circle is broken." Almost desperately, Wideman seeks words to fill the void of "the emptiness [that] has no name, no place": "the parent who grieves for the lost child owns an emptiness as tangible as a photo"; "think of a leg that's been amputated" (119). Absence replaces presence, confusion replaces assurance, lack of words replaces words: "No word for the space where the absence of a leg is real, the pain is real. No word for the confusion. My life forming around an absence we've been in the habit of calling one thing, but now it's another without a name, but I must speak to it, of it, exist with the pain of its presence and absence speaking to me a hundred times a day, every day" (120). Metaphorically, Cudjoe feels dismembered after the MOVE fire and the disappearance of Simba, "the child who is brother, son, lost limb" (7–8), and he cannot be re-membered until he brings the boy back into the community: "he must find the child to be whole again" (8).

Shocked by the breakdown of community and family, each of the novel's protagonists—Cudjoe, Wideman's persona, and J. B.—is alienated and self-divided. Cudjoe, divorced and having spent the last twelve years in self-imposed exile in Greece, cannot understand what has happened to the Philadelphia he once knew. He tries but fails to learn about Simba from Margaret Jones, a resident of the shattered neighborhood, and he is out of place in the new political atmosphere in which his old friend Timbo thrives. Cudjoe's "confus[ion]" is expressed as a temporal displacement: "he's a generation behind, lost in time" (117), and he is "out of phase again" (192). Cudjoe also feels out of joint spatially, as if he were "actually someplace else, in a dimension where the stink of this stale cabinet didn't exist" (53). Like Cudjoe, J. B. is dislocated, "inhabit[ing] many places, no place"; "he is no one, no where" (184).

Besides anger and confusion, the protagonists also feel guilt, as if each one is responsible for the breakdowns. Like Wideman, Cudjoe feels guilty for having abandoned his home community and for being far away when the MOVE bombing occurred. Like Wideman, he married a white woman and now feels both racial betrayal for having done so and guilt for the marriage's failure: "How did they know he's failed his wife and failed those kids, that his betrayal was double, about blackness and about being a man?" (9–10). Wideman's persona, the second variant, mocks his own curiosity when he first heard about the bombing two thousand miles away in Wyoming, blaming himself for "always know

[ing] next to nothing about [his son, Jake]" (98). Even J. B. feels guilty—for having betrayed the MOVE leader, King, and more generally for having "no life worth thinking about" and yet for insisting on "hanging on when no reason to hang on" (186).

As a result, each protagonist nearly loses the power of language. When Wideman's persona tries to talk on the telephone with his imprisoned son, Jake, they "don't get on" (98), for "words between us have become useless" (99). The "loss" of Jake, coupled with the tragedy of the MOVE fire and the loss of Simba, nearly paralyzes Wideman the writer. Just as words are useless between him and his son, his writing almost ceases, he frets over his "frightening" failure to remember the name of a friend's daughter (122), he laments that "words fail me because there are no words for what's happening" (118). He compares himself to L. Zasetsky in A. R. Luria's *The Man with a Shattered World,* who could not narrate his own story, his own power to tell nearly reduced to zero: "Not as bad as pitiful Zasetsky but I do feel my narrative faculty weakening. A continuous, underlying distraction so that if I look away from what I'm doing, I lose my place" (115).[6]

Despite this dominance of loss, breakdown, alienation, and paralysis, *Philadelphia Fire* also manages to convey Wideman's theme of integration, in particular through the faith that mental creations have more significance than physical ones. Physically, the world has collapsed—the needle appears to have no eye—but, even in the face of such calamity, Wideman asserts his belief in the power of the mind to make meaning and therefore for meaning to continue to exist. The city, still present in its inhabitants' minds and hence rebuildable, urges Cudjoe to speak it back into existence—"All you have to do is speak and you reveal me, complete me" (44). Cudjoe imagines the city's founders "dreaming the vast emptiness into the shape of the city" (45), and he enacts the rebuilding by mentally constructing a room for the shoes he remembers, "a row house to hold the room," a street for the house, a neighborhood of streets, and "a city to hold the neighborhood" (46–47). Cudjoe further imagines himself creating the city through the act of seeing it: "Didn't you need a million windows opening, framing views of the city every morning in order for a city to come to life? Wasn't a city millions of eyes that are windows opening on scenes invisible till the eyes construct them, till the eyes remember and set out in meticulous detail the city that was there before they closed for sleep?" (53–54).

Despite Jake's imprisonment, or perhaps because of it, Wideman's persona is awed by the continuities of the generations of his family. Thinking about photographs of five generations of women in his family and of four generations of males, he becomes "dizzy from the intersection, the connection" (118). He is overwhelmed by the "nexus," the "bridge," and the "touching" that "link" people over generations within a family (118). Paralleling that process, the mind goes back and forth between past and future, weaving them together: "Years coded. Flashing across the screen of this dark room. Forward and backward" (102).

Stunned by the overwhelming reality of the bombing and his son's incarceration and thereby by the unyielding exigencies of life, Wideman counters with an emphasis on the power of subjectivity. Wideman's privileging of the perception of reality over external events is evident in his contention that "the central event" of the novel is the staging of *The Tempest* by his persona and the child actors: "Though it comes here, wandering like a Flying Dutchman in and out of the narrative, many places at once, *The Tempest* sits dead center, the storm in the eye of the storm, figure within a figure, play within play, it is the bounty and hub of all else written about the fire" (132). Yet this central event never takes place, all the performances having been rained out. A nonevent can be so crucial because of Wideman's epistemology: events, or external reality, are far less significant than mind. What matters is the imagining of *The Tempest* by Wideman the author, Wideman's persona, the children, the anonymous adults who offer suggestions and criticisms, and readers. If external events like the MOVE bombing sunder community ties, mental re-creations can forge new ones.

A second result of this collective imagining is the transcendence of time, of *tempestas* (107), the "other" meaning of *tempest:* "Begin with a double meaning. If Cudjoe did not live to see his play hatched, he did spin from the endless circles of its possibility that second meaning cached in the drama's title: time. Borrowed time, bought time, saved time" (133). The focus on *The Tempest,* and on its imagined production, means that the novel turns time inside out, moves in it, through it, and beyond it: "So this narrative is a sport of time, what it's about is stopping time, catching time. Watch how the play works like an engine, a heart in the story's chest, churning, pumping, tying something to something else, that sign by which we know time's conspiring, expiring" (133).

Because of Wideman's privileging of subjective realities, the preferred mental condition for the protagonists becomes a semiconscious dream state in which external reality is fully open to the mind's re-creations. In part 1, Cudjoe's odd state of mind, in which he can barely believe the reality of the Philadelphia to which he has returned, leads him to the edge of hallucination, particularly when he equates the woman in the park with Teresa (27) and wonders if she is only "an invention, one more lie he'd told himself" (28), and again when he thinks he hears kids' voices in the park and wonders if he "is slipping in and out of a dream" (50). Much of part 2 revolves around the attempted production of *The Tempest,* which we watch (139) but which never occurs. In part 3, J. B. recalls going to the movies with Cynthia (168), but then Richard Corey recalls being embarrassed by her "unladylike panty show" (173), and J. B. appears to be set on fire and to dive into a dry fountain (189).

Wideman calls into question the boundary between "reality" and "imagination" for the same reasons he calls into question other boundaries: to transcend such limiting categories, to probe the endless complexities of infinite gradations of reality and imagination, and to assert the primacy of the imagination over external reality. Hence, it doesn't matter whether Richard Corey's body lies at the corner of Sixth and Market (179) or "in the center of

Eighteenth Street" (182); what does matter is the mental impact of the suicide both for the novel's characters, who tell and retell the incident, and for the novel's readers, who must try to assess its impact in the tangled contexts of the stories of Cudjoe, Wideman's persona, and J. B.

In this novel, as in Wideman's other novels, the multiplicity of consciousnesses reproduces the communal web of minds creating meaning. *Philadelphia Fire* is an extremely nonlinear, confusing montage of four males—Cudjoe, Wideman's persona, J. B., and Richard Corey. The interrelated stories in the mind are like the result of channel surfing: "cut and paste images, [when] you are the director, driver, pilot, boss hoss, captain" and when you can freely indulge in "flashes forward and flashes backward and fast shuffles" (100). Such mental gymnastics are necessary because to survive the trauma Wideman and his protagonists must freely invent, but in the crumbled psychological space of this novel their inventions can only be chaotic.

Cudjoe is another storyteller, a writer, who is both like and unlike Wideman. Just as this novel, like each of Wideman's volumes, focuses on connections across times and among consciousnesses, Cudjoe "is exploring the connection" between his present and his past, between reality and memory, as he tries to recall his wife, Sam, Rachel, and Cassy as well as Simba and the MOVE victims (67–68). Like Wideman's, Cudjoe's storytelling is open-ended, but Cudjoe's is so open-ended that he cannot write at all, cannot come to grips with his sense of personal and communal confusion: "Cudjoe's getting confused, his stories mixed up" (65). Like Wideman, he wants his stories to transcend the limitations of time ("first step is always out of time" [23]) and space ("he must always write about many places at once" [23]), but for him the stance leads to paralysis, not creation. Lacking confidence in his ability to invent or to understand the value of invention, he cannot tell Timbo the story of his dream about the boy lynched on a basketball rim, for the dream is truncated, merely a fragment: "The dream stops there. Everything surrounding it's gone. I want to know the rest, too. Thought telling you might help. But it doesn't. I feel myself beginning to invent. Filling in the blanks but the blanks are real. Part of the dream" (94). Even though he is stuck, he is on the right track, for in "beginning to invent" he becomes more like Wideman, who, even after the wreckage of Jake's imprisonment and the bombing, is able to invent, to build in the mind a new city, a new community, a new self.

Like the socially and psychologically devastated world of *Philadelphia Fire*, the fictional landscape of Wideman's 1996 novel, *The Cattle Killing*, is bleak. Zhosa cattle are slaughtered, as are various animals in the elder Stubbs's slaughterhouse; cadavers, such as that of a pregnant African woman, are dissected; eighteenth-century Philadelphia is ravaged by plague; a man nears death in his isolated cabin where his wife's corpse molders. As in *Philadelphia Fire*, individual isolation and broken communities predominate. Every character is isolated, even minor ones such as Bishop Allen and socially privileged ones such as Dr. Thrush and his wife. Some partially recover from their isolation: Liam regains his interest in talking and making love, and the young preacher is buoyed by his efforts to cure the sick lady. But such revival is short lived, for Liam and Mrs. Stubbs are soon murdered, and when the orphans are killed the young preacher loses his faith and his ability to narrate. Communities fail or become anticommunities: by killing their cattle, the Zhosa tribe mistakenly hastens its own downfall; Philadelphia citizens turn against themselves in response to the plague; the racially mixed congregation of St. Matthew's splits along racial lines; the healthy African-American community of Radnor is destroyed; locked in the cellar at night, the orphans become an anticommunity where individuality is erased and brutality thrives. For African-American characters, "this New World [is] a graveyard for African people" and "a country where madness reigns" (127), and "God's absence [is] confirmed by evil everywhere raging" (157). The young preacher cannot think of a story with a happy ending, because for him the world is "upside-down" (31) and a "vale of tears" (107), in which, echoing the slaughterhouse imagery, "people

[are] an unbroken chain of sausages fed in one end and pulled out the other" (149).

In this grim world, characters have visions and dreams that resemble traditional Christian imagery of apocalyptic purging and an earthly paradise to come, as in the young preacher's post-epileptic visions during which he "glimpse[s] a world sweet as it must have been, and still is, if we had but eyes to see it, before the Fall" (57). The boy preacher also chooses an apocalyptic passage from the Book of Jeremiah for his worship service ("Behold, I am making my words in your mouth a fire, and this people wood, and the fire shall devour them"), and, echoing Revelation, he hears the approaching beast ready to "lay waste this sinful land" (67). He is convinced that "the broken kingdom" will be "restored" (144), that an idyllic new order will follow the purging: "A day is coming, soon enough, in God's good time, when wolf and lion and lamb shall lie down together" (99). The projection of an apocalypse followed by a new order is also voiced by Bishop Allen, who leads his black congregation to its separate church, as he "calls on Heaven to purge whatever it is the whites fear and hate in him" in his "prayer for sweet annihilation" (159).

These evocations of a purging apocalypse, however traditional and appealing, are called into question in several respects. First, at the end of his narration the boy preacher loses his faith in God and presumably therefore in his belief in such a redemptive future. Second, the clearly disprivileged Mrs. Thrush uses similar imagery to explain the plague to the black orphans: "God sent the fever to purge us. To cleanse. To humble us, the blind one said. We who have survived must struggle to build a new city. A better city" (194). In the mouth of a hypocrite, such a vision is not terribly appealing. Third, at the beginning of part 2, Wideman quotes Ezekiel's warning against false prophets, suggesting that predictions of a redemptive apocalypse, like the Zhosa girl's unfortunate prophesy that all the cattle should be killed, should not be trusted. The ending of the boy's narration resolves the ambiguity by rejecting prophecies that urge self-destruction or that tolerate suffering as preparation for a visionary future. In a voice that sounds much more like Wideman than the boy, he warns of impending doom in modernistic terms: "I must warn you there are always machines hovering in the air, giant insects with the power to swoop down spattering death, clean out the square in a matter of instants" (206). But he then asserts that the air is also filled with prophecies that are "deadlier than machines" and mocks the prophets who predict that "a better world will be born" if "you deny yourselves, transform yourselves, destroy yourselves" (207). He denounces all such prophets, like those of "the cattle killing," those of "Kool-Aid" (a reference to the senseless slaughter of the Jim Jones cult), and those of all the other prophets urging people to "bend over and take it in your ear," to put up with misery and mistreatment, to accept less than they deserve. Wideman rejects the traditional African-American narrative of a future apocalypse and a new day because that narrative is too linear, too formulaic, too deterministic. It is a one-way track from the present, based on the past, into the future. Wideman is more interested in open orientations toward time, perspectives that allow ultimate transcendence of chronology rather than the following of a monologic script.

Whereas prophecy is often destructive, storytelling allows Wideman such transcendence and therefore is the most potent, and necessary, response to the novel's dehumanizing conditions. By proliferating stories, storytellers, listeners, settings, and times, he develops this theme, and the associated technique of tangling his own narrative threads, more fully than in his previous novels. He surrounds the main narrative with frame stories. In the first of these, his persona is at a conference where he will read some of his fiction and where he visits his father, who he hopes will listen to him read and "be part of the story" (14). In the closing frame story, his son, Dan, having already read the embedded novel, comments on it, both to himself (209) and in his letter to his father (210). Within the tale proper, the primary storyteller is the boy preacher and the primary listener is Kathryn as the boy tells her the stories related to their finding each other. In addition, the young preacher is an effective listener, enabling Liam to identify with the preacher as he listens to Liam's stories about spying on young Stubbs and feeling the power of listening when "every morning I listen for [Mrs. Stubbs's] listening. Teaching myself the shape, the texture of her listening, how it changes the silence" (138).

Especially in this novel, Wideman requires the reader's concentration. He often changes tenses unexpectedly, sometimes in the same paragraph, usually moving from the past into the more immediate present. He routinely shifts between first and third person for the same narrator, and identification of narrators, characters, and settings is often delayed or ambiguous. Besides blurring these traditional boundaries, Wideman also blends apparent biography and fiction, historical research and fiction, and fantasy and reality. The shifting narration, the Chinese-box like narrations and subnarrations, and the metafictional conflation of fiction and autobiography create a rich collage of voices, perspectives, and stories. Like other Wideman texts, this one is richly intertextual, with references to several of Wideman's own works; allusions to other literary works, such as Samuel Richardson's *Pamela* and Phillis Wheatley's poetry; and inclusion of historical figures, such as the painter George Stubbs and the physician John Burton.

Such narrative complexity has a purpose. Since each person is a composite of multiple selves and since communities are composed of the infinite relationships among their members, stories that accurately reflect individuals and communities must be correspondingly complex. Thus, the "author" mixes his present identity as an accomplished writer with himself as a fifteen-year-old like the boy about whose murder he has just read (13), and "Mrs. Stubbs," known only by her alias, is repeatedly described as not merely her present "self" but her many younger selves as well. More convoluted is the identity, or identities, of the young preacher's lover and auditor, who, rather than a single person, is a composite drawn from multiple, related stories: the beautiful young woman who gives the preacher a drink of water after one of his epileptic fits; the young woman with the baby; Kathryn, the Thrushes' maid, who becomes the preacher's lover and is raped by Dr. Thrush; and the "sick lady" whom the preacher hopes to cure by telling the stories.

Readers are led to hope that all these characters are the same woman, but the chronology does not work. It does not work because for Wideman linear time inaccurately represents the complexities of human experience. Since human consciousness constantly roams backward in memory and forward in hopes, fears, and visions, his novels are emphatically nonlinear. Consequently, *The Cattle Killing* abounds in foreshadowing, flashbacks, and interpolated times, often moving backward in chronological time rather than forward. When the preacher's auditor surmises, "I thought stories always go backward," the preacher responds, "Backward to go forward. Forward to go back" (54). Because for Wideman the intricate webs of individual and communal consciousness never begin or end, the novel, like the preacher's stories, must be "untidy," must have "No beginnings nor ends" (29).

The young preacher's stories deepen the mutual empathy and love between him and his "sick lady," for he, like Wideman, knows that "all stories" are returns to "memory, possibility, life" (55). Here, as in other Wideman novels, there are endless stories and endless versions of stories, for example in the several renditions of the story of the black maid and the blond baby. Like Doot in *Sent for You Yesterday,* the young preacher has learned Wideman's principle: he "believed each story" about the baby, for he had learned from "the old African people, who said all stories are true" (53).

Wideman himself, as listener to all the voices and then as teller of his stories, embodies the entwined roles of witness/testifier, a position he makes explicit in the prologue: "What he shared with the eighteenth-century African boy whose story he wanted to tell, the thing he would try to write . . . would be testimony witnessing what surrounds them at this very moment, an encompassing silence forgetting them both, silence untouched by their passing, by the countless passings of so many others like them, a world distant and abiding and memoryless" (13). Wideman's persona can be a witness/testifier because he shares the African-American experience with the young preacher, and he must be a witness/testifier because otherwise no one might remember and silence might prevail.

Convinced of the necessity of storytelling and listening, Wideman extends his exploration by contemplating the end of the storytelling power and of the existence of stories. Like the near paralysis of each protagonist in *Philadelphia Fire,* the boy preacher also loses the power to tell stories after the orphanage burns. First, he loses his faith in God (203), and then he begins to stutter, "losing [his] facility in this language" (205). His collapse is more foreboding than are those in *Philadelphia Fire* because in that novel Wideman's persona recovers to continue writing and narrating, but here the boy does stop. Moreover, he stops after concluding that his stories are not doing any good, are not curing Kathryn, despite her affirmation that "they save me" (203): "Time now to give it up. This speaking in a strange tongue, this stranger's voice I struggle to assume in order to keep you alive. The stories are not working. I talk, maybe you listen, but you're not better, not stronger" (205). "The language [is] coming apart in [his] hands" (205), a disaster for a storyteller. Readers do not know if Kathryn is physically ill or if the boy's stories could actually save her, but when he stops telling them, she perforce stops listening. Her fictional existence depends on his continuing to narrate, so, when he stops telling, she does "die." Much earlier, the boy narrator speculates on the ontological status of his auditor during the gaps in his stories: "When I omit parts of the story, do I relinquish my hold on you. When the tale jumps to a different place, where do you go" (39). At that point he "can't bear to think this single telling is my last chance, my only chance to be here with you" (39). Both passages call the reader's attention to the interdependence of listener and speaker and to the dependence of the former's existence on the latter's telling. Therefore, the narrator's loss of language at the end of the novel symbolically kills both the narrator and the helpless listener. This pessimistic mood is exacerbated by the ensuing shift to the "time to tell the last story" (206). If such a time really came, the last story itself might end, which would mean the deaths of all storytellers and all listeners—in effect, the end of human life.

But Wideman and the boy avoid that dire situation by affirming that the last story will be continuously passed on from speaker to speaker and will join and save speaker and listener, living and dead: sounding very like Wideman, the boy preacher lyrically promises to tell his listener, and therefore the reader, all the stories, "to bring you as gifts, stories of my dead to keep you alive" (206). The stories of each of the cities of the United States are "different stories over and over again that are one story," each one passing on the memory and the life "in one of the cities where I search for you, to join you, save you, save myself, tell you stories so my dead are not strangers, so they walk and talk, so they will know us and welcome us. Free us. To love" (207). For Wideman, only our stories can cure us, unify us, teach us to be human: "Aren't we lovers first, spirits sharing an uncharted space, a space our stories tell, a space chanted, written upon again and again, yet one story never quite erased by the next, each story saving the space, saving itself, saving us. If someone is listening" (208).

The shift out of linear time into Great Time coalesces with Wideman's abiding interests in community, in the tensions between individual isolation and communal unity. It also becomes a vehicle for Wideman's vision of the power of people to make and remake the world through their imaginations, their seeing. Only in Great Time—"one day neither in the past nor future and not this moment either" (*Fatheralong* 177)—can the myth of the people telling the stories that shape the world be actualized. In *The Cattle Killing*, Wideman lifts his narrative into Great Time, so that it exists simultaneously with the novel itself, like the stories that the boy preacher tells to Kathryn and that Liam tells to the boy, like the manuscript that Dan has "just" read, and like the "last story" continuing forever in the reader's mind. In such mythic time and space, the potential of merging one's consciousness with the cosmos reaches perfection as self and Other become indivisible: "the world was one sight, one luminous presence inventing his eyes" (69).

"Always yes and always no" encapsulates Wideman's open-ended vision of the complications of life. Even in *Sent for You Yesterday*, perhaps his most optimistic novel, the current of fear and doubt runs deep. Correspondingly, in his bleakest novel, *Philadelphia Fire*, he finds the hope to live on, as at the end of the novel Cudjoe is able "to turn to face whatever it is rumbling over the stones of Independence Square" (199). Imagining the destruction of a community and the loss of its youth is nightmarish but is not the end of life's story. Reimmersing oneself in one's home, family, and community, as in *Sent for You Yesterday*, is cause for celebration but likewise is not the end of the story.

It makes sense for Wideman that stories should have open endings and multiple meanings and layers, like onions (*Fatheralong* 61), for the greater the number of versions, possible answers, and interpretations, the thicker the communal and cultural web of connected subjectivities. Even a simple sentence cannot be pinned down to a simple "answer" or meaning: "Like a sentence with seven clear, simple words and you understand each word but the meaning of the sentence totally eludes you" (*Fatheralong* 61). Wideman wants sentences to elude him, his characters, and his readers, just as he wants his endings open, for answers are endpoints, boundaries in the otherwise seamless fabric of individual and communal consciousnesses.

Wideman's desire for openness is also expressed in his preference for an inclusive both/and approach rather than a dichotomous either/or one.[7] His writing is suffused with assertions that anything can be simultaneously one thing and its opposite: it was "easy" and "impossible" for "John" and his brother to talk (*Brothers* 80), Reuben being in jail was funny and not funny (*Reuben* 184), the rain is "there and not there" (*Cattle* 133). Frequently, such embracing of both sides of a supposed opposition involves the dichotomy between material presence or absence—with Albert Wilkes "it's not a matter of being gone but being here and being gone both" (*Sent* 70). By accepting both sides, Wideman asserts that the material/nonmaterial opposition is not really an opposition, that only thinking makes it so, and that therefore thinking can make it not so. The oppositions dissolve as the primacy of the mind's power is realized.

Wideman wants to replace the traditional Western orientation toward an either/or perspective with a more African and holistic orientation. He rejects the former: "With the same blind, relentless logic of the computer whirring through the billion off/on choices of its circuitry, the Western mind set seems disposed to conquer by dividing, apprehending the world in polarized terms of either/or" (*Fatheralong* 68). He worries when his mother drifts into a Manichean worldview in response to Robby's imprisonment: "Everything was clean and clear. No room for her sense that things like good and evil, right and wrong bleed into each other and create a dreadful margin of ambiguity no one could name but could only enter" (*Brothers* 71). Racial distinctions in America are inseparable from this concern, for race is the central limiting opposition for African Americans. Living with race is not something that happens again, that stops and starts, that has discrete boundaries; instead, it is continuous: "the burden of our personal and collective history" is "that these things never stop" (*Fatheralong* 107). As Wideman asserts, "race can mean everything or nothing" (*Fatheralong* xii), and as the enlightened boy preacher knows when asked if he is black, "Yes, madam. And no" (*Cattle* 168).

For Wideman, the necessity of a both/and perspective is more general than race. For his epigraph to *Fatheralong,* he quotes Goethe on the unity of all things: "Ever splitting the light! How often do they strive to divide that which, despite everything, would always remain single and whole." The riddle can be ethical (King, the leader of MOVE, is "always" "right *and* wrong" [*Philadelphia* 15]) or historical (the circles of civilizations are "expanding and contracting at once" [*Cattle* 149]). Life requires the embrace of both sides of alleged oppositions: neither yes nor no but "always yes and always no" (*Sent* 115; *Reuben* 199); not somewhere or somewhere else but "everywhere" and "no where"

(*Philadelphia* 184). The boy preacher in *The Cattle Killing* is Wideman's most recent spokesman: "No time. All time. Rain transparent as the years. Nowhere, everywhere, escaping the canvas" (133). In Wideman's web of interconnected consciousnesses, a both/and perspective is necessary: not one version over another, but all versions; not one preferred story, but all stories; not one mind, but all minds; not one mode of consciousness, but all modes. Only then is there a possibility of overcoming isolation, of passing through the needle's eye of external exigencies into the holistic web of interconnected minds that comprises community, binds families, and nourishes identities.

3

"ACROSS THE BORDERS"

Imagining the Future in Toni Cade Bambara's
The Salt Eaters

As in Wideman's fiction, Toni Cade Bambara's 1980 novel depicts the struggle between isolation and breakdown on the one hand and community and wholeness on the other. For Bambara, the crisis is not as biographical as it is for Wideman but is more explicitly endemic, encompassing individuals, families, communities, American society, and the entire globe and involving psychological, social, economic, political, and environmental dimensions. Because the crisis is universal, the forces needed for recovery must be eclectic. To restore balance and harmony at all levels, people must tap into all possible sources of energy, must value all cultural forms, must study all disciplines, must acquire all possible forms of knowledge. For human beings to go forth into a revitalized future, they must reexamine and revalue everything from the past. Recovery depends on the combined mental and spiritual efforts of all human beings, as they reassemble their shattered psyches and reconnect the damaged communal fabric. Bambara's vision leads to the certainty of passage into an unknown future. That passage will be difficult and violent, it will require more work than anyone can imagine, and it will transcend all known limits. But the work will be productive and satisfying, replacing the meaninglessness of the present with the harmonious and fulfilling integration of individuals and society.

The Salt Eaters takes place during one afternoon in the fictional, southern city of Claybourne, during which individuals, couples, groups, and community institutions—and by extension the whole city, African-American culture, American society, and all human beings—endure their crises and approach their dangerous passages to an uncharted but radically new future. Through the interlocking stories of dozens of residents, Bambara enumerates the problems causing disunity in the community, in the society, and within individuals; suggests numerous forces and skills that may help restore wholeness; and hints at the parameters of the visionary city of the future.

Critics of *The Salt Eaters* have established several points of consensus. The movement of the novel is from social and psychological fragmentation toward spiritual wholeness. The novel's chaotic form, which shifts radically from consciousness to consciousness and from locale to locale, parallels its content. Both form and content privilege nonlinearity and multiplicity, and both require open-endedness, an open-endedness that prevents Bambara from being specific about the imagined future.[1] In addition to this consensus, Margot Anne Kelley ("Damballah") applies chaos theory to the novel, which provides a useful frame for interpreting its structure and themes. In his analysis, Elliott Butler-Evans comes closest to my approach. He sees the paradoxical representation of both a utopia and a dystopia in the novel's "deconstruction and reconstruction of the immediate historical past, and its questioning and subverting of its own enterprise" (177). For me, the novel's depiction of utopian and dystopian elements is not paradoxical but progressive—that is, the essential thrust of the novel is not the simultaneity of such elements but the sequential movement from problems to constructive energies and finally to a futuristic vision.

The problems in Claybourne are legion. At all levels—from the cosmic to the social to the individual—disruption, fragmentation, imbalance, and uncertainty prevail. The world, Claybourne, and most of the characters are out of kilter: like Lorraine's pottery wheel, they are spinning, but "something ain't right" (115), they are "off-balance" and "the beat's just off. . . . Way off" (116). The world has become a wasteland,[2] a "waste-howling wilderness" (46), characterized by "body/mind/spirit out of nexus, out of tune, out of line, off beat, off color, in a spin off its axis, affairs aslant, wisdom at a tangent" (49). Community, families, and individuals have suffered "an accumulation of fissures in the fabric" (232), for, as Susan Willis puts it, "the people have become a sundered memory whose lives are as irretrievable as a whole bottle from its shards" (138).

The novel's social and psychological wasteland is figured by images of war. Differing community factions become divided into "camps" (147), and "abstractionists make good bombardiers, good military beasts" (31). Velma Henry dreams of war (218), and her memories of civil rights demonstrations resemble war scenes, complete with her bleeding (38). She pictures herself as the "borderguard" (5), posted on the frontier to ward off all enemies, whether of the family, the movement, or the self.[3]

The dominant symbol for this wasteland is poisoning and disease. The world and its people have become sick and need to be healed, hence the setting in the Infirmary and the plot's focus on Minnie Ransom's attempt to heal Velma. Various characters express concerns about poisons and disease: "Legionnaires' disease is just the beginning" (69); "we are dying from overexposure to some kind of wasting shit—the radioactive crap, asbestos particles, noise, smog, lies" (79); and "as if the big shots cared a hoot about safety gloves and ventilation and special ways to deal with asbestos and them poisons down there" (108–9). The air is polluted by smoke from the city's largest factory, the Transchemical plant (207, 233), and even a bad tooth can become an "abscess, poisoning your system" (227).

Nuclear poisoning is the most frequently mentioned environmental danger. The groundwater in nearby Barnwell is being poisoned by radioactive leaching (225, 234, 245); the chemical plant is rumored to be shipping trainloads of radioactive sludge through town (69, 207); Fred Holt's friend, Porter, suffered from nuclear radiation ("Some kind of wasting disease was eating him up. Yucca Flats, 1955, atomic test blasts" [80]); and Velma has a waking nightmare about children digging up contaminated clothing and instruments (274). Minnie, the novel's primary healer, is concerned about healing not just Velma but the whole earth: "How we gonna rescue this planet from them radioactive mutants?" (46).

In addition to such environmental threats, Claybourne suffers economically. Two characters—Fred and Jan—remark on the deteriorating factories built after World War II (71, 243). Fred, seeing homeless men along the highway, frets that "it could be the Depression all over again" (70), and, barely earning enough to live on, he is anxious about keeping his job. Economic development consists of destruction rather than construction, pictured in the "huge plain of mud" littered with the detritus of a former neighborhood by which Fred drives (71), reminding him of Pruitt-Igo, the infamous public housing project in St. Louis that had to be razed soon after it was built (73). Behind the economic stagnation are tense labor-management relations, particularly at Transchemical. Characters express their antagonism against the "big shots" who run the factory (71, 108), Velma is in trouble for destroying many of the company's computer files, and the plant allegedly is sending "goons" to infiltrate Claybourne neighborhoods (187). Claybourne as a whole is said to be "on edge" (257) and unsure of its identity (181), like "the back wards of the asylum" (216).

At the same time that the town is politically fragmented, the African-American movement is undergoing a crisis. Obie remembers when "everyone seemed to be pulling in the same direction" (98) and laments the current "factions," "intrigue," and "old ideological splits" (90). His world—not just the movement and the community but also his psyche and his marriage to Velma—seem irremediably fragmented to the extent that, early in the novel, he can foresee only widening gaps: "And tomorrow the polarities would have sharpened, the splits widened" (90).

Obie's perceptions are verified throughout the novel. The previous year's spring festival was disrupted by a riot. Leaders like Obie and Velma seem unsure of their ability to lead, and the people seem unsure of where and by whom they want to be led. The 7 Arts Academy is split by warring factions, and its functions,

even its name, are in dispute (92–93). The worst fracture is between African-American men and African-American women, the
women having become fed up with doing all the work while the
men do all the posturing. In response to the polished but empty
rhetoric of Jay Patterson, the women form their own group,
Women for Action.

Possible causes for the splintering of the movement are only
hinted at, but the novel, published in 1980, is set in the disillu-
sionment that followed the black power movement. Previous African-American heroes are cited (such as Harriet Tubman,
Frederick Douglass, and W. E. B. Du Bois), as are contemporary
African-American leaders like Martin Luther King, Jr., Malcolm
X, and Stokely Carmichael, but Claybourne residents seem to
have no meaningful connections with such heros. Activism, like
the town itself, seems to be suspended, poised between one era's
identity and another's. Speaking about Women for Action, Ruby
says, "We're at the crossroads and we gonna have to decide the
shape, scope, thrust, and general whatnot and so forth of this
group" (37). As with so much in this novel, her words apply
equally well at other levels. The city—and by extension the
whole country—is similarly at a crossroads, on the brink.

In parallel fashion, individual characters are at various turning
points, all ready for another passage, a shift to a new condition.
They are thus at a collective and individual moment, as chaos
theory describes, when change will occur, but the characteristics
of the change cannot be foreseen.[4] Collectively and individually,
all have suffered the "loss of trust, breakdowns on the afrophone,
misleadings and misreadings" (232) that Velma and Obie have
endured. All need a restored sense of unity and community.

In short, they need to eat salt with each other. For, as Sophie
Heywood wisely opines, "you never really know a person until
you've eaten salt together" (147). Salt brings people together, and
it helps integrate each individual by keeping the body's chemis-
try in harmony. With just the right amount of salt, the body can
maintain its equilibrium, so Ahiro advises Obie that crying is
therapeutic: "the body needs to throw off its excess salt for bal-

ance" (164). Too much salt also upsets the body's balance, leading to ossification in the extreme case of Lot's wife (257, 259). Salt is also touted as an antidote for snakebite (8, 257–58), which seems especially useful in a setting where snakes abound. But salt is two edged—it is an antidote for physical wounds from literal snakes, but it is no remedy for the serpent's venom and, in excess, is equivalent to "succumbing to the serpent" (8). As opposed to flesh-and-blood snakes, serpents are cultural or mythic constructs. Folk wisdom in Claybourne's African-American community can provide antidotes for the physical bites of real snakes, but remedies for culturally created "monsters" are not so readily found.

Snakes themselves are also curiously ambiguous in this novel, both part of the novel's multileveled crisis and a potential source of healing and new energy. One must stomp the ground to drive them away (52), and a passenger's basket of snakes disgusts and frightens Fred Holt (78). Insidiously, they can get inside people's heads, becoming metaphors for insanity or at least torment (60). They are most frequently associated with women's heads and hair, à la Medusa, but this image is particularly double. Early in the novel, Velma "fight[s] off the woman with snakes in her hair" (8), but then Minnie describes Velma as like a "basket of snakes on a pole" (42), and Campbell, infatuated with Jan, says that "it looked like she carried a basket of snakes on her head" (195). At the end of the novel, the Medusa allusion becomes explicit, first when Velma identifies with the mythical woman ("She would not have cut Medusa's head off" [257]), and then when she imagines infinite energy and sublime oneness with the cosmos when she would "dance off into space with snakes in her hair and tusks sprouting from her gums and her head thrown back" (265). The doubleness of both salt and snakes is significant: either can destroy or empower. Regaining a balance, getting just the right proportions, handling them just right, is crucial.

Since *The Salt Eaters* is based on parallels among the cosmos, society, community, individuals, and the novel's form, many of the problems affecting Claybourne as a whole are also manifested in individuals. Many of the characters are physically tight, unable to relax or to move freely. As the novel and Velma's healing session begin, she is physically bound up: "Velma Henry turned stiffly on the stool, the gown ties tight across her back, the knots hard. So taut for so long, she could not swivel. Neck, back hip joints dry, stiff. Face frozen" (3). She is so tight that she is not herself: "She could not glower, suck her teeth, roll her eyes, do any of the Velma-things by way of answering Minnie Ransom" (3). Later, she reports in flashbacks that she "felt like the lump of clay" (115) that Lorraine was trying to throw, and she recalls the bad feeling "at the pit of her stomach" (231) when she accused Obie of adultery. Similar language describes the physical tightness of other characters. Obie is almost as tense as Velma: he feels "a sack of stones swaying in his chest" (94) and "tight muscles and joints" (160). Fred's stomach is so upset from the chili he had for lunch that he vomits and his stomach is still "throbbing" (160) when he reaches the Infirmary. Even Sophie, one of the healers, is almost overcome by "weariness," "a wave of nausea" (146), and "the buzzing throb in her temples and the lift and drop in her stomach" (147).

Like Sophie, many of the characters are weary, not so much physically tired as tired of their political struggles. Ruby is tired of "taking on everything" (243) and "tired of worrying about Velma" (216). Obie is stressed out because of the excessive demands he feels: "Velma wanted him. The folks wanted him. His brother Roland wanted him. And oh did the cops want him" (286). Velma tried to kill herself and has now retreated into herself because she too is weary of her life and the demands placed on her. The characters' burnout results from their overcommitment, particularly Velma and Obie, who have unsuccessfully tried to do too much in balancing their individual identities, their family, their jobs, and the community.

One reaction to this stress is to seal oneself off from everyone else in a deathlike stasis. Fred recalls being told that "he was a four," lots of whom were too "busy feeling boxed in by the four sides of their nature" (77). Since his loss of his friend, Porter, and his first wife, Wanda, he has boxed himself into his own reflections and memories, bound in a moribund relationship with his second wife, Margie, and alienated from his job and his passengers.[5] More extremely than Fred, Velma has withdrawn into herself in a destructively defensive posture, "steeling herself against intrusion" and reverting to her childhood role of guardian, formerly to ward off bill collectors from Mama Mae's house, now to "throw up the barrier and place the borderguard" against Minnie (5). Congruent with her attempted suicide, she fantasizes total isolation in an airtight glass jar: "To be that sealed—sound, taste, air, nothing seeping in. To be that unavailable at last, sealed in and the noise of the world, the garbage, locked out" (19).

Characters exhibit numerous isolating traits. Many do not talk: Velma is silent throughout almost the entire novel, so silent that her growl is a significant sign (40); Fred, in contrast to his loquacious passengers, drives in silence and in town says almost nothing. Other characters, such as Ruby and Cora Rider, although not socially isolated, nevertheless withdraw into egotistical attitudes. Even Doc Serge, a community leader and potential healer, places his ego first in his rambling speech to Buster (126) and in his paean to self-love (152). Julius Meadows and Fred Holt demonstrate their narrow perspectives by stereotyping others, and Ruby and Fred take out their frustrations in anger at others. Not surprisingly, many characters have difficulty in their relationships to others. Obie and Velma's marriage is in serious trouble, Fred cannot stand Margie, Jan and Ruby spend most of their time arguing, and Buster and Nadeen seem to be heading in opposite directions.

In such physically tight, mentally locked-in, and egotistical states, the characters are not only isolated from the community but also cut off from the past and the future. They deny both as they try to escape from the present, and yet, overwhelmed, they cannot imagine the unknown of another passage. They exist in a temporal, psychological, and communal limbo in which the past is inaccessible, the present intolerable, and the future unimaginable and in which the intersubjective web and their individual identities are unraveling.

Given their preoccupations with self, the characters might be expected to have considerable self-knowledge, but many do not. Just as Velma can not recognize herself as she sits tensely on Minnie's stool, Obie "didn't recognize himself" and "didn't recognize [Velma] either" (94). His life and self are in shambles: "His whole johnson was getting raggedy—his home, his work. . . . He was not taking care of business." Similarly, Fred realizes that he has come to the Infirmary "to figure out where he was and who was who" (270).

One reason for such difficulties of self-recognition is that many characters are divided into two or more selves. Meadows listens to his "country self" with his "city mind" (122). Obie lingers in a doubled, semiconscious state, "trying to coax the subconscious to surrender the plan, to surface, take over, and reveal something he knew he must know to pull it all together. But dodging it too" (285). Velma is the most seriously split. While Minnie speaks to her, she remains partially "in a telepathic visit with her former self who seemed to be still there in the kitchen reenacting the scene" of her attempted suicide (18). That she is double is confirmed by Buster, who "saw two faces at once on Mrs. Henry" (58). Later, as she apparently progresses back toward sanity, the problem is to restore her whole self: "the divinely healthy whole Velma waited to be called out of its chamber, embraced and directed down the hall to claim her life from the split imposter" (148). Near the end of the novel, she is still double, and, like Violet in Toni Morrison's *Jazz*, she contemplates her other self, "the woman next to her" (259), and speculates that "maybe the thing to do was invite the self by for coffee and a chat." Even as she recovers, she may be splitting apart: "She could be coming apart, totally losing her self. That woman in the park, who was that but another her, a part?" (262). The novel's troubled characters are torn apart by self-doubt and failure of will, and Doc Serge is worried about them, for "there was no charge, no tension, no stuff in these young people's passage" (135).

As a result of such internal division, Velma feels unbalanced and uncentered. As the novel begins she "perche[s] uneasily on the edge of her stool" (6), a precarious position that expresses her individual mental fragility and her community's lack of connectedness. Her flashbacks of herself participating in demonstrations and marches focus on her physical, emotional, and spiritual disarray. In one memory she "had no control over her feet. No control over her head either" (40), and her problematic menstrual bleeding suggests her bodily chaos. Jan realizes that "Velma's never been the center of her own life" (240), and Velma herself comes to understand her difficulties of "maintain[ing] the right balance there, the personal and the public" (241), even though she thought "she knew how to build resistance, make the journey to the center of the circle, stay poised and centered in the work and not fly off, stay centered in the best of her people's traditions" (258). Velma's husband, Obie, has had a similar problem, "trying to maintain equilibrium, trying to find a balance between the longing for clarity and the dread of finding too great a challenge of reunion" (285). Both Velma and Obie have been thrown off balance in their attempts to lead the community and to have satisfactory personal lives, but Bambara implies that to succeed as a leader, personal balance and self-knowledge are essential. Before continuing the journey, before undertaking the next passage, one must center oneself.

Such internal splits and imbalances create a sense that characters are confused about their lives and values. In addition to Velma and Fred, who are most obviously suffering life crises, Palma, Velma's sister, is puzzled about her life and values. She is part of the Seven Sisters but also is falling in love with Marcus Hampden, and she is pulled toward Velma in the latter's crisis but is simultaneously critical of her. Psychologically disoriented, Palma "could not quite get her bearings" (141). Meadows, uncomfortable with his profession and the Hippocratic oath, does not know whether to stay at the healing session or leave (54–55) and feels socially worthless: "his presence or absence mattered to no one, not even to his patients he worried over through the nights" (58). Like Velma and Fred, he has lost himself, and later when he becomes literally lost in a poor neighborhood of Claybourne, that confusion serves as an emblem for his identity confusion. When Thurston or Hull asks, "You lost? . . . In some kind of trouble?" (186), he has no response because he is deeply lost and in serious psychological trouble.

Meadows's failure to respond is part of a strong motif of unanswered questions throughout the novel.[6] Characters frequently ask questions of themselves or of their interlocutors, and in both cases there are seldom any answers. The novel starts with one such question and nonreply: "Are you sure, sweetheart, that you want to be well?" (3). The pattern is reinforced when Minnie repeatedly asks Velma similar questions and Velma repeatedly does not answer: "You ready?" (8); "Are you sure, sweetheart?" (15); "Can you afford to be whole?" (106); and "What will you do when you are well?" (220).

As in Minnie's series of questions, many of the unanswered questions ask about the future. An unnamed visitor watching the healing wonders aloud what everyone's course of action should be: "So whadda we supposed to do, stand here for this comedy?" (17). Obie wonders, "Where to take the Academy? And where was his partnership going? What was he to do about Roland, about Velma, about anybody?" (99). Such questions intimate the novel's more pervasive speculations about the future—not merely what someone should do about the healing or what Obie should do about his life, but more universally, what all people should do about their lives and about all humanity.

Other questions ask about the present, in the form of either "What's happening?" or "What's wrong?" When Fred slows the bus down, one of the musicians on board asks him, "What's happening, my man?" (73), a question Fred does not answer because, taking the question in its broadest form, Fred has no idea. Like Meadows, Fred is lost and in trouble and therefore cannot respond to the question. In his thoughts he considers the wider sense of the question: "Exactly. What? Everything ruined and wrecked, made old and garbage before its time." At the healing, on the bus, throughout the novel, characters cannot answer basic questions because they are confused about themselves and the events around them.

Reflecting such concerns, many characters are worried about each other: Jan wonders "What's the matter with you here lately, Ruby?" (193), Palma is anxious about Velma (141), and Sophie (147) and Minnie (42) continually fret about Velma. These specific anxieties reflect the characters' general nervousness about their own lives. When Palma is greeted by Marcus, her series of unanswered questions about what is happening to Velma leads to her underlying fear: "Was everything really all right?" (141). And Minnie's concern for Velma is part of her broader concern for all women: "What is wrong with the women? . . . What is wrong, Old Wife? What is happening to the daughters of the yam?" (43–44).

This pattern of unanswered questions extends the characters' anxieties about each other and their lives to the reader. The reader also wonders what is happening and what is wrong. When Minnie asks Velma "What's your story?" (9), the reader, reading a novel with Velma as the central character, also questions what Velma's story is—that is, what the novel's story and meanings are. But since no answers are provided for the characters, none are provided for the reader, so that the reader shares in the novel's indeterminedness, its chaos, its sense of crisis. Near the beginning of the novel, Velma reflects twice that "anything could happen" (5), which refers not only to her situation but also to the novel as a whole. The reader is thus warned to expect the unexpected and is promised the novel's openness. On all levels and among all participants, questions must be asked to help move participants beyond their paralyzing stasis, yet answers cannot be given, cannot even be known, for known answers would produce merely a new stagnation, a different stasis.

That openness is reiterated in two exchanges between Minnie and Old Wife. In the first, Old Wife twice responds to Minnie's questions with more questions. When Minnie asks, " 'What ought I do about the Henry gal, Old Wife?', Old Wife counters with

'Don't you know?' "; and when Minnie asks, " 'You studying?', Old Wife is again evasive: 'You? You making the most of your situation, Min?' " (49). Minnie then calls attention to this evasive strategy: "I ask a question, you answer with a question." Then, at the novel's end Minnie asks Old Wife a series of questions, again unanswered, about time and reality: "None of this ain't happened yet? Some of this is happening now? All of this is going on, but I ain't here? All of the above? None of the above? Will you at least tell me, is it raining or not?" (295). The force of these questions is not directed at Minnie herself, for she has shown throughout the novel her levelheadedness and secure sense of self. Instead, they apply more fully to the novel itself. In this novel, not only can anything happen and not only do questions have further questions rather than answers, but also things may not have happened, may happen in the future, and/or may happen to other characters than those depicted. The pattern of question and nonresponse is thus paradigmatic of the novel.

Paul Grice's theory of conversational implicature is relevant here. Grice argues that conversations are usually governed by the "Cooperative Principle," namely "make your conversational contribution such as is required, at the stage at which it occurs, by the accepted purpose or direction of the talk exchange in which you are engaged" (26). He then defines four categories that yield maxims by which one obeys the Cooperative Principle: Quantity requires one to "make [one's] contribution as informative as is required" for the current purposes of the exchange; Quality is "do not say what you believe to be false" and "do not say that for which you lack adequate evidence" (27); Relation dictates that one "be relevant"; and Manner simply means "Avoid ambiguity." Not answering another's question appears to violate the maxims of Quantity, for the nonresponding respondent is quite uninformative, and of Manner, for not answering usually creates ambiguity. Responding with another question or with a nonanswer may also violate the maxim of Relation. Conversely, if the respondent "lacks adequate evidence"—in other words, has no valid answer—then answering would violate the maxim of

Quality. Presumably, the cooperative response to unanswerable questions would be to acknowledge, "I don't know." In any case, the prevalence of the question/nonresponse pattern, augmented by the absences of such acknowledgments, is evidence that the text of *The Salt Eaters* radically violates Grice's maxims, that it is not a cooperative text. It lacks Grice's sense of cooperation because the multitiered crisis enveloping the residents of Claybourne has disconnected them from the intersubjective social web and severely disrupted the web itself. Since they are out of touch with the past, confused in the present, worried about the future, mixed up in their identities, and at odds with each other, their conversations and therefore the novel's discourse cannot be cooperative.

To explore alternatives to this disharmony, Bambara strives for different kinds of engagement with reality and with the reader, types of engagement that are apparent in the healing forces in the novel. Characters, Claybourne, and by implication American society as well as the entire cosmos, move gradually toward health and wholeness, but the process is nonlinear, moving sometimes forward, sometimes backward, and sometimes aimlessly. In similar fashion, many of the forces of recovery are not wholly separable from the problems themselves. Just as the form of the book is nonlinear, so any presumed cause-and-effect logic between problems and potential solutions is not one dimensional.

Multiplicity is a prime example of such a two-edged parameter. As discussed earlier, for many characters—principally Velma—internal division into multiple selves or parts of the self is indicative of their psychological confusion. Conversely, multiplicity is often a powerful, eclectic force. For several characters—characters who are "together" and who help heal others and the community—openness to multiplicity is strongly valued.

One such character is Campbell, who emerges in the last third of the book as a unifying influence. Physically, as he waits on their tables, he links isolated groups of characters, thereby creating an informal community at the cafe. He is a jack-of-all-trades: a waiter, a writer, an inventor, a wooer. Carrying coins from many countries (173) and understanding allusions to a potpourri of cultures and disciplines (210), he embodies multiplicity and global interconnectedness. He can explain such things as fission and thermonuclear dynamics "in the language of down-home Bible-quoting folks" (210), and he can integrate the material and spiritual realms, meshing spirits and mythical deities with environmental reports on the weather (210–11). Able to bridge the rift between the material and spiritual realms (92), he becomes one of Bambara's spokespersons, expressing two of her key themes. First, he grasps the underlying unity of all human ideas: "all the systems were the same at base—voodoo, thermodynamics, I Ching, astrology, numerology, alchemy, metaphysics, everybody's ancient myths—they were interchangeable, not at all separate much less conflicting" (210). Second, and closely related, he has the epiphany that "everything was everything" (249), and he writes down, just as Bambara has done, that "everything that is now has been before and will be again in a new way, in a changed form, in a timeless time."

More obviously than Campbell, the Seven Sisters represent the strengths of multiplicity. They are multiple, with seven personalities and heritages, yet they are one, just as, over time, they are the same group even though the participants change. Appropriately, it is often hard to distinguish among them or to know which one says what.[7] One of their performance pieces is a particularly telling metaphor for the novel itself: "There was a long piece they'd ended with, a colored sister solidarity piece, operatic almost, a fugue-like interweaving of the voices, the histories, the lore of Caribbean, African, Native American" (214). They believe in multiple planes: "the material without the spiritual and psychic does not a dialectic make" (64). And they perform multiple operations, equally at home with a screwdriver (65), a dance (238), and a waking vision (221, 238).

The novel's primary healers—Doc Serge, Minnie Ransom, and Sophie Heywood—model multiplicity.[8] Serge, a legend in his own time, has had multiple lives: before becoming administrator of the Infirmary, he ran a gambling joint as "Faro," went by other names such as "Candy Man" and "Sweet Bear" (131), and still dresses like a gambler (135, 269). As head of the Infirmary, he brings together traditional medicine and alternative healing, he is a successful administrator, and he talks philosophy and religion to Buster. He is an actual and a potential community leader; when Ruby wonders, "who could effectively pull together the folks—the campus forces, the street forces, the prison forces, workers, women, the aged, the gay" (193), Jan thinks of him. Serge is also multiple because he is both real and larger than life. Like the legendary African-American hero "Stagolee" (268), he is connected with legend and magic, keeping the Infirmary going without paying the bills (81), retaining the myth of his "magic stetson" (268), and satisfying ordinary people's "need for magic, for legend, for the extraordinary so big, the courage to pursue so small," especially their desire to believe in his superhuman sexual capacities. He is also compared to the Magician in the Tarot deck, the figure most associated with the power of the human spirit, the unity of the individual, and the union of the divine and the human (Waite 72–75). He exudes confidence and self-love, even to the point of supreme egotism: "I am one beautiful and powerful son of a bitch" (136). His "litany" of self-love is oppressive, but Bambara privileges his acceptance of himself in all his roles and phases, "in error and in correctness," and in his conclusion "that self-love produces the gods and the gods are genius" (137).

The novel's other two healers—Sophie and Minnie—exemplify the virtues of multiplicity by their mental abilities to transcend boundaries. For Sophie, related to the leader of a slave rebellion (127, 241), time is fluid, as she steps easily back into her childhood (14). She can exist simultaneously in multiple planes, merging the physical and the spiritual, as when she undergoes out-of-body experiences (149, 151–52, 217) or interprets Velma's dreams (219). Through her mind, she is connected to the heart of the cosmos and therefore can help restore Velma: "And at the very core of the earthworks her stomach dropped down to and at the center of the universe her temples throbbed toward and somewhere in between where her heart beat, the divinely healthy whole Velma waited to be called out of its chamber" (148).

Minnie Ransom is even more explicitly enriched by multiplicity. She can heal anyone because "she knew each way of being in the world" (48). She is unbounded by time (51, 295) and space, "Free to go anywhere at all in the universe" (60) and able to build and visit "the chapel in The Mind" (53). Her spiritual strength derives from her ability to receive messages from multiple sources, including Saturn's rings, the Ring of Wisdom, CBs, and traffic waves (276). She can also cross the border between life and death, as she converses with Old Wife, the spirit of her now-dead friend, Karen Wilder. She knows, as Old Wife reminds her, that "There is no death in spirit" (62). As the healing session dramatizes, Minnie is in both the physical, present world trying to help Velma and the spiritual, timeless world communing with Old Wife, loa (spirits), and energy fields. Minnie's powers as primary healer in this novel about healing derive from her ability to transcend all boundaries, to live on multiple planes, and therefore to connect all disparate threads. She personifies the infinite connections that Bambara insists do link all consciousnesses on all levels without any restrictions.

Multiplicity in these healing characters is significant because it is a primary source of their renewing energy. Energy sources themselves are just as emphatically multiple but often double edged. Although some can have damaging consequences, such as the radioactive poisoning repeatedly associated with nuclear power, connecting with various kinds of energy is therapeutic. Characters must link the multiple energy sources, just as they must try to combine all other apparent differences and dichotomies. Very early, as Velma is "perched uneasily" (6), she is unable to make such connections or even to be in contact with any energy forces: "scrambling to piece together key bits of high school physics, freshman philo, and lessons M'Dear Sophie and Mama Mae had tried to impart. The reliability of stools? Solids, liquids, gases, the dance of atoms, the bounce and race of molecules, ethers, electrical charges. The eyes and habits of illusion. Retinal images, bogus images, traveling to the brain. The pupils trying to tell the truth to the inner eye. The eye of the heart. The eye of the head. The eye of the mind. All seeing differently" (6–7). As the fragmented sentences enact, Velma's thoughts are broken up, and they are broken up because she cannot synthesize the multiple energy fields—personal, spiritual, and physical—and therefore cannot gather herself to focus clearly. She needs to "piece together key bits" (6) not only of earlier lessons but of her life and self. Like Velma, each character must piece together his or her self, and the reader must piece together the disparate bits of the novel, for, although multiplicity and multiple energy sources are valued, they can also lead to chaotic disintegration.

The first principal type of energy is personal. Minnie recalls healing a woman by "zapp[ing] a little energy up there near the pineal" (45), Sophie pauses to "let her soul get on with its gathering and return with greater force to its usual place" (152), Campbell seems to overflow with personal energy (172–73), and Minnie tells Velma that "the source of health is never outside" (220). This locus of power in the individual reinforces the novel's focus on the psychological disarray of Velma, Fred, and many of the other characters and on their gradual passages toward personal and communal recovery.

A second major kind of energy is spiritual. This energy can affect communities, for example in the rumor that Claybourne is "a major energy center, one of the chakras of this country" (163), and it affects the United States itself, as in Doc Serge's convictions about this country's "latent destiny, its occult destiny" (134). The personal applications of spiritual power are demonstrated throughout by Minnie. She communicates directly with the world of loas. She heals by "clearing the channels, putting herself aside" and becoming "available to a healing force no one had yet, to her satisfaction, captured in a name" (47). It is a force like electricity, accompanied by a "corona of light," "a petaled rainbow," and "a single white flame." She can absorb the hidden energies in nature and transfer them to people; she can "read the auras of trees and stones and plants and neighbors" (48). In one lyrical passage, Bambara captures the sheer energy of Minnie's talent:

On the stool or in the chair with this patient or that, Minnie could dance their dance and match their beat and echo their pitch and know their frequency as if her own. Eyes closed and the mind dropping down to the heart, bubbling in the blood then beating, fanning out, flooded and shining, she knew each way of being in the world and could welcome them home again, open to wholeness. Eyes wide open to the swing from expand to contract, dissolve congeal, release restrict, foot tapping, throat throbbing in song to the ebb and flow of renewal, she would welcome them healed into her arms. (48)

Minnie's power is conveyed through the passage's content as well as through its rhythmical flow and its piling up of active verbs and participles.

These first two kinds of healing energy—personal and spiritual—are linked to an even broader power source: cosmic energy. Everyone on Fred's bus experiences the influence of cosmic forces in a frozen moment when Fred finally speaks: "Claybourne in five minutes. Last stop" (85). The narration then veers into an alternate version of reality in which the characters "might have been" in many other places, including being in the bus in Fred's fantasy of driving it into the marsh. In this alternate plane, they would have felt the unleashed power of the cosmos:

Silence on the bus as at a momentous event. But an event more massive and gripping than the spoken word or an accident. A sonic boom, a gross tampering of the weights, a shift off the axis, triggered perhaps by the diabolics at the controls, or by asteroids powerfully colliding. Earth spun off its pin, the quadrants slipping the leash, the rock plates sliding, the magnetic fields altered, and all, previously pinned to the crosses of the zodiac and lashed to the earth by the fixing laws, released. A change in the charge of the field so extreme that all things stop and are silent until the shift's complete and new radiations open the third eye. (87)

In this illusory moment, a fiction within the fiction, Fred and the passengers are exposed to the limitless power of the universe and are "released" by the sudden modifications of that power. "New radiations" replace harmful radioactive pollution, and the change redounds inwardly to all the characters as their "third eye," their inward spirituality, is opened.

Later, this same moment is described as the removal of an inner blockage, "like the barrier that dropped away for the passengers on the highway" and as a force that transcends time, coming at the characters from the future: "silent and still in the sonic boom echoing back from a blasting event to occur several years hence, and to occur with so powerful an impact, its after-effect ripples backward and spreads over them now" (104). Later still, Velma seems to be waiting for a similar force to release and energize her: "waiting for a word from within, from above, from world events, from a shift in the power configurations of the globe, waiting for a new pattern to assemble and reveal itself" (170).

The release of cosmic energy accelerates in the last third of the novel. Velma's passage to recovery is associated with the cosmos: "She could dance right off the stool, right off the edge of the world and collide with comets" (265). Her "Day of Restoration" (263) results from the combination of such cosmic dimensions, personal power, and connections to multiple spiritual powers, such as Christianity ("in the direction of resurrection" [264]) and native American religions ("the Spirits of Blessing way" [264]).

The cosmic energy is concentrated in the sudden storm that breaks over Claybourne. Characters all over the city hear the mysterious sound and wonder whether it is thunder (200, 223, 245, 278), drums (200), an earthquake (223, 245, 278), a strange march (223), a "cataclysmic event" (245), cannons (245), angry gods (245), a volcanic eruption (245), or an explosion at Transchemical (245). The energy and its potential multiplicity imply its powers of revitalization, for even though the sound is ominous, it and the ensuing storm galvanize the city. Campbell associates the power of the storm with Damballah, the venerable and benevolent father deity in African and Haitian mythology (245).

Caught in the storm on his way to the Infirmary to help his wife, Obie is transfigured. Two children become "odd beings sent to earth at the moment encased and then peeled to walk among the people as kin and bring them through the passage" (288). At that moment he, like the characters on the bus, feels the power of the third eye: "There was an eye poised on him, an energy focused on him from somewhere, an eye clarifying him, arresting him" (289). Because of this transfusion of cosmic energy, Obie now has an answer for the book's repeated but heretofore unanswered question, asked here by an unnamed character, "Brother Obeah, what's going on?" (290): "Looks like everything's going on." "Everything" is happening because of the confluence of multiple energy sources—personal, spiritual, and cosmic—and because "everything is everything," because multiplicity is highly valued, and because energies are desperately needed.

If recovery depends on turning multiplicity and diffuse sources of energy in positive directions, it also requires reversing the destructive patterns underlying personal and social problems. The physical and emotional tightness felt by several characters must be loosened. Hence, as he tries "to get out the knots," Ahiro, Obie's masseur and counselor, urges his patient to "Relax, breathe deep" (162). In parallel fashion, Jan responds to the mysterious thunder by "flexing her hands against Ruby's back" (248) to loosen both her hands and her friend's muscles. Concomitantly, she relaxes her taut mind: "A muscular response to some dimly heard instruction in her mind to loosen her grip now on all notions of the seemingly complete world, release her hold on notions that might lock her to the old." Likewise, Velma hears in the drums from the park the message of a "barrier dropping" (251), which echoes the personal, cosmic, and temporal "barrier falling away" (104) experienced by the characters on the bus. Obie, Jan, and Velma thus head toward recovery as they move toward Minnie's position of openness—"I'm available to any and every adventure of the human breath" (56)—and to the novel's message that "anything could happen" (5).

The word *up*, used in such expressions as *loosen up* or *shape up* and usually connoting an improved situation or status, becomes a subtle motif for characters' recoveries and in its repetition implicitly interweaves those recoveries. When Nadeen sees a sign of Velma's impending recovery, "She felt a straightening" because "What she caught . . . made her stretch up" (102). The metaphor within *up* is reinforced, for at the same moment, "Minnie, too, was feeling up." Minnie and Velma then are "holding each other up out of the fall" (103), which echoes in the next paragraph when the bus passengers' eyes are "throwing up images on the walls of the mind" and Cecile and Nilda, two of the Seven Sisters, "fly up out of the roof of that bus and are back on the road in another." Later, while heading toward recovery, Velma imagines "Giant teachers," despite overwhelming obstacles, "standing up in their genius anyhow ready to speak the unpronounceable" (265). The motif culminates in the physical image of Obie, undergoing his epiphany during the storm, slipping on wet leaves and then being urged to "Get on up, Brother" (292). He first cannot get up, but then he "couldn't get up and so he did get up." The heroic effort is reinforced by the simultaneous start up of an electric generator, as Obie is transformed into myth: "And he saluted [the couples] in a daze, the sky opening and the Regal releasing molten gold into the fog, the drums sounding in a playoff with the thunder. Saluted the future, gold splashing in his eyes" (292).

Personal recovery is also enhanced by characters' vocal expressiveness. Fred's silent anguish on the bus is ameliorated when he finally speaks. Ahiro counsels Obie not only to relax his muscles but also to vent his emotions by having "a good cry" (164) and by being "never . . . too tired to laugh" (165). Velma's suicidal retreat into the silence of her hermetic jar begins to be reversed when she audibly growls, as Minnie recognizes: "Growl all you want, sweetheart. . . . You gonna be all right" (41). Later, Velma's recovery is reinforced when she audibly releases some of her emotion, confessing, "I might have died" (267). And in the final paragraph of the novel, Velma's eventual recovery is assured because she is "turning smoothly on the stool, head thrown back about to shout, to laugh, to sing" (295).

Music is also a therapeutic and unifying force throughout the novel. From the beginning, Minnie is associated with music, "spinning out a song" (4) and playing music to help Velma and her audience, in particular "some saying-it music" for "these crazy folks" (47). Later Velma is "spinning in the music" (114), which places her within Minnie's orbit. Minnie's music for Velma becomes interspersed with the pan man's drumming, "music [that] drifted out over the trees toward the Infirmary" (168), the same music that Velma tries "to lift, to sing with." As this music spreads over and unifies the town, music from a variety of sources begins to be heard. Small and large drums from the park mix with the jukebox inside the cafe (200), and the drums convey the "call and response" of "one side of the Hill calling to the other" (250). Meanwhile, three of Jan's former students, "noisy but harmonious" (234), serenade her outside the cafe. Finally, under the influence of the blues song "Wild Women Don't Get the Blues," Velma senses that she is ready "to surrender it up whatever it was" (267).

Along with music, dancing is therapeutic. Fred hears the dance class at the Regal, where "elderly women freed up from girdles and strict church upbringing bumped, glided and rolled to the variation of cheft telli that the four musicians on drum, oud, finger cymbals, chekere and the pan fashioned" (166). Inspired by this eclectic mix of instruments, the multicultural group of women is loosened from the paralysis of their conventional restraints, and they can therefore renew their souls as well as exercise their bodies: as their instructor urges, "Don't cheat the body, don't cheat the spirit, ladies. Do the whole movement." Old Wife realizes that the same lesson applies to Velma: "Dancing is her way to learn now. Let her go" (264). Indeed, Velma intuitively feels the desire "to dance right off the stool" (265), a release that appears about to be fulfilled in the novel's last sentence, when Velma "rising on steady legs, throws off the shawl" (295).

Once characters have unwound their tightness, they can extend their healing by interacting more positively with others. The Seven Sisters and the three healers are relaxed and well centered and consequently love, empathize with, and help others. For example, Old Wife knows that Minnie is bound by love to Velma, to all her patients, to everyone: "Love, Min. Love won't let you let her go" (61). Toward the end, Velma in finding her own harmony relearns the necessity of empathy: "To have dominion was not to knock out, downpress, bruise, but to understand, to love, make at home" (267). Internal balance is inseparable from love of others: "The hunt for balance and kinship was the thing. A mutual courtesy." She then imagines her invisible ties to all other human beings: "The silvery tendrils that fluttered between her fingers, extending out like tiny webs of invisible thread. The strands that flowed from her to Minnie Ransom to faintly outlined witnesses by the windows" (267).

Such personal connections with other people are part of the novel's broader emphasis on social and worldwide connections. The threads not only go out from individuals to other individuals but link everything to everything, as Campbell realizes (249). Minnie is the most privileged character because she most fully understands and exhibits the widest connections. Meadows moves toward greater appreciation of interpersonal and community ties. Isolated in the Infirmary, he enters the African-American community to find a place there with Thurston, Hull, and their friends. Along the way, he hears the social message of a street philosopher urging the need for "synthesizers" and "new alliances," which helps him refocus his own personality: "His city and his country mind drew together to ponder it all" (126).

The connections go beyond individual links to other individuals. They involve the community-building work of the 7 Arts Academy, as Obie realizes: "The work was the same: to develop, to de-mystify, to build, to consolidate and escalate" (93). They also involve parallels among seemingly diverse parameters, for example, "pressure points of the human body . . . pressure points of the system . . . the U.S. . . . presence" (162). Jan similarly realizes that nuclear energy, pollution, ecology, and communities are "connected" (242).

The necessary connections also cut across time to incorporate the past and thereby to dispel the characters' former temporal limbo. On a personal level, Velma's recovery depends on her reworking her own past, including the traumas of past political demonstrations but more importantly the memory of parental love, the feeling that "she'd never been more cared for" (225). The past may be dominated by painful memories of loss (as for Fred) and may seem overwhelmingly chaotic (as for Velma), but, however painful, it must be rehearsed, regained, and savored.

Correspondingly, understanding the past but not being controlled by it is important for the community and society. Ruby recalls the past, only to be frustrated by the lack of progress or resolution: "When the Europeans stopped killing Christians and became Christians, that was the end of Christianity and the beginning of Christendom and Christidolatry. And when the white boy quit lynching niggers and became a nigger, that was the beginning of the Wild Bill Dogget revival and the beginning of Bloods wearing Blues Brothers emblems. When O when will confusion end, my sistuh" (201). The narrator, not confused, links the historical moment when the cosmic storm hits Claybourne with a series of other memorable moments in recent U.S. history, such as the assassinations of John F. Kennedy, Malcolm X, and Martin Luther King, Jr. (246). And throughout the book, African-American heros from the past, such as Harriet Tubman and Crispus Attucks, are invoked.

The symbol of this venerated past is the Old Tree, planted by free coloreds in 1871 and still frequented by spirits (145). The tree contains the living past and present of the African-American community, "its roots fed by the mulch and compost and hope the children gathered from the districts' farms." Its new growth also portends the community's future strength, "The flowers . . . promising the perfect fruit of communal actions" (146). The Old Tree, whose name jibes with Old Wife, is even more significant because it represents "the collective mind" (146) of the community. It is "attended each generation by a certain few drawn to the tree, or drawn to the [Infirmary], called to their vocation and their roots—messenger, teacher, healer, clairvoyant, clairaudient, clairfeelant, clairdoent." It represents the mental forces of the community that communicate, teach, feel, see, hear, and act. It symbolizes therefore the rich intersubjective web of African-American culture, developed over the past by the collective efforts of that culture's participants and even more necessary now for a passage into a new future.

This power of the mind is the most powerful healing force in the novel. I have already pointed out some manifestations of mental power, such as Minnie's spiritual transcendence of the life/death barrier and her healing empathy for Velma and all her patients, the mutual cooperation that creates the intimate community of the Seven Sisters, and the critical importance of memory in the healing process for individuals and the community. But there are many more modes in which mind power is demonstrated, and, like other recovery forces, this power gains momentum in the last third of the novel.

Paralleling the Old Tree, The Master's Mind represents the mental power of the community. Like the zodiac and Christ's disciples, the twelve secondary healers of The Master's Mind encircle the primary healer (Minnie) and her patient, supplementing Minnie's individual mind power with their collective mind power. They in turn are encircled by a much looser layer of visitors and medical staff and beyond that layer by the city itself. Although many in these outer layers are skeptical about the healing, the concentric circles imply that Velma's recovery requires not only Minnie's therapy but the combined efforts of the entire community. Her problems are inseparable from the community's, and her recovery is impossible without the community's help and in turn its recovery. As in West African philosophy, harmony for the individual is inseparable from harmony between the individual and the community and from the harmony of the whole community.

Characters' mental powers are manifested throughout the

novel in many ways. Characters can read each other's minds, as when Minnie cures by "touch[ing] mind on mind" (48) and even when Campbell, preoccupied with Jan, knows that "she would want toasted banana nut bread" (195). Characters have collective mental experiences: for example, when the other eleven members of The Master's Mind wish that Sophie would return to their circle ("What did bounce around the circle of eleven was the opinion that Sophie should return and restore the group intact" [13–14]), and when everyone feels the same chill "up the collective spine" at the moment when Jan and Ruby "thought the same thoughts but could not speak" (248). The most arresting of these collective experiences is when the bus passengers pass into alternate realities after the illusionary experience of sinking into the swamp. This communal mental activity eludes language and thought: "No one remarked on any of this or on any of the other remarkable things each senses but had no habit of language for, though felt often and deeply, privately. That moment of correspondence—phenomena, noumena—when the glimpse of the life script is called dream, déjà vu, clairvoyance, intuition, hysteria, hunger, or called nothing at all" (89). The experience is mutual, clairvoyant, and transcendent, like the collective mind power of the Old Tree and the synthesizing power of Minnie Ransom.

Individually, characters' thought processes stretch ordinary limits. Twice, Cora Rider has a thought, but the thought is overheard by others as if she had spoken it (17, 109). In his anxiety about his brother, Obie "hears" him speak (96–98). Although Portia Patterson is not present at the organizational meeting, her words are present for Velma (31). Thoughts are almost tangible objects, as Minnie repeatedly urges Velma to "hold that thought" (e.g., 62) and as several characters—Mai (221), Velma (226), Campbell (245), and Obie (285)—are shown in the midst of mentally digging to find a memory or to grasp a thought. As in *Sent for You Yesterday*, the usual borderline between thoughts and reality is blurred, for example, when Minnie's thought of what Meadows is doing becomes what he is doing (60), when Jan and the other women affect the clay by concentrating on it (116), and when Meadows's mental reconstruction of welfare men becomes what they are (182–84). Similarly, waking thoughts and dreams merge: Palma's dream of Velma in trouble merges with both "premonitions" of the future and "replays" of the past (140), and Obie, floating in the pool, also floats among dream, dozing, and wakefulness (285–86).

When Fred fantasizes steering the bus into the swamp, not only do the passengers experience a collective transfer into another plane, but many of them also have individual out-of-body experiences that transcend the ordinary limits of reality. For example, J. D. "connects" with the music "in a moment when speech, movement, thought were not possible" (87), Mai "com[es] unstuck from the web of time and place," Fred is reunited with Wanda (88), and Palma is transported to the Infirmary, where she "pass[es] right through [Buster and Nadeen's] bodies."

Like the bus passengers, Minnie, Sophie, and later Velma transcend the border between mind and reality in their out-of-body experiences. Minnie and Old Wife construct "the chapel in The Mind" (53), complete with cliff, trees, rainbow, fountain, candles, and altar. During the healing session, they mentally return to this chapel and to Minnie's memories of her acquaintance with the living Karen Wilder. Sophie, relaxing in Doc Serge's chair, is mentally transported first through "circles of a surrealistic landscape replete with 'Mighty Titans'" and with "the grinding of the earth's plates" (149) and then to an amusement park and a desert landscape where she continues her mental search for a way to help heal Velma (217–18). Velma, her mind loosening as the healing forces revive her, mentally projects herself out the window of the Infirmary and then synchronizes with Sophie's out-of-body circling (220). This brief projection prepares the way for her sustained imaginative vision when, according to Old Wife, she is "off again" (251) but at the end of which Minnie knows that she "is coming through" (262). During this mental ramble, Velma's thoughts range chaotically over her whole life, including childhood, Daddy Dolphy, Obie, her political work, and the riot at last year's festival. Thinking about salt as a cure for snakebite and about the absence of an antidote for the serpent's venom, she reaches an epiphany about herself and the movement. Recalling the African-American historical and artistic traditions, she "thought she knew how to build immunity to the sting of the serpent . . . thought she knew how to build resistance, make the journey to the center of the circle, stay poised and centered in the work and not fly off, stay centered in the best of her people's traditions" (258). But the effort was too much, for no individual can defang the serpent: "heart/brain/gut muscles atrophied any-how," and "something crucial had been missing" (259). Conse-quently, she now realizes, "she had fled" and had become two selves, in a sense had lost herself, her balance, her purpose.

As in such mental flights, inner vision is a prominent metaphor for the power of the mind. Four times readers are explicitly re-minded of the importance of inward sight: when Velma recalls Sophie's and Mama Mae's lessons ("The pupils trying to tell the truth to the inner eye" [6–7]); when the narrator describes the bus passengers' change of consciousness ("A change in the charge of the field so extreme that all things stop and are silent until the shift's complete and new radiations open the third eye" [87]); when "Maazda explained what it was to stalk, to take over the hunted, but not with arrows or bullets but with the eye of the mind" (266); and when Obie feels that "There was an eye poised on him, an energy focused on him from somewhere, an eye clari-fying him, arresting him" (289). Through such mental (re)envi-sioning, characters open themselves to the creative energies of the cosmos, through which they can reintegrate themselves and reestablish their ties to others.

Many characters exhibit the power to see beyond ordinary vi-sion. Fred feels that Porter "might've pointed out what there was to see, what was escaping his eye" (68), Fred can see the bus sinking into the marsh (80), and Campbell "could actually see the unbonded atoms on the table" (213). Sometimes this inner vision takes the form of seeing the lives of other characters, as when

Fred mentally imagines the activities of the newspaper boy, Lil James (154), when Meadows projects a detailed picture of the welfare men (182–85), and when Campbell fantasizes names and identities for the six engineers (205). Twice, characters create a mental fantasy of themselves. Meadows sees himself as Crispus Attucks in the bicentennial pageant (181), and Velma, distant from her bodily self, "could see herself: hair matted and dusty, bandages unraveled and curled at the foot of the stool like a sleeping snake" (4). This shared ability to see beyond literal vision suggests both the characters' power of mind and their desire to see what they want to see. Their visual projections reflect their subconscious desires. Campbell can see the atoms because he wants to be able to, Fred sees the bus in the swamp because he wants to crash it, and Fred later sees Porter outside the Infirmary because he desperately wants Porter alive again (279). As Sophie taught Velma, "You see nothing but what you're looking for" (18).

Besides having the power of inner vision, the characters also demonstrate the power of their minds by attempting to interpret events and other characters. Given the extraordinary number of questions they and the narrator ask, it is not surprising that the characters try to answer some of them. For example, Meadows tries to interpret the three men in drag ("What was that all about?" [180]), and "eavesdropp[ing] on the conversations" (65), Fred freely interprets his passengers. Interpretations, and the plot, focus on two notably mysterious phenomena: Velma's breakdown and the thunderlike sound in the last third of the novel.

In several ways the motif of interpretation is particularly highlighted. When Meadows meets Thurston and Hull, they engage in a double dance of mutual interpretation. Meadows, having stepped on Thurston's feet and feeling nervous in the strange neighborhood, interprets Thurston's and Hull's movements as threatening: "He felt himself coming into focus for them. . . . And now they were checking out his clothes, the cat in the cap eying his watch" (186). At the same time, the other two are mystified by Meadows, asking repeated questions, such as "You lost?" (186), "Whatcha doin round here?" and "What's your name and who you work for?" (187). Moreover, Meadows is acutely aware that they are interpreting him: "They were studying him. By now they'd know he was not a honky. He felt himself coming into focus for them. . . . Now the grain of his skin would be coming into view" (186).

Sophie, one of the privileged characters, asserts the necessity and ubiquity of interpretation: she "was forever reading signs before they were even so," and she asserts that "every event is preceded by a sign" (13). As if to bear out Sophie's dictum, the front of the Infirmary bears "all manner of messages," some easily read and others "to be read by initiates of the order only" (121). A further reminder of the necessity of interpreting difficult signs is the reference to the Rosetta Stone (196). More radically, the motif is underscored when Velma fantasizes several surrealistic images and is unable to understand them: "A crab had attacked a fisherman and held on or dropped off into the sand meaning. A fig unripe had dropped from a tree and burst open, mud oozing smelling like stink fish meaning. A mushroom cap toppling like a severed head meaning. A wheel falling off its axis face down meaning" (273). The open-ended syntax, ending with the unresolved *meaning,* forces recognition of the ultimate impossibility of any final interpretation. Thus, the characters, as well as the reader, engage in interpretation, in reading all kinds of signs, but they can never complete their interpretations. Ongoing, open-ended interpreting constitutes part of the healing process, for, like inner vision, it is the exercise of individual and collective mental power by which the damaged cultural web is rebuilt and reinforced.

The Salt Eaters not only details the problems confronting contemporary African-American and American cultures and depicts potential healing forces in action but also projects a visionary future. That future is offered only through hints and fragments, for, since one of the future's most dominant features is its open-endedness, Bambara cannot spell out its details. As in black theology, Bambara posits that a new future is coming that will radically change every character's life; for her that future is coming now, it will mean unprecedented change, it will require more of everyone, and it will bring individuals and communities together in meaningful productivity.

That the characters have any future at all is slightly problematic. The uninterpretable, thunderlike noise seems to be ushering in a dangerous new era of some sort, an era marked by Resettlement Centers (279), radiation counts (" 'rad' and 'rem' would riddle everyday speech" [246]), and very different "assumptions on which 'security' had once been built" (247). But throughout the novel's final twenty-five pages, assorted details document not only that the characters do have futures but also that their futures will be far better than their pasts. Palma and Marcus will be together and will intimately understand each other, "decod[ing] the look that passed between them" (285). Jan's future begins with her unfinished sentence about the storm, "I hope it's not . . ." (248), and "that thought unfinished but intuited got fixed and would hold its shape for decades to come." She will be Mrs. Janice Campbell (282), and Campbell will speak at "blue-ribbon panels and organized seminars" (280). Meadows will renew his commitment to the Hippocratic oath, will find meaning in community involvement, will work at the Infirmary, and will be converted to a more holistic view of medicine and life (281–82). Fred, already feeling much better once he reaches the Infirmary (270), will be reunited with his son and will then be able to describe the change that came over him (279). Obie will remember the details of the day of the thunder when he felt "an energy focused on him from somewhere" (289) and will recount how he was "stripped by lightning" (292) down to his soul. Velma "would remember [the beginning] as the moment she started back toward life" (278) and will in time be ready for further training by Sophie (293).

As these glimpses indicate, the future will be shaped by many of the forces of recovery that I have discussed. The new era will be dominated by the power of the mind and by individual and communal energy, and it will be characterized by new understandings of the past. Tina Mason, with Sophie's help, "plans to revive the ancient Earth Mother cult" (241), which suggests that connections with the community's female heritage, the mud mothers, will be reestablished.[9] Connections with the entire spiritual world will be remade, and the appropriate initiation rites will be relearned (247). Historical and mythical heros from all cultures will re-remembered (246–49) and will help "regenerate the life of the world" (249). As Obie realizes, silence will not be "the way" (290), but instead the past will be remembered and all the stories will be told. By implication, the future will revalue the past, as embodied by Old Wife and the Old Tree, and it will be shaped by the values and strengths of the novel's healers.

A primary trait of the imagined future is its newness. The day of the thunder will be remembered as the beginning of a new life. That new future will require growth for individuals, "for the Academy, for the national community, for the planet" (98). It will embody Velma's "belief in ordinary folks' capacity to change the self and transform society" (259–60). New meaning will be given to old vows. As Campbell understands, the future will incorporate the past, but it will also be new: "everything that is now has been before and will be again in a new way, in a changed form, in a timeless time" (249). This apocalyptic future will be more like Great Time than linear time. Initiation rites will be necessary because "initiation was the beginning of transformation" (247). As in black theology, the present is intolerable, the past must be revalued, and the future will bring a restructuring of society and individuals that will redress the injustices and misalignments of the past.

The changes will be in the direction of wholeness. Individuals, communities, and the planet must be reunited: "the ecology of the self, the tribe, the species, the earth depended on" transformation (247). People in the future will make every effort "to remember the whole in time and make things whole again" (248). They will connect all mythologies, all disciplines, all sources of energy, all modes of knowing. As Campbell already realizes, "all the systems were the same at base . . . were interchangeable" (210), and "everything was everything" (249).

As Bambara's cryptic formulations suggest, the future will transcend the material limits of the present. As implied by Velma's revival, in which she is reborn from a "burst cocoon" (295), "human beings [will] becom[e] something else" (292). They will "race across the border to new frontiers" (280). These borders are not material but are passages beyond ordinary reality: "no one would say 'across the border', for that entailed tiring explanations, obliged the speaker to be precise about what border was meant" (246). Instead, the borders would be metaphysical ones, crossroads between this life and some other life, "Where Legba stood at the gate? Where Isis lifted the veil?"[10] The new regions would be "beyond the limits of scientific certainty," would be "the uncharted territory beyond the danger zone of 'safe' dosage." For Bambara, change must be radical and total and therefore cannot be accomplished within the existing borders of ordinary space but must be projected in an alternative reality.

Crossing the border also means transcending the conventional Euro-American experience of time. The narrative form of the novel repeatedly embodies such transcendence, for example, in its suspension of time in the fantasy of the bus sinking in the swamp and in its free fluctuations among past, present, and future. Velma, like the novel, is often free of temporal restraints, as when "time . . . open[s] up to take her inside" (171) and when "time stream[s] along below her in the tree" (251). In the novel's last few pages, both Sophie and Minnie reiterate their understanding that "everything" will come "in time" (293, 295), but, given the novel's temporal improvisizations, "in time" acquires more than its conventional meaning. It suggests not so much that, if one is patient, everything will come to pass, but that everything will exist in a transcendent future, "in a timeless time" (249). "In time" also expresses Minnie's unraveling of the distinctions among past, present, and future. She wonders if she is having a "flash forward" (295), which is what the novel itself does as it presents premonitions and glimpses of the future. Then, after Old Wife reminds Minnie that she always says, "everything in time," she steps out of time: "None of this ain't happened yet?

Some of this is happening now? All of this is going on, but I ain't here? All of the above? None of the above?" (295). Since this most privileged character in the novel is loosened from the parameters of time and space, the novel itself, all its characters, and its readers are similarly cut free. Everyone and everything must be liberated in Bambara's vision of revolutionary change at all levels of existence.

This transcendence of time is suggestive of another trait of the projected future: its open-endedness. Readers are repeatedly told that the day of the thunder marked a new beginning, but they are never told what is beginning. Instead, the vague pronoun *it* substitutes for any precise identification, as when the narrator foresees that "many would mark the beginning of it all as this moment" and when characters in the future will ask each other "when did it begin for you?" (246). The openness of the future is also figured by the insistent message that the characters have and will have choices. From the novel's opening line—"Are you sure, sweetheart, that you want to be well?"—Minnie's primary message to Velma is that the latter has choices. Later she tells Velma to "choose your own cure" (103) and asks her "What will you do when you are well?" (220). To Old Wife, Minnie repeats several times that everyone "got options. . . . Always got options" (44).

Minnie's lesson is not lost on Velma. Early in the novel she is confused by the concept of choice, as when she groans incoherently, "Afford . . . Choose . . ." (111). But her recovery is couched partially in terms of her recognition of her choice to live: "And she standing now in the wet streets as if there were a choice available now that she'd been rescued from the scissors and the oven's gas" (264). Her recovery is even more assured after she rediscovers her past and realizes that, in her childhood desire to learn from Sophie, she had already made her choice: "her choice made long ago" (275). For Velma, as for Bambara, recovery is indistinguishable from a coalescing of past, present, and future into a transcendent and unified time, place, and state of being.

Reinforcing Minnie's privileged position, the narrator confirms Minnie's advice by pronouncing that everyone has important choices: "There were choices to be noted. Decisions to be made" (248). This same judgment forms the core of a curious paragraph, separated from the rest of the text by line breaks:

> A barrier falling away between adulthood and child. Like the barrier that dropped away for the passengers on the highway silent and still in the hum of the wheels over asphalt, silent and still in the sonic boom echoing back from a blasting event to occur several years hence, and to occur with so powerful an impact, its aftereffect ripples backward and spreads over their moment now, giving them a glimpse of their scripts which they can acknowledge and use, or ignore and have to reexperience as new. Always the choice. But with attention able to change directions as sharply and as matter-of-factly as the birds winging toward Claybourne. (105)

This passage anticipates the new beginning on the day of the thunder, a day on which many barriers fall away, and it is the first explicit indication of the transcendence of time. But the narrator's lesson is that the characters have and must use the potential to choose. They can choose. They can be flexible enough to "change directions." They can renew themselves by participating in the carnivalesque ritual of burning their lists of "all the things they wanted out of their lives" (157) and correspondingly dedicating to carnival their "list of dreams." On the day of the cataclysm, during the "downpour [that] was no spring shower" (294), the cosmos opens up a multicultural cornucopia of options: "Choices were being tossed into the street like dice, like shells, like kola nuts, like jackstones." As Gloria Hull asserts, the novel offers a choice of two futures for humankind, one projecting an evolving humanitarian society and the other characterized by increasing warfare and nuclear contamination (228).

Significantly, this apocalyptic day is also the day of preparation for Claybourne's annual festival, for the onset of carnival is the traditional time for conventional authority to be temporarily lifted (Kelley, "Damballah" 487–88). The lifting of such barriers allows new energies to be released, energies that for Bambara are necessary for the city's inhabitants and by extension all human beings to be reborn. Bambara radically extends this liberating effect of carnival by suggesting that this time there will be no return to the preexisting order but instead that everything—individuals, human society, and natural systems—will be permanently restructured. Instead of the conventional circular pattern of carnival—old order, temporary release from it, and return to the previous order—Bambara uses carnival to propel her fictional world beyond the borders of the old order and into an indefinite, open-ended, and expansive vision of a radically altered world.

For Bambara, the future is neither utopia nor dystopia but opportunity. It will offer a myriad of choices. It will necessitate continued learning, as Minnie recognizes (54). It will require harder work than the past: Velma "didn't know the half of it. Of what awaited her in years to come" (278); and Sophie knows that "what had driven Velma into the oven . . . was nothing compared to what awaited her, was to come" (294). It can be utopian, can end "the authoritarian age" and begin "the new humanism, the new spiritism," but only if "attention could be riveted on the simplicity of the karmic law—cause and effect" (248).

The future is thus similar to the novel itself. For the reader, as for the characters, "anything could happen" (5) and "everything" is included. For readers and characters, it is a novel of many questions and few answers, of many things to be interpreted and few solid interpretations. The novel, like the characters' lives, appears to be a "Scattered, fragmented, uncoordinated mess" (201), in which it is all too easy to "los[e] the thread of [the] story" (20) and in which "the thread of the conversation [is] interrupted" (236). It is a Foucauldian heterotopia, a place defined by "the disorder in which fragments of a larger number of possible orders glisten separately" (Foucault xviii). Yet, just as Meadows's confusing experience ultimately "come[s] together as a coherent and focused narrative" (282), so the novel gradually coheres for the reader. Meadows only makes sense of his life in the future, and the novel eludes total comprehension in the reader's present but always seems to be coming into focus in the next reading.

This novel probes many of the traditional themes of African-

American fiction, such as rediscovery of the past, reconstitution of identity, and incorporation of multiple perspectives. More emphatically than other contemporary novels, it also risks consideration of the future, even though the imagined future cannot be—and, by the novel's own premises, should not be—clearly focused. Like the characters' own dangerous passages into the unknown future, the novel is confusing, unsettling, and never finished, for it too is an experiment, a leap, a passage.

4

"AS WITHIN, SO IT IS WITHOUT"

The Composite Self in Charles Johnson's *Oxherding Tale* and *Middle Passage*

In his novels *Oxherding Tale* (1982) and *Middle Passage* (1991), Charles Johnson, like Wideman and Bambara, pursues questions related to participation in the intersubjective web of community. Unlike Bambara's targeting of changes across society, Johnson focuses on transformations of the individual that enable that individual to accept love and thereby join the community. Johnson's protagonists, in contrast to most of Wideman's, resolve their tensions between alienation and community membership. Traveling the historic paths of the Middle Passage and the northward escape from slavery, they journey metaphorically from a world and a perspective of inflexible binary oppositions to tolerance, empathy, and fluidity. Because of Johnson's radical epistemology, they gain maturity, a secure place in the community, and even enlightenment by encountering other characters' perspectives, trying them on for size, and finally developing personal worldviews. The protagonists join the intersubjective web by virtually becoming all the threads.

Oxherding Tale and *Middle Passage* overtly explore Johnson's interests in phenomenology. Based on his reading of Edmund Husserl, Martin Heidegger, Jean-Paul Sartre, and especially Maurice Merleau-Ponty, Johnson believes that the centrality of the human mind is the crucial factor in our attempts to understand experience. When asked about the central themes in his work, he replied that "consciousness is primary for all 'experience'—that the nature of the *I* is the deepest of mysteries, and that all other questions arise from this primordial one, *What am I?*" (Boccia 615). For Johnson, the most important quality of Richard Wright's fiction is that it teaches us "that the world we live in is, first and foremost, one shaped by the mind" (*Being* 14). Because the human mind is so wonderfully complex, we are able to perceive reality as infinitely complex, multiple, and fluctuating: it is "consciousness itself that allows us infinitely to perceive meaning as a phenomenon of change, transformation, and process; it is Mind (the subject pole of experience), not Matter (the object pole), that gives the perceived world a polymorphous character" (*Being* 16). Consequently, each individual identity is not "fixed or static" but a continual "process," "dominated by change and transformation" (Little 161).

Our most ethical and effective course is to align ourselves with this multiplicity by projecting ourselves into as many other perspectives as possible. If we fail to do so, we become locked in our narrow, private perspectives, unable to change, unable to empathize. When we project ourselves, we understand Merleau-Ponty's concept of the Lifeworld, "a common situation, a common history in which all meanings evolve" (C. Johnson, "Phenomenology" 151; Johnson, *Being* 44). In that commonality, as Johnson quotes Merleau-Ponty, "Our experiences thus have lateral relationships of truth: all together, each possessing clearly what is secret to the Other, in our combined functionings we form a totality which moves toward enlightenment and completion" ("Phenomenology" 152; *Being* 44). By constantly broadening our individual perspectives to assimilate other points of view, "what is entirely subjective becomes intersubjective" (Little 163) as we achieve "the transcendence of relativism" (C. Johnson, *Being* 44). Paraphrasing Herbert Spiegelberg, Johnson wants us to "try to occupy the real place of the other and view from this standpoint the world as it is present in all its texture, limitations, and possibilities"; to "divest ourselves of our own historically acquired peculiarities by adopting as much as we can of the other's viewpoint"; and to "move back and forth between the other's perspective and our own, comparing evidence, collating profiles, criticizing the other's perspective for what it lacks, and, according to what we find, amending our own" (*Being* 43). The best "analogue" for this situation is "truly great actors because they have a knack for disappearing into any number of difficult roles" (*Being* 40). For Johnson, human enlightenment depends on this ability to imagine ourselves as others; actors in particular, but also writers, "and all of us really, . . . believe in the interchangeability of standpoints," in "a form of phenomenological 'free' variation" (*Being* 43).

Johnson's imperative for the individual meshes perfectly with the moral duties of the fiction writer and the fiction reader. Since the real is in doubt, "the artist is obliged . . . to reconstruct as best he can perspectives on the Real" (C. Johnson, "Phenomenology" 150). The "process of truth" is to "throw ourselves with a character toward his projects, divest ourselves of our own historically acquired peculiarities, and reconstruct his world" (151). Language, especially fiction, is particularly valuable, for, through it, "suddenly our subjectivity is merged with that of a stranger" (C. Johnson, *Being* 39). Reading, which allows us "to inhabit the role and real place of others, and writing," which requires an "act of self-surrender" (39), both create a complex "we-relation" that "strives for interpretative *completeness*" ("Phenomenology" 152). To stretch toward such completeness and therefore toward enlightenment, the writer must try to "embod[y] as many perceptions as possible in a fiction, slighting none" (153), and, correspondingly, the reader must try to experience the perceptions of as many characters as possible. Johnson's ideal novel would be "the process novel where everybody mentioned is a main character in the process of evolution" (Little 172), where all the threads, and all their connecting entanglements, would be depicted and assimilated.

American experience and especially African-American experience are particularly relevant to Johnson's program because they incorporate so many varied positions and perceptions. Since America is a "genetically mongrelized" country in which all lives "are a tissue of cross-cultural influences" (C. Johnson, *Being* 43), Americans find ready at hand a wide array of other people whose perspectives they can sample. African-American experience is exceptionally multiple—"a tree branching forth innumerable appendages in an endless explosion of meaning," "a kaleidoscope of meanings, rich, multi-sided" ("Philosophy" 58). Because of the "nightmare" of African-American history, identity has been the most important theme of African-American literature: "The black American writer begins his or her career with—and continues to exhibit—a crisis of identity. If anything, black fiction is *about* the troubled quest for identity and liberty, the agony of social alienation, the longing for a real and at times a mythical home" (*Being* 8). Denied a past, lacking a place, looking for a secure future, African Americans, in history and in fiction, struggle to find meaningful selves. But, given Johnson's theory that the self must continually try on other selves, such a predicament becomes a metaphysical advantage. Forced out of a viable place, denied access to both African cyclical time and European linear time, and thrust into an American experience that continually kept identities off balance, African Americans of necessity adopted approaches similar to Johnson's. Since no individual position was ever secure, the tendency was to adopt a multiplicity of other positions—in short, to approximate the intersubjective web. In *Oxherding Tale* and *Middle Passage*, Johnson delineates how that process might work.

The two novels are parallel allegories, two fictional renderings of Johnson's ideas about the self and the world. Each is narrated by a young male protagonist who starts from a position of naïveté and moves toward enlightenment. Given Johnson's views, this means that each progresses from a one-dimensional and self-centered sense of self through an absorption of other characters' identities to a polymorphous, empathetic, and enlightened being. Correspondingly, the social milieu surrounding the protagonists is at first rigidly controlled by bipolar oppositions and later characterized by greater fluidity and multiplicity, as boundaries and oppositions are gradually transcended. Each novel is a picaresque adventure, a hero's quest, in which the protagonist moves physically, psychologically, and philosophically through a series of passages on his journey toward enlightenment. Each protagonist is separated from home and family, undergoes various tests, encounters a mixture of unusual characters, gains self-knowledge, marries wisely, and settles down to middle-class respectability. Each is heavily influenced by members of a fictional African tribe, the Allmuseris, who personify many of Johnson's philosophical ideas. Each reveals his ethical goodness in caring for a helpless female: for Andrew, his mortally ill former girlfriend, Minty; for Rutherford, the Allmuseri child, Baleka. As a result of his ordeal, each develops an abnormal heartbeat, indicating not only his suffering but also his growing compassion. In creating these structures, Johnson plays off traditional European novelistic forms, such as the novel of education, or bildungsroman; the novel of testing, or *prufungsroman;* and the battle over the hero's soul, or *psychomachia.* He also imitates and modifies traditional African-American forms: the slave narrative, the novel of passing, and the Middle Passage. Through a dazzling array of motifs and techniques, both novels exhibit Johnson's beliefs about the primacy of intersubjectivity.

Both Andrew Hawkins and Rutherford Calhoun are cut off from the traditional bonds of parents and family. Andrew's life begins, literally, with a reversal when, on a whim, his father and his father's owner sleep with each other's wives. Although Andrew is raised in the slave quarters by his stepmother and his father, George, his status is ambiguous, and he is light skinned enough to pass for white. He is only partially welcome at the master's house, where his white mother refuses to acknowledge his existence but where his stepfather accepts some responsibility for him and provides him with a tutor. From the tutor, Ezekiel Sykes-Withers, he receives an education in Western philosophy, and then, at age twenty, he leaves home with the hope of earning enough money to free his parents and his girlfriend, Minty. Rutherford Calhoun also receives a philosophical education, in his case from his master, Reverend Chandler, and then leaves home at about the same age as Andrew. He leaves because he cannot abide by his brother Jackson's decision to divide their dying master's fortune among all the plantation's workers. Compared with Andrew, he starts more clearly from a narrow position of self-interest and disenlightenment as he seeks his fortune in New Orleans.

The world both characters encounter is dominated by rigid binary oppositions. In *Oxherding Tale,* the dichotomies of race and gender nearly overwhelm Andrew. The "joke" of his conception hinges on the racial barriers between his black slave family and his white owner family and on the gender disparities that allow the swapping of wives to be enticing for the men but anathema for the women. Throughout, the novel refers to unbridgeable gaps between blacks and whites and between men and women. Andrew believes that the black world "was, had always been, and might ever be a slaughterhouse—a style of being characterized by stasis, denial, humiliation, thinghood" (70)—and relations between the sexes are characterized as a war (28, 50, and 136). Controlled by white males, "again and again, and yet again, the New World said to blacks and women, 'You are nothing' " (75). Racial oppression leads to narrow preoccupation with race, as for George, a "flinty old Race Man" (21) whose life is ruined after he loses favor with his master, and for Patrick, Flo Hatfield's former lover, who fears every other black man as a rival and consequently becomes "this warped and twisted profile of the black (male) spirit" (50). Likewise, gender oppression generates Flo's narrow obsession with sexuality and sensuality, making her, in Reb's terms, "a slave like you'n me, Freshmeat" (62) and in Andrew's terms, "in bondage" (71) and "the creature of men" (72).[1]

In *Middle Passage,* Rutherford's binary world begins in Illinois, where he feels diametrically opposed to his brother, who is "like a negative of myself": "He was (to me) the possible-me that lived my life's alternative options, the me I fled. Me. Yet not me" (112). Unready to accept that alternative self, he flees to New Orleans, which in its depravity is the opposite of the intellectual North where Rutherford was raised. As Celestin Walby enumerates, the oppositions between Rutherford and Jackson and between New Orleans and Illinois continue in the contrast between Madame Toulouse, who presides over Rutherford's sensual life in New Orleans, and Isadora, the proper young woman from the North who truly loves Rutherford (662–63).[2] The opposing forces become more stringent on board the *Republic,* where the battle lines are drawn between whites and blacks and between the captain's party and the mutineers. The captain, Ebenezer Falcon, embodies the binary perspective. For him, the self is defined by its conflicts with the Other: "For a self to act, it must have somethin' to act *on*" (97). Opposition to a thing, or to another self, is the natural condition of humans: "And the final test of truth is war on foreign soil. War in your front yard. War in your bedroom. War in your own heart, if you listen too much to other people" (97). For him, opposition runs so deep that it is endemic within each person—"a bloody structure of the mind" and "a deep crack in consciousness itself" (98) that predisposes humans to such acts as murder and slavery. As Daniel M. Scott, III, puts it, Falcon "is the spirit of opposition, dualism, repression, and conflict" (649).

In their sharply dichotomous worlds, Andrew and Rutherford are noticeably free from the constraints of any fixed position. Andrew can pass for white; Rutherford is black yet part of the *Republic*'s white crew. At first each is bewildered by the freedom his position allows him. Andrew "belonged . . . to both house and field" and felt "caught . . . in [the] crossfire" between his black family and his white one (*Oxherding* 8). Later he worries that he will never be comfortable as a white or a black, "forever poised between two worlds" (17). Initially, Rutherford feels that for him, born "in bondage," "there are only two ways you can go: outright sedition or plodding reform" (*Middle* 114). Choosing the former, he heads for New Orleans, where he is trapped between his attraction for Isadora and his desire for an untrammeled life of fast living. Isadora's agreement with Papa Zeringue threatens to force him to choose, which throws him into "a lather of confusion" (17) and leads to his hasty decision to stow away on the *Republic*. On board, however, his suspension between opposing forces becomes dangerously intense when the ship divides into three factions: the Allmuseri slaves, the mutineers, and the captain. Rutherford feels loyalties to all three because he is confused about all loyalties and about his own identity. He spies for the captain but objects when McGaffin, one of the mutineers, calls him a spy (87). As McGaffin says, Rutherford has gone "his own way . . . believin' in nothin', belongin' to nobody" (88), but he rejects that description as well. Trying to sort out his feelings, he is completely confused, "too pitchkettled to trust in my own speech" and unable to "find my loyalties" or to know "what were my interests" (92). As Brian Fagel argues, Rutherford is caught in the middle, in the space between the factions, between America and Africa, between white and black (626).

Despite the turmoil it causes, however, the suspension between bipolar oppositions eventually leads each protagonist toward enlightenment. As Johnson phrases it, "In each one of the novels there is a progression from ignorance to knowledge, or from a lack of understanding to some greater understanding" (Little 160).[3] The movement is from self-interest to love, from alienation to commitment, from self to community. Andrew finds happiness with Peggy Undercliff and a secure role in middle-class society, and Rutherford discovers his love for Isadora and plans to return with her to the family farm in Illinois. In *Oxherding Tale* the progression is explicit, as Andrew acknowledges but rejects the Ways to enlightenment followed by Reb and Bannon and consciously realizes that he has found his own Way. The last chapter is titled "Moksha," which, as Johnson says, means "enlightenment" or "liberation" (Little 161). In *Middle Passage* Rutherford's transformation is more complete, as he emerges from the ravages of the voyage as a new person, physically altered and morally rebuilt, able to "recognize the reciprocal, intersubjective nature of experience" (O'Keefe 635) and having acquired a sense of "polyhistory" (Smith 672).

These transformations are possible for several reasons. Because each hero is initially set free from the binary oppositions that characterize his social world, he is not bound by them. Not being aligned clearly with any of the known positions in those oppositions causes each character considerable confusion and anxiety, but being placed in the interstices, in the *différance*, also allows each the freedom eventually to transcend the system, to grow to the realization that, in Johnson's words, "the little boxes and categories into which we sort 'experience' do not exist" (Boccia 618).[4] Their difficult passage to and through this transcendence requires them to endure many trials—their *bildung* is inseparable from their *prufung*. Reflecting Johnson's ideas about intersubjectivity, their passages are characterized by their encounters with a series of other characters whose perspectives they must understand, empathize with, and even emulate as they progress from their initial one-dimensional selves to more inclusive selves.

Andrew's encounters with other characters constitute a symposium on the relationship between the self and the Other. As he gets to know the others, he absorbs their approaches to the problem, learning from them and learning that their Way is not his Way, modifying each but not adopting any. Ezekiel illustrates the extreme case of a person with no significant relationship to the Other, and consequently his self is "emotionally bankrupt," "empty," and needing "something to serve" (91). His only way of relating to another is to try to buy a relationship, as when he is duped by Shem Moses into paying for the latter's daughter, Althea. Flo Hatfield does buy her relationships with others, using her financial and social power to entrap young black men in sensual relationships that primarily serve her bankrupt ego. Gerald Undercliff, a "crypto-Schopenhauerean" (120), attests to an abiding negativism about human beings—they are either Annoying or Very Annoying—yet his love for his daughter and his empathy for his patients belie his crustiness. Minty, Andrew's young lover, shows Andrew the Allmuseri extreme of subsuming oneself in the service of others. Peggy Undercliff comes closer to Andrew's, and Johnson's, preferred position, which combines a strong individual identity with love for another. She maintains her own self and identifies with Andrew: "I want what you want, even if your pleasure means I experience pain" (162). In Andrew's and Peggy's joint care of the dying Minty, Peggy, like Andrew, grows through her fears: "With Peggy, whose fear of sharing love was tested, then transcended, we made it through more bad nights than I care to recall" (164).

The symposium becomes peculiarly Johnsonian with the inclusion of Reb, the coffinmaker, and Horace Bannon, the soulcatcher. For Reb, an Allmuseri, the solution to the self/Other problem is to eliminate the self by denying the self's desires. He advises Andrew that "if you got no power . . . you have to think like the people who *do* so you kin make y'self over into what they want" (62). Instead of enjoying what he needs, he "rejoiced at what he *didn't* need" (46); instead of feeling pride in his work, he asserts that "*I* didn't *do* anythin'. . . . Things are done, that's all" (47). He learned his worldview from a beggar named Jupiter, who told him "Boy, you don't git *nothin'* 'til you *don't* want it" (76). Reb's position is one of "surrender," "nihilation," "sacrifice," and absolute "self-denial" (75). Bannon confirms Reb's absence of self when he reports his inability to become Reb and thus capture him: "yo friend . . . didn't have no place inside him fo' me to settle. He wasn't *positioned* nowhere" (174). Although Andrew must add Reb's position to those he absorbs, Reb's self-denial leads him to social isolation, whereas Andrew must combine elements of every character's position to fulfill his identity within the community.

Bannon is a parody of the Allmuseris, for like them he gives up his identity as he becomes each of his victims, but he does so not to create community but to destroy it. Rather than a cipher, like Reb, he becomes a polymorphic personality, made up of the many persons, mostly fugitive slaves, he has murdered. Before learning Bannon's secrets, Andrew notes that Bannon is "a racial mongrel" with a striking "collage of features" (67) and that his clothes likewise are a patchwork—"Rob Roy jeans, a redingote, cartridge belts, and Ivanhoe Cap" (68). Bannon's success as a slave catcher is based on his uncanny ability to know his victims so well as to literally absorb them into his self: "Yo mind has to soak hup his mind. His heart" (114–15). The victim's Achilles' heel is his or her innermost desire: "You *become* a Negro by lettin' yoself see what he sees, feel what he feels, want what he wants. What does he want?" (115). Not only is Bannon a figurative "crazyquilt of other's features" (169), but his polymorphism is actualized in his tattoos, living pieces of each of his many victims, "an impossible flesh tapestry of a thousand individualities no longer static, mere drawings, but if you looked at them long enough, bodies moving like Lilliputians over the surface of his skin" (175). Having killed hundreds of people and having become each of his victims, Bannon exemplifies Johnson's philosophy of intersubjectivity, but he has inverted the idea by using his knowledge to kill rather than to love. Since he tries to become the intersubjective web by destroying its individual threads rather than loving and validating them, his parodic quest leads to alienation rather than enlightenment.

Andrew, the initiate, learns from each of these members of the symposium, seeing the world from each other perspective and thereby developing his own mature perspective. He understands each other Way, realizing that it is not his: "I had seen so many Ways since leaving Hodges—the student in Ezekiel, the senses in Flo Hatfield, the holy murderer in Bannon (Shiva's hitman), and Reb, who was surely a Never-Returner; but in all these well-worn trails—none better than another—I discovered that my dharma, such as it was, was that of the householder" (147). Thinking that Bannon is about to kill him, Andrew has his deepest epiphany, enabling him for the first time to see clearly: "the Soulcatcher's presence drove out every false possibility, stripped perception clean as whalebone, freed it from the private, egoistic interests that normally colored my vision" (173). Through Bannon's role as Krishna, the vehicle for Andrew's achievement of enlightenment (Byrd 556), Andrew transcends all the other one-dimensional perspectives to merge with the Other: "I could hear—*was*—the sound of a raincrow's song ringing in the tree we approached" (173). Adept now at "seeing distinctions," he realizes that the woman he has long sought is "Being" (173).

Whether he lives or dies does not matter, for in this discovery he has transcended ordinary earthly desire; it is enough to contemplate Being, "bountiful without end" and "so extravagantly plentiful the everyday mind closed to this explosion, this efflorescence of sense" (173).

This merging with Being prepares Andrew for his final epiphany, a spiritual identification with his father. In Bannon's "theatre of tattoos," he sees his father in a composite image of a dead boy, a dying steer, and "several others" (176). In that image he perceives and understands "the profound mystery of the One and the Many" (176), thus cementing his earlier identification with Being. This spiritual linkage with his father—"I was my father's father, and he my child"—equates Andrew's identity not only with Being in general but also with the past and the future, with his lost heritage and with his ancestors to come. His Way is the Way of the householder, the steady survivor in the now endlessly linked generations of his family, community, and race. This Way enables Andrew to find the elusive African-American home, to locate himself in American space, and to orient himself in both Western and African time.

Rutherford Calhoun's relationships with other characters is less like a symposium on self and Other than a *psychomachia,* a battle for his soul. In Illinois, he feels that his brother and his master want him to adopt their attitude of selfless generosity. Then in New Orleans Papa Zeringue and his enforcer, Santos, attempt to own Rutherford, and even Isadora's love is expressed through her plot to force him to marry her. On the *Republic* he is the unaligned neutral whose allegiance all three factions seek.

Of the factions, Captain Falcon depicts the extreme version of the willful self in total and hostile opposition to the Other. He, like all would-be world conquerors, is ego writ large: "the desire to be fascinating objects in the eyes of others" (33). The same age as the United States (49) and captain of a ship called the *Republic,* his "burning passion was the manifest destiny of the United States to Americanize the entire planet" (30). He is thus a microcosm of the United States (Scott 649) and a vehicle for Johnson's satire of America's dualistic orientation. His destructive willfulness is reminiscent of Bannon (Gysin 291), but his insistence on the individual's inviolate separation from all others is the opposite of Bannon's absorption of others into himself. Together, Falcon and Bannon reveal the negative possibilities of either extreme.

Rather than simply rejecting Falcon's predation, Rutherford tries out Falcon's perspective on his journey toward enlightenment. Stealing from the captain, Rutherford wants "to know his heart" (48), in Falcon's room feels that he has "fallen into another man's nightmare" (54), and as Falcon's spy becomes his "eyes and ears" (57). Later, having incorporated the philosophies of everyone on board and thereby gained valuable empathy, Rutherford can pity the captain, can pity him "for his incompleteness" (143)—that is, for his single-minded perspective as opposed to the intersubjective position that Rutherford is acquiring.

The leaders of the second faction, the mutineers Peter Cringle and Josiah Squibb, are closest to Rutherford's perspective and therefore serve as foils for him. Like Falcon and the unenlightened Rutherford, Cringle wants to believe in human rationality but, to his credit, lacks Falcon's brutal insistence on it. He worries that humans are surrounded by "the formless Naught" of the ocean and that "all our reasoning and works are so provisional" (42). He shares Rutherford's sense of precariousness, of not belonging anywhere, and of being always "contrary" (159). Like Rutherford, he speculates about the human condition, but he does not absorb others' perspectives as the protagonist does and must be content with a vague relativism ("Truth is what *works*, pragmatically in the sphere of commerce" [160]) as opposed to Rutherford's ascension toward enlightenment.

Squibb, the alcoholic cook, appears to be very unlike Rutherford but like the latter is tested, assimilates the Allmuseri perspective, and achieves a degree of enlightenment. The ordeal of near starvation on the helpless ship forces Squibb into the shameful act of stealing food from the surviving children, an act that associates him with Rutherford, who had been a professional and pathological thief. But, like Rutherford, Squibb is changed for the better by his association with the Allmuseris. Required to become the ship's surgeon, he suddenly and inexplicably wields his lancet with the dexterity of the Africans. "His breathing even resembled that of the Allmuseri" (76), and he acquires the mixture of individuals and cultures that the Allmuseris possess, Johnson advocates, and Rutherford also acquires. As Rutherford says of Squibb, "I felt perfectly balanced crosscurrents of culture in him, each a pool of possibilities from which he was unconsciously drawing, moment by moment, to solve whatever problem was at hand" (176). Not surprisingly, Squibb, but not Cringle, survives.

The Allmuseris on the *Republic*, the third faction, are diametrically opposed to Falcon. Instead of his insistence on the individual and combative self, their tribe is a collective, "as close-knit as cells in the body" (58). Whereas Falcon is convinced of the duality of the world, for them, hell is "the failure to experience the unity of Being everywhere" (65), and they fear that their forced passage to America and slavery is a fall into that hell, "into the madness of multiplicity" (65). Because of their belief in absolute unity, they are also the opposite of Falcon in their abhorrence of harming any other creature (78). Unlike Falcon but like Reb in *Oxherding Tale*, they try to eliminate all desire, labeling one day a month as a Day of Renunciation (180). Reflecting their belief in unity, they are an amalgam of many peoples, including Egypt and the sub-Sahara (61) as well as India, Central America, the Caribbean, and South America (76–77). They are as close as one can come to an epitome of the human race—an "old people" (43), "the Ur-tribe of humanity itself" (61), in whom Rutherford feels "the presence of countless others" (61).

As Rutherford becomes acquainted with Ngonyama, Baleka, and the other Allmuseris, he adds their perspective to those of Falcon, his brother, Isadora, Papa Zeringue, and everyone else he encounters. Like Andrew, he does not adopt wholesale any of these perspectives but modifies what he sees in each of them as he becomes a broader, composite self. Although he does not fully realize the value of his behavior, he is on the right track when he sets aside his own self to borrow from others' identities: "I was a parasite to the core. . . . I was open, like a hingeless door, to everything" (162). As such, he often feels the chaos of the lack of a secure identity, but he is unwittingly gaining the polymorphic, intersubjective self that Johnson endorses: "for in myself I found nothing I could rightly call Rutherford Calhoun, only pieces and fragments of all the people who had touched me, all the places I had seen, all the homes I had broken into. The 'I' that I was, was a mosaic of many countries, a patchwork of others and objects stretching backward to perhaps the beginning of time" (162–63).

The mysterious god of the Allmuseris, also on board the ship, personifies the tribe's qualities. Like a living black hole, it is an almost unspeakable, indescribable unity, absorbing unto itself all other identities, creatures, and objects. When the cabin boy, Tommy, descends to its cage, self and Other become one: "singer, listener, and song, light spilling into light, the boundaries of inside and outside, here and there, today and tomorrow, obliterated as in the penetralia of the densest stars, or at the farthest hem of Heaven" (69). Like Melville's weaver god in *Moby-Dick*, this god "sustains everythin' in the universe . . . like a weaver" (100). The god is the "heart of things hidden" (69), a composite of all living things: it "had other beings, whole cultures of them, living parasitically on its body" (168). It is perfect yet it is always becoming, "contained in a silence where all was possibility, perfection, preformed" (168). Absorbing Tommy and then Rutherford as it links each individual to all others, it symbolizes Johnson's ideal of intersubjectivity: it is a living locus—an infinite web—where the individual self intersects all other selves, past, present, and future.

Just as Andrew is spiritually reunited with his father in the polymorphic tattoos on Bannon's body, Rutherford has an epiphanic vision of his father in the presence of the Allmuseri deity, who, like Bannon, is covered with tattoos. Through "a seriality of images," the god brings forth Riley Calhoun's life as part of Riley and Rutherford's entire heritage—"the *complete* content of the antecedent universe to which my father, as a single thread, belonged" (169).[5] Like Andrew, Rutherford is also linked to his for-bears, his culture, and his nearly lost past by connection to his father. Rutherford's vision of his father and his past, conveyed by the god, is a mystical union of the one and the many: "A thousand soft undervoices that jumped my jangling senses from his last, weakly syllabled wind to a mosaic of voices within voices, each one immanent in the other, none his but all strangely his" (171).

The epiphany climaxes with Rutherford's realization that he and the god are inseparable, that he, the individual, and the god, incorporating everything, are all part of one unity: "Suddenly I knew the god's name: Rutherford" (171). Rutherford thereupon begins his ritualistic death—"Then I fainted. Or died. What-ever"—which is further represented by the sudden whitening of his hair (172), his physical purging of "black clumps" like "an afterbirth or a living thing aborted from the body" (178), his near-death illness (180) in which he lies "as in a chrysalis" (181) await-ing rebirth, and his near drowning after the ship breaks up (184). He is then reborn as a new Rutherford—barely recognized by Isadora, Zeringue, and Santos—with a new personality capable of outwitting Zeringue, of truly loving Isadora, of accepting San-tos's fealty, and of settling down with his brother in Illinois. Like Andrew, he has achieved a high state of Johnsonian enlighten-ment, characterized by empathy, love, wholeness, and commu-nity. To achieve this state of contentment, both Andrew and Rutherford must absorb the principles embodied by the Allmus-eris but, curiously, must not wholeheartedly adopt those princi-ples. Intuiting the absolute unity of everything in the cosmos is an essential element in their development, but fully embracing such unity carries the risk of reducing their perspectives to a limiting monologism, albeit the privileged Allmuseri one. Rather than becoming Allmuseri, both protagonists must add the All-museri perspective to the array of other perspectives they have experienced and assimilated.

In both novels, Johnson deepens his theme of intersubjectivity through motifs and techniques that reinforce the principle. For example, by telling lies and stories, the characters, primarily Andrew and Rutherford, temporarily try on new identities. If one should try to see the world from the perspectives of other people, one should also see the world from a perspective that one invents. Because of his dual white/black identity, Andrew feels that he is a "living lie" (*Oxherding* 17). Before he creates his new identity as a white man, he toys with the idea of a different name when he evades Bannon's question ("What might yo name be, son?") with a near lie ("It might be James") (68). Then, to pass for white, he makes up a new self, William Harris, complete with "a wonderful biography" (109). Not only are this fictional self and biography expedient—they keep Andrew and Reb out of the deadly Cripplegate mine and lead to Andrew's successful life as a teacher, husband, and father—but the self-invention is also consistent with Johnson's belief that the individual should experience other perspectives. Other characters also lie to help themselves reinterpret the world: Andrew's father, George, lies to cover up his fall from Mr. Polkinghorne's favor, and Peggy Underhill creates her own version of her mother's absence (123, 127). Even though lying can help characters broaden their identities, Johnson also knows that telling the truth is essential, as when Andrew owns up to his obligation to Minty.

Rutherford is a more extravagant and consistent liar than Andrew, and, as with Andrew, lying enables Rutherford to escape the narrow confines of a single-dimensioned identity. As a child, frustrated by the rectitude of his brother and his master, he told "preposterous lies for the hell of it" (*Middle* 3), and later he admits to readers that "I always lied" (90). In his wild life in New Orleans he is enmeshed in a world of lies, his own as well as Papa Zeringue's and virtually everyone else's. Needing a temporary escape, he quickly forges the lie of attempting to become Josiah Squibb. On the ship, lies predominate—Rutherford lies about his cooking ability (25) and about the ring Falcon gave him (90); Falcon (presumably) lies about cannibalism (33); sailors, we are reminded, are "careless with the truth" (58); and stories abound about the Allmuseri god (67). As Rutherford struggles to expand his identity and to weigh his allegiances to the different factions, he questions the possibility of any honest commitments between people. He worries that "all bonds . . . were a lie forged briefly in the name of convenience and just as quickly broken when they no longer served one's interests" (92), and he wonders "Were all loyalties here a lie?" (105). Even though lies have their purposes, Rutherford must mature to the point of developing true empathy and thereby forging a true bond, a true loyalty, with others, as he does eventually with Isadora, Baleka, Santos, and his brother.

Just as each protagonist uses lies to grow out of his monologic self, each novel enacts the values of "lying." Like all fiction, each novel is, like a lie, made up. It is Johnson's story by which he and the reader imaginatively become each character, thereby releasing themselves from confining one dimensionality and participating, at least vicariously, in a broadening intersubjectivity. Johnson and the reader thus replicate the protagonists' progress toward enlightenment, as all the novels' participants move from their isolating individual perspectives toward the unity of Being.

Johnson calls attention to this status of his texts as lies by embedding stories within the novels, fictions within the fiction. Some of these embedded stories are Andrew's and Rutherford's acknowledged fantasies, evidence of their growing abilities to project other perspectives, as when Andrew pictures the scene of Bannon killing his father (*Oxherding* 174–75) and when Rutherford imagines Cringle's upbringing (*Middle* 25). Other embedded stories are accounts by minor characters that Andrew and Rutherford then renarrate, such as George's story about Flo Hatfield and her appetites (*Oxherding* 20), Reb's story of his attempts to beg money to help his dying daughter (*Oxherding* 76), Squibb's story of his marriage to Maud (*Middle* 39), and the Allmuseri stories of atrocities they have endured (*Middle* 134). Some have obvious parallels to the novels, such as Ezekiel's story of Trishanka's quest for *Samsara,* the highest knowledge, which parodies Andrew's journey to enlightenment (*Oxherding* 32–34). In *Oxherding Tale* some of the stories involve historical figures, such as the account of Karl Marx's visit to Ezekiel at Cripplegate (81–88); Andrew's footnote on the allegedly real life of James Travis,

Jr., the boy guarding the turnpike; and Peggy's anecdote about Evelyn Pomeroy's acquaintance with Harriet Beecher Stowe (143). As James W. Coleman persuasively argues, these embedded stories, as well as allusions to Thomas Hobbes's *Leviathan* and Laurence Sterne's *Tristram Shandy*, break down readers' preconceptions about the novel, African-American fiction, and the figures and intertexts alluded to (632, 639). As Johnson's text is modified by the allusions and the allusions are modified by Johnson's text, these mutual influences parallel Johnson's ideas about the benefits of mutual influences among people and the ultimate value of intersubjectivity: all texts, like all minds, are ultimately interrelated, part of the tangled but unified web of Being.

Both novels radically allude to their problematic status as fictions. Both first-person narrators frequently remind readers of their narrations, through references to themselves as narrators (such as "if I may speak freely" [*Oxherding* 61] and "I must add" [*Middle* 163]) and to the text as the product of their narration (such as "to shorten the story" [*Oxherding* 139] and "Of all the players who promenade through this narrative" [*Middle* 75]). In *Oxherding Tale* many self-references are heavily underscored, for example when Andrew ends the text with a separate paragraph consisting of "This is my tale" and when he breaks his narration between chapters, interjecting first that "this had best commence a new chapter" (66), titling the next chapter "A New Chapter," and then beginning that chapter with a repetition of the interrupted sentence at the end of the preceding chapter.

One thrust of these self-references is to cast doubt on each narrator's ability to convey accurately all the details of his story. In *Middle Passage* Rutherford declares to Falcon, "I'm no writer" (146), which creates doubt about "his" text that we are reading. Furthermore, Rutherford insists that he will "tell the story," not only of "everything [he] can remember" and not merely "what [Falcon] told [him]," but "first and foremost, as I saw it" (146). As with any first-person novel, the text is biased by the subjectivity of the narrator, but here that narrator is a confessed liar, and his limitations are explicit. In *Oxherding Tale* such limits are even more emphatic. Several times Andrew admits his inability to remember accurately (101, 110) or to express adequately what transpires (102, 107, 157), and at one point he "confess[es] . . . that this account is a tale woven partly from fact, partly from fancy" (94). Even more noticeably, Andrew's entire narration is embedded in the metanarration of an omniscient, external narrator who interrupts Andrew's tale with two short "intermissions" (118–19 and 152–53). This authorial-like narrator, reminiscent of conventional eighteenth- and nineteenth-century narrators, provides historical, philosophical, and theoretical ruminations on the form of slave narratives in the first intermission and on the limitations of first-person narrators in the second.

Johnson achieves a similar effect of calling attention to and calling into question the text of *Middle Passage* by equating the text with the ship's log. Starting with one of the epigraphs, which appears to introduce the *Republic*'s log—"Laud Deo / Journal of a Voyage intended / by God's permission / in the *Republic,* African / from New Orleans to the Windward / Coast of Africa"—and continuing with the novel's dated chapter titles ("Entry, the first" through "Entry, the ninth"), numerous references establish the idea that the novel is the ship's log: for example, "the log in which I now write" (27), "what I am about to say must go no farther than the pages of this logbook" (175), and "I opened the logbook you presently hold in your hands" (200).

Such an equation, however, raises doubts about the status of the text. If the text is the ship's log, why does it include Rutherford's adventures in New Orleans prior to sailing? Why does it include Rutherford's recovery, dealings with Zeringue, and reunion with Isadora after the *Republic* sinks? Why does it include embedded stories about Jackson and Chandler, about Squibb's marriage, about Cringle's father, and so on? Moreover, a ship's log is ostensibly an objective record of a voyage, yet Rutherford declares that he will tell the story "as I saw it" (146)—that is, subjectively. This subjectivity is also suggested by his admission that he wrote "furiously and without direction" to "free myself from the voices in my head, to pour onto these water-stained pages as much of the pain as I could" (189).

As Scott argues, such narrative "dislocations" (650) create a "textual fluidity" (651) that echoes the novel's investigation of the fluctuations in identity.[6] Rutherford must experience the world from other characters' perspectives, and, similarly, the doubts about the status and validity of the text force readers to experience the novel from a sliding perspective. In addition, the act of writing, of reformulating the events into the log, enables Rutherford to view them differently: "Then, as our days aboard the *Juno* wore on, I came to [the writing] with a different, stranger compulsion—a need to transcribe and thereby transfigure all we had experienced, and somehow through all this I found a way to make my peace with the recent past by turning it into Word" (189–90). Since writing is a transformative act, by definition giving Rutherford a different perspective on the events, it is analogous to his taking on another character's viewpoint. Either kind of expansion is therapeutic. Virginia Whatley Smith accurately describes the multiplicity inherent in Rutherford's role as writer: "As a recorder/historian, he blends autobiographical with biographical accounts and first- with third-person perspectives, ultimately becoming an omniscient, first-person narrator. . . . His log synthesizes Falcon's knowledge of polyhistory and his linguistic adeptness, Calhoun's own biblical and classical training, and the Allmuseris' ancient history and customs" (672–73).[7] Moreover, Rutherford's act of writing doubles Johnson's own act: by turning these imaginative events into Word, Johnson also takes on the perspective of the written language even as he imaginatively takes on the perspectives of each character, and he projects the hope that readers will imaginatively try on the perspectives of the characters as well as the author.

In several respects the style of the two novels is also designed to unsettle and involve readers. One such technique occurs when Johnson runs a string of words together with no punctuation, as in Flo's list of what she wants in a lover—"I *also* want sexual satisfaction compliments gifts fidelity a great body cleverness sophistication yet boyish exuberance a full head of hair good teeth and the ability to know my moods" (*Oxherding* 60)—or in Rutherford's description of the *Republic*'s crew—"thirty-two sopping-wet cutthroats black-toothed rakes traitors drunkards rapscallions thieves poltroons forgers clotpolls sots lobcocks sodomists prison escapees and debauchees" (*Middle* 82).[8] These catalogs convey a sense of energy and urgency to the narrative, and they call readers' attention to the acts of reading and writing, making them shift away from their usual perspective toward a more flexible and plural viewpoint. Johnson also sprinkles both novels with slang words, such as "clotpolls" and "lobcocks," and neologisms, such as "ostrobogulous" (*Oxherding* 124), "flinderjigs" (*Oxherding* 131), "mubblefubbled" (*Middle* 92), and "gaposis" (*Middle* 193). Like the unpunctuated series, such diction forces the reader to notice the text and to adopt a more active perspective simply to extrapolate meaning from the unfamiliar language.

In both novels, Johnson attempts to extend the readers' identity expansion by frequently referring to them. Both narrators often acknowledge their readers' presence, ostensibly to keep them comfortable but more likely having the opposite effect. The first paragraph of *Middle Passage* ends with Rutherford's warning that what lies ahead in his narrative, "as I shall tell you," will be "far worse than the fortune I'd fled in New Orleans" (1). He cares about readers' interests, as when he starts to digress about Squibb's transformed personality but then surmises that readers do not care: "Don't care about that? Okay, we shall push on" (176). He assumes that readers inhabit his world and are holding the water-stained pages of the logbook in their hands, and so he tells them not to "bother to call on" him on Sunday evenings (187). In *Oxherding Tale* Andrew similarly assumes the readers' close presence, as he regularly refers to their probable reactions, as in "you will agree" (109), "you are wondering" (132), and "as you've probably guessed" (147).

Often, each narrator-protagonist is defensive, worried about his readers' reactions: Andrew is afraid that readers will not believe him (*Oxherding* 101), are frowning (119), or do not understand (163), and Rutherford requests that readers not judge him too harshly (*Middle* 90) and not think poorly of him (95–96). Andrew often addresses his readers, usually as "sir" (e.g., *Oxherding* 40), once as "brothers" (162), and once as "friend" (166), and Rutherford once addresses the reader as "brother" (*Middle* 155). These terms of address are unsettling, creating both distance ("sir") and closeness ("brother," "friend"), and even the possible closeness is offset by the distinctly masculine quality of most of the terms and by the potential racial exclusiveness of *brother(s)*.

Readers are also likely to be unsettled because, in the midst of each narrator's familiarity and concern, each manipulates readers' emotions. Andrew tricks readers by making them assume that the return of Reb's ring means that Bannon has killed Reb, and then, in the climactic pages of the narrative, he makes readers anticipate that Bannon is about to murder Andrew as well. Andrew, of course, knows that his life will be spared, but he puts readers through the emotional wringer of expecting his death. Rutherford similarly plays with readers' expectations when, in his 28 June log entry, he reports that the mutineers plan to take over the ship "tomorrow at noon" (*Middle* 83), but then there is no log entry for that day. While readers wonder about the proposed mutiny, Rutherford's next entry—for 30 June—blithely digresses to Falcon's ideas about the Allmuseri god and to Rutherford's relations with Jackson and Chandler. Only in the following entry—for 3 July—do readers hear about the slaves' revolt, which supersedes the mutiny. Johnson imposes these manipulations on readers to force them, like his protagonists, to broaden their perspectives, to engage in their own vicarious middle passage and their own escape from a vicarious slavery. Readers must move beyond their expectations of linear narrative time, of foreshadowing that always predicts accurately, and of conventional distinctions among first- and third-person narrators and among limited and omniscient ones. Readers are thus jarred loose from their confining but comfortable monologisms just as the protagonists are forced to relinquish theirs.[9]

As much of the previous discussion suggests, time in both nov-

els is complex. The picaresque narrations of Andrew and Rutherford on the one hand proceed in the linear chronology of their
lives but on the other hand are constantly interpolated with "flash
forwards" (Bambara 295) to future times and with embedded stories that are often told by secondary narrators and that usually
involve flashbacks to earlier times in the characters' lives. In *Oxherding Tale,* for example, the narration leaps ahead to the twentieth century in a footnote that summarizes the life and death of
a minor character's great-granddaughter, and the future is invoked in *Middle Passage* in such anachronistic moments as the
references to science fiction (29) and to Claude Lévi-Strauss's
concept of the raw and the cooked (75).

In *Middle Passage* the tension between linear and nonlinear
time is exacerbated by the contrast between the linear sequence
of "entries" in the logbook that the novel purportedly replicates
and the nonlinear nature of the actual text. For example, in addition to the suspension of time regarding the mutiny, Rutherford
ends his second 3 July entry with his confrontation with the Allmuseri god (166–67), yet his next entry skips to 1 August, leaving
readers to wonder about the unreported twenty-eight days. More
unsettling, as he begins the 1 August entry, Rutherford is still in
the presence of the god.

In *Oxherding Tale* flashbacks and foreshadowings proliferate.
The ostensible forward direction of the narrative is repeatedly
interrupted with stories from the past (such as Andrew's bizarre
conception, Ezekiel's life before coming to Cripplegate, and
Marx's visit to Cripplegate) and hints of the future (such as the
reference to Ezekiel's death "ten years later" [11], Bannon's anticipated presence [28], and Bannon's quitting the slave-catching
business [116]). But several such intimations of future events
prove false: Andrew feels "a foretaste of a death sentence" (74)
but does not die, and Bannon murders neither Reb nor Andrew.
At one point Andrew imagines his future as a householder, then
tells us that "what came to pass . . . was quite another story"
(147). Yet in the narrative, he does become a householder. The
presumed chronology of this narration is also compromised by its

tendency to make sharp breaks in time or place. As Andrew and George ride to Flo Hatfield's estate, the narration is interrupted by Andrew's memory of Ezekiel's story about Trishanku, and then the narrative, and Andrew, are abruptly shifted back to the "present" when George wakes him up (34). Another sudden shift occurs, again manipulating the reader, when, as Andrew and Reb approach the dreaded Yellowdog Mine, Andrew announces that he has a plan (81), but the plan and the action must wait for fourteen pages while Andrew recalls the stories of Marx's visit and Ezekiel's subsequent effort to buy Shem Moses' daughter.

Such dislocations in the temporal sequencing of each narrative have thematic implications. Each protagonist begins his journey with the unenlightened sense that time is uncomplicated, that it simply moves forward chronologically. Neither thinks about time, naively expecting the onward sequence of events to create his future. Their spiritual education requires them, however, to become conscious of their much more complex immersion in the multiplicity of time. Andrew at first thinks that he can remake his confused past by simply earning enough money from Flo to free George, Mattie, and Minty. But his perilous affair with Flo, the necessity of his decision to pass for white, and his attempts to evade Bannon embroil him in a much more complicated sense of time, a complexity reinforced later by the return of the now help-less Minty. Even more radically, Rutherford at first thinks that he has no past, expressing this simplistic sense of freedom to Cringle—"In a way, I have no past, Peter" (160). For much of the novel, Rutherford denies that past, repudiating his brother, ignoring his feelings for his father, and running away from his love for Isadora. But as he learns in his encounter with the All-museri god, he does have a past, a relationship with his father that is central to his own identity, and that expanding identity moves in the direction of commitment to his brother and Isadora.

As each hero progresses from a simplistic to a more mature sense of time and identity, each experiences odd moments of freedom from the usual sense of temporal continuity. At his wed-ding, Andrew momentarily escapes "clock time": "all through a ceremony that suspended Time. The heart knew nothing of hours" (*Oxherding* 140). Later, in a much less happy "moment," Bannon's arrival, which, Andrew fears, means his capture and death, seems also to suspend ordinary time: "Climbing down, Bannon moved like the Coffinmaker, as if Time were fiction, all that was and would be held suspended in this single moment, which was forever" (172). Ordinary time also opens out for Rutherford, once when Falcon tells him that one of the ship's owners is the same Papa Zeringue who "owned" Rutherford in New Orleans ("My months on the *Republic* seemed to dissolve" [*Middle* 150]) and once when his consciousness expands to include his ancestors ("the *complete* content of the antecedent universe to which my father . . . belonged" [169]).

As the forms of the two novels demonstrate, time within fiction is itself a fiction that can be readily manipulated, and, during that manipulation, each hero develops a broader understanding of the complexities of time and of his interwoven roles in the past, present, and future lives of his family and community. The novels destabilize chronological time because the protagonists must comprehend its instability; protagonists as well as readers are thereby encouraged to experience time differently, to move beyond their conventional sense of linear time, and thereby to try on this form of "phenomenological 'free' variation" (C. Johnson, *Being* 43), just as they must broaden their narrow individual selves by trying on other perspectives.

In *Middle Passage*, Johnson develops the motif of stealing to symbolize his ideas about intersubjectivity. Rutherford starts as "a petty thief" (2) who does not think twice about stealing Squibb's papers, who cannot help breaking into Falcon's cabin, and for whom "stealing was a nervous habit" (103). Like lying, stealing has its negative ramifications, but, also like lying, it elucidates Johnson's philosophy. When Rutherford steals Squibb's papers, he steals, or borrows, Squibb's identity, even though at that early stage in his journey he does not realize the value of such interpersonal borrowing. When he breaks into Falcon's cabin, Rutherford is more thrilled by the pleasure of breaking "the power of the propertied class" (47) than in the feeling of "transcendence" (46) afforded by his break-ins, but he enunciates the deeper principle: breaking into someone's home always made him feel "as if I were slipping inside another's soul" (46).

But after the rebellion, when Rutherford successfully ministers to the hurt and despondent survivors, he plumbs more deeply into the metaphor: he realizes that "everything of value lay outside me" and that he needed to "steal things others were 'experiencing'" (162). He sees himself as "a parasite to the core" (162), not merely in the earlier sense of a social parasite but now partially in Johnson's sense of a polymorphic self composed of fragments from others. He recalls that as a child he had literally stolen objects from Chandler and Jackson—"watches from Chandler's bureau and biscuits from his kitchen" (162) and change from Jackson's trousers. And much more significantly, he had "stolen" everyone's words, ideas, and, in short, identities: "I listened to everyone and took notes: I was open, like a hingeless door, to everything" (162). Now, as savior of the *Republic*'s survivors, he consciously transforms that parasitism into therapy both for himself and everyone around him: "And to comfort the weary on the *Republic* I peered deep into memory and called forth all that had ever given me solace, scraps and rags of language too" (162). In one sense he can do so because he does not yet have his own identity—"for in myself I found nothing I could rightly call Rutherford Calhoun." But in Johnson's view, he is clearly headed toward enlightenment. For Johnson it is destructive to have a fully formed, complete identity; it is always necessary to borrow from others. Rutherford has that fluidity, in chaotic excess at this point, but he is oriented properly in his multiplicity, since he "was a mosaic of many countries, a patchwork of others and objects stretching backward to perhaps the beginning of time" (162–63). After the rescue, Rutherford again uses the metaphor of stealing to express his guilt for surviving when others around him died: "By surviving, I sometimes felt I'd stolen life from Cringle, or was living on time belonging to Ngonyama and the other mates; I felt like a thief to the bitter end" (188). Johnson does not recommend actually stealing someone's life, but experiencing another's perspective is analogous to stealing from him or her, and Rutherford's strength of character in besting Zeringue and uniting with Isadora implies that he has incorporated the lives of Cringle, Ngonyama, and the others who died.

A formal counterpart to Rutherford's literal and psychic stealing is Johnson's extensive use of allusions and intertexts in both novels. The abundance of references to other texts is overwhelming: *Oxherding Tale* is based on such prior texts as the series of ten oxherder pictures, slave narratives, *Tristram Shandy* and other eighteenth-century picaresque novels, and Hobbes's *Leviathan* and the works of Karl Marx; *Middle Passage* depends on such preceding texts as Plato's *Republic* and many sea voyage texts from Western civilization.[10] A list of the novels' epigraphs suggests the eclecticism of the texts and figures mentioned: for *Oxherding Tale*, St. Augustine, *Rig Veda, Ten Oxherding Pictures,* and Franz Kafka's *The Great Wall of China;* for *Middle Passage,* St. Thomas Aquinas, Robert Hayden's poem "Middle Passage," and *Brihad-aranyaka Upanishad.* In both novels, the allusions demonstrate the protagonists' broad education, focusing on Western philosophy and literature and including some Eastern philosophy.

What Johnson does with these prior texts is what he believes people should do with other people: "steal" from them, try out their perspectives, modify them, and consequently enrich one's own perspective. Both the individual and the enriched text then can attain the Lifeworld. As Scott puts it, "Johnson's examination of identity (human and textual) depends on appropriation for its literal and philosophical method" (646). For his enlightenment, the character must steal the perspectives of other characters, and for its enlightenment, the text must "steal" other texts.[11] The writer must give up the self to be open to the appropriation of others' words, for writing "involves a corresponding act of self-surrender such that my perceptions and experiences are allowed to coincide with those who came before me . . . until my life and the life of others 'intersect and engage each other like gears'"

(C. Johnson, *Being* 39). Any word is "like a palimpsest," "a tissue of interpretations," and the attempt to use words throws the writer "suddenly into the midst of a crowd" (*Being* 39) of previous users and uses of those words, just as any person or character, faced with any event in life, is thrown into the midst of a crowd of others. By liberating ourselves from the outmoded conventions of a freestanding text or a unitary self, we can turn the situation into advantage, can strengthen ourselves and others by uniting with them in a transcendent multiplicity.

In both novels Johnson further probes his theme of intersubjectivity by depicting characters in varying degrees of merging, or commingling, with each other. The commingling can be physical, as when Andrew and Flo share tastes and bodily fluids (*Oxherding* 65). It can involve shared gestures, as when Rutherford throws Santos using moves he had observed in McGaffin and Atufal (*Middle* 193) and when Isadora imitates Rutherford's old habit by pulling at her earlobe (*Middle* 196). It can be a conscious imitation, as when Meadows acts out caricatures of Rutherford and Cringle (*Middle* 104–5). More often the commingling is spiritual: Peggy wants to desire and to feel what Andrew desires and feels (*Oxherding* 162), Rutherford senses that he has entered Falcon's nightmare (*Middle* 54), and Rutherford feels "bruised . . . if [Baleka] bruises herself" (*Middle* 195).

This interpenetration of souls can be total. To track down and kill his victims, Bannon becomes them: "You *become* a Negro by lettin' yoself see what he sees, feel what he feels, want what he wants. . . . You nail his soul so he can't slip away" (*Oxherding* 115). Exposure to the Allmuseri god takes Tommy and then Rutherford out of themselves and into immersion with cosmic Unity. For Tommy, as for Melville's Pip, the effect is madness, "himself chained now yet somehow unchained from all else . . . the boundaries of inside and outside, here and there, today and tomorrow, obliterated as in the penetralia of the densest stars, or at the farthest hem of Heaven" (*Middle* 69). For Rutherford, the effect is near madness—"it's safe to say I was hardly in my right mind" (168). But when the god takes the form of Rutherford's father—"I could no more separate the two, deserting father and divine monster, than I could sort wave from sea" (168–69)—Rutherford finds unity with both father and god. This near-death experience is also Rutherford's most powerful epiphany, leading to his liberation from his old, one-dimensional self and his growth into a new, polymorphic one.

These comminglings of one character with another also take the form of the merger of one character with a group or class of characters. According to Andrew, the Negro is "the finest student of the White World," because he/she borrows traits from that world, "the one pupil in the classroom who watches himself watching the others, absorbing the habits and body language of his teachers, his fellow students" (*Oxherding* 128). Similarly, the crew of the *Republic* is forced to resemble Falcon: the crew "was perpetually angry and dissatisfied" but "it wasn't *their* anger at all—it was Falcon's" (*Middle* 53), and "in a sense we *all* were ringed to the skipper in cruel wedlock" (144).

The most striking commingling aboard the *Republic* is the mutual influence of the Allmuseris and the crew. Unconsciously, each becomes like the other. Squibb is transformed by the voyage, able to perform surgery as well as Ngonyama had carved the pig and even breathing like the Allmuseris (176), and Rutherford acquires not only an Allmuserian empathy and egolessness but also "their accent" and their incapacity to generalize (194). For their part, the Allmuseris, like Rutherford, are "remade by virtue of [their] contact with the crew" (124). Rutherford realizes that, "like any men," they are "not fixed but evolving" and that they "were not wholly Allmuseri anymore" (124), just as he, Squibb, and the rest of the crew are not wholly American anymore. The Allmuseris regret this contagion, grieving over their fall into violence, murder, and "the world of multiplicity, of *me* versus *thee*" (140). But from Johnson's perspective, even the Allmuseri way of life is only one way; mutual influence, borrowing, and commingling are always necessary since that is the path toward the desired intersubjectivity.

The theme of contagion, or mutual influence, is conveyed by

the motif of smells, particularly in *Middle Passage*. When we smell something, we sense, even ingest, a physical trace of that thing, thereby experiencing and even partially becoming the thing. A character's dominating presence in a place can be expressed by his or her permeating odor, as when we are told that Patrick's presence is "worked into the texture of [Flo's] house . . . like an odor" (*Oxherding* 54) or that Falcon's "emotions permeated the ship like the smell of rum and rotting wood" (*Middle* 53). Odors often identify a place, as for the "toadstool smell" of Shem Moses' farmhouse (*Oxherding* 94), the "petroleum stench of the marketplace" (*Oxherding* 167), the "assault of smells" of New Orleans (*Middle* 2), and the "violent" smells of "medicaments, lotions, and disinfectants" of Reverend Chandler's bedroom (*Middle* 115). The smell of disease and death is noticeable in Minty—"She smelled sour. Sweat. A seaweed odor, as if her cells were breaking down into more basic elements" (*Oxherding* 165). A similar stench permeates the *Republic,* which "smells like a pesthouse" (*Middle* 116), worsens with the rotting body of the young slave "in the first stages of stench and putrefaction" (122), and further intensifies after the slave rebellion, when Squibb can "detect plague by its sweet scent" (156).

Hiram Groll, the strange veterinarian in *Oxherding Tale*, tends to stick "his nose right inside your clothes (almost) when talking to you, like an Arab, as if how you smelled was partly what you were" (57). Although Andrew finds this habit "damned peculiar," the two novels corroborate the idea that one's odor is part of one's identity. Peggy only needs "a whiff of" Bannon (*Oxherding* 169) to intuit his evilness. The Allmuseris carry "the smell of old temples" (*Middle* 61), suggesting their ancientness and their religiosity. Since a person's room is often indicative of the inhabitant, its smell also conveys a sense of the person: Flo's room, when Andrew is at odds with her, "swam with a smell so strong, so thick, [his] eyes began to water" (*Oxherding* 51); Isadora's hotel room has a "sweet, atticlike odor" (*Middle* 6), indicating her pleasant disposition and her old-fashioned demeanor; and Falcon's cabin has "the clamlike, bacterial odor of tabooed plea-sures" (*Middle* 27). Odors do not merely reflect characters' identities, but they also suggest that the boundary between self and Other is not as distinct as ordinarily assumed. Since characters' odors permeate the objects around them, allowing other characters to experience them, to know them, to ingest them, and thus partially to become them, the mutual interchanging of odors parallels the development of a composite self.

The ability to transcend the relative and thus to achieve intersubjectivity and community depends on the ability to efface the self (C. Johnson, *Being* 44). The Allmuseris demonstrate this ability in their tribal behavior that is "so ritualized, seasoned, and spiced by the palm oil, the presence of others it virtually rendered the single performer invisible—or, put another way, blended them into an action so common the one and many were as indistinguishable as ocean and wave" (*Middle* 166). Reb, an Allmuseri, achieves this subsuming of the self into the Other when his song "swelled, expanded, ate space, filled the woods like a splash of wind, blended with the air" (*Oxherding* 56) and when his skin and his ring become inseparable: "metal worked painfully, like scarification, into the skin during infancy and, like skin, was impleached until cartilage and metal melted back into a common field" (148). For the Allmuseris there is only unity, including unity between the self and the world: "as within, so it was without" (*Middle* 164). Moreover, what happens within the soul has a determining effect on what happens outside, as expressed by the Allmuseri concept of "outpicturing": "as if a man's soul was an alchemical cauldron where material events were fashioned from the raw stuff of feelings and ideas" (*Middle* 164). By projecting oneself outward into the world, one can achieve internal harmony: "It took up ten thousand hosts, this I, slipped into men, women, giraffes, gibbering monkeys. . . . [Reb] learned intimately the life of these objects and others, died their unrecorded deaths, and ever returned to himself richer, ready to assume a sorcerer's role" (*Oxherding* 49–50). Self and Other—other human beings, animals, and objects—are not dichotomous but unified, as the self incorporates all, becomes all.

The opposite of this progress toward unity and harmony is conveyed through the imagery of traps. Both Andrew and Rutherford are initially caught in the cross fires of binary worlds in which each has no place. Trying to break out of his racial trap, Andrew goes to Flo Hatfield's only to become more tightly bound in her binary perspective. He then escapes the surely fatal trap of the Yellowdog Mine, and he must subsequently use his wits to avoid being caught in his white disguise. Bannon then represents the most sinister trap because he preys on his victims' souls, and Andrew acutely feels this danger: "In weariness, I would welcome the kill as a wish. Could the trap be tighter?" (159).

Rutherford also begins in what he perceives to be an entrapping world. He sees his brother and his master's philanthropy as a debilitating cage that allows no room for his ego or desires. Unenlightened, he can see marriage, even to the sweet Isadora, only as "a hole" (7), as a way "to shackle myself" (10), and as "bondage" (19). On the *Republic* he continues to use marriage as a negative metaphor connoting entrapment: "as if, heaven help me, [Falcon and I] were married, and the very thing I'd escaped in New Orleans had, here off the unlighted coast of Senegambia, overtaken me" (58). But his transformation aboard the ship enlightens him to the realization that commitment to another person does not have to be a cruel trap but can be a fulfilling bond: "I wanted [Isadora and my] futures blended . . . our histories perfectly twined for all time" (208). Similarly, he progresses from his entanglements in Falcon's literal booby traps as well as the captain's egocentric rationalism to the epiphany that Falcon is also trapped, not a free man but under the thumb of the ship's investors, in fact "no freer than the Africans" (147). Such realizations liberate Rutherford from his narrow modes of thinking and pave the way for his ability to entrap the trappers, as when he blackmails the blackmailer, Papa Zeringue.

As Andrew and Rutherford journey from naïveté and division toward enlightenment and unity, they glimpse but do not fully attain the Allmuseri orientation. For Andrew, opium breaks down the usual boundary between self and other: "opium . . . *lowered* the senses, slowed them down and, in doing so, expanded the skin's sensitivity to the point where the body's edge vanished and blended into other bodies, objects" (*Oxherding* 63). The result is a temporary "clairvoyance" by which Andrew "could see . . . the interior of objects" (63). Twice, Rutherford briefly senses the identity of his internal state with external conditions, once when, internally diseased and dissolving, he reflects on the "dissolving, diseased world" (*Middle* 180) and again when he equates his personal debilitation with the destroyed ship—"I could not hide what I was: a wreck of the *Republic*" (190).

Although neither hero fully realizes the interconnections between his inner state and the objects around him, Johnson subtly privileges the Allmuseri position by repeatedly depicting the similarity between characters' inner selves and the rooms and houses they inhabit. In *Oxherding Tale* Ezekiel's two tiny rooms are filled with an eclectic potpourri of furniture, unfinished papers, and "a catastrophe of books, periodicals," newspapers, and sculpture (29). To Andrew, the rooms are "an extension of my tutor's mind" (29). In other words, Ezekiel's rooms exemplify the Allmuseri philosophy of unity between the internal and the external. The same can be said for numerous other rooms and houses throughout both novels. Flo Hatfield, whose clothes are "like a landscape," is as "decadent," "lush," and like "Dionysus" as her boudoir (*Oxherding* 37). Gerald Undercliff's "splendid house" (*Oxherding* 121) and Reverend Chandler's "manor house" (*Middle* 110) reflect their comfortable personalities and middle-class prosperity. Neither Isadora nor her hotel room are "much to look at" (*Middle* 6), but the very plainness of that room, as well as her cabin on the *Juno* and her ever-present menagerie of injured pets, accurately mirrors her unpretentiousness and generosity. In contrast, Papa Zeringue's cabin on the *Juno*, reflecting his crass materialism, is overstocked with "all the comforts Papa enjoyed on shore, including enough clothes "to fill the hold of a merchantman" and many pieces of "ornate furniture" (199). Similarly, Falcon's cabin on the *Republic* is a perfect metonym for its inhabitant, as it is characterized by "the odor of tabooed plea-sures," "dense" air, a low ceiling, navigational clutter (27), and "plunder from every culture conceivable" (48). Most significantly, it is "ingeniously rigged with exploding, trip-lever booby traps" (48), an external manifestation of the captain's worldview.

One apparent exception to this equation of person and domicile is Reb, the Allmuseri coffinmaker in *Oxherding Tale*, whose "quarters left no residue of its lodger" (75). But this exception proves the rule, for Reb has so completely eliminated the self, has so fully separated himself from the world, that he is not there: "He was not in the shed. Not in his work. Not truly in the thickness of the world-web" (75). Within is still the same as without, for Reb is effaced both internally and externally.

Another extreme case is the space occupied by the Allmuseri god in the hold of the *Republic*. Because the god is everything and everyone—the unity of the cosmos—details of the space cannot be described. The room is absolutely dark, the air "stale, potted," and the silence "heavy" (*Middle* 166). In that space, one is loosened from the normal parameters of space and time: Tommy reports that the creature "did not so much occupy a place as it bent space and time around itself like a greatcoat" (69). When he approaches the god, Rutherford senses that "something was off," that there was "an edge on the air," that some "catastrophe" was about to happen (166). "As within, so it is without," for the "gathering chaos" is transferred to Rutherford's soul as the god steps toward him in the form of Riley Calhoun.

In addition to mirroring the psyches of their inhabitants, rooms and places sometimes have marked symbolic values. In *Oxherding Tale* Andrew's room at Flo Hatfield's is a "catchall space, full of luggage" (41) because it has housed and will continue to house Flo's endless series of young lovers. The farmhouse deserted by Shem Moses and his alleged daughter is disheveled, tomblike, inhuman, its ruin suggesting both Shem's treatment of Ezekiel and Ezekiel's emotional collapse (94). The church where Andrew and Peggy marry is, like their relationship, "awash with sunlight" and "constructed such that light rippled, ever richer, as it neared the pulpit" (140).

The most fully developed space in these two novels, and one that further explores the symmetries between inner and outer, is the *Republic*. Both ship and crew are motley, composed of a hodgepodge of parts. The ship is "like a crazy-quilt house built by a hundred carpenters, each with a different plan" (21), and the crew members are "like social misfits" (40) and an assorted band of vagabonds (82). Just as the ship is "physically unstable" (35), so relationships among the factions on board this "house divided" (53) are constantly shifting. The ship is "a process, . . . perpetually flying apart and re-forming during the voyage" (35–36), like the shifting social relationships among its inhabitants and like the processes of psychological change in Rutherford, Squibb, and the Allmuseris. But, as the positive changes in Rutherford and Squibb suggest, the *Republic* is also a site of philosophical opportunity. Every physical part of the ship is interrelated with every other part: "you cannot touch a single rope without altering the intricate tracery of the whole design" (152), just as all the crew members are "dependent . . . on each other" (72). Since, as Falcon says, "a ship is a society" (175), experience on board provides a chance to glimpse the intersubjectivity of the Lifeworld, to entwine oneself in the tangled threads of the communal web, to expand one's self in conjunction with the Other.

This symbolic opportunity becomes especially pronounced after the slaves' rebellion. As in the carnivalesque mode, the revolt releases the society on the ship from conventional order, so that individual growth can occur before order is reestablished, in this case a much more benign order on the *Juno*. This loosening of social bonds is paralleled by the ship's temporary freedom from ordinary navigation. Like Melville's *Pequod*, it reverses direction (79), moves "in a circle, without direction [or] destination" (130), and drifts "aimlessly like men lost in the desert" (152). The ship and the surviving crew and slaves are like Reb, cut loose from any fixed position, home, or destination in this world. On one level, such a plight is horrific, as most people on board die, the survivors suffer extreme hardships, and the ship seems like the *Flying Dutchman* or the Ancient Mariner's ship, "cursed" and "damned never to touch shore" (158). But on another level the *Republic*'s open-ended journey symbolizes the philosophical freedom of the Allmuseri position, for ship and passengers have slipped between the cracks of the multiplicity of ordinary human purpose and thereby approach the oneness of unity. As in carnival, the break in the conventional routine of established authority, linear time, and ordinary space allows for development of community and individual growth, in particular a clarifying epiphany and a rebirth for Rutherford.

This theme is further developed by Johnson's characterization of the sea, most notably its formlessness, its "bottomless chaos" (42). On the sea one is often "deprived of such basic directions as left and right, up and down" (45), and one is beyond not only the Euro-American presumption of the directional nature of reality but also beyond "civilized law" (32). During one furious squall, the ship seems to leave known reality, to plunge "as if into Hell" between two "solid walls of water, during which "the sun stood still. The moon stayed" (81). Experiencing such apocalyptic chaos transforms one, as Falcon explains to Rutherford: "The sea does things to your head, Calhoun, terrible unravelings of belief that aren't in a cultured man's metaphysic" (33). Rutherford is "hypnotized by this theatre of transformations" (79), and after his heart stops during the squall, like the sun and moon, "it has never worked exactly right since" (81). Like the voyage itself, such a sea evokes terror and produces suffering, but, also like the voyage, this sea has the potential of liberating those who experience it. It is akin to the Allmuseri god: like the latter, it is associated with "impenetrable darkness" (83), and it is monstrous, all-powerful, formless, polymorphic, and abundant: "it seemed to be some monster of energy, without start or finish, a shifting cauldron of thalassic force, form superimposed upon form, which grew neither bigger nor smaller, which endlessly spawned all creatures conceivable yet never consumed itself, and contained a hundred kinds of waters, if one could but see them all" (79). Like the mysterious, thunderlike sound in *The Salt Eaters*, the sea vaults the characters into a future that is unknown, terrifying, and liberating.

Both god and sea are sites of access to the "unity of Being" (65) to which the Allmuseris are linked but from which Euro-Americans, particularly as personified by Falcon, have separated themselves. To be placed at such a site is terrifying to the Americans—their journey kills nearly all of them and radically transforms Squibb and Rutherford—for it undermines their rational methodology. After the rebellion, Cringle, assuming that the ship has entered "a rogue sea," cannot navigate because all his Western perspectives are lost—"the heavens are all wrong" and "the world [is] tilted" (158). But, from Johnson's position, this journey into the unknown, like Bambara's thunder, allows the survivors, including Squibb and Rutherford, to pass beyond the usual boundaries, to try on others' perspectives, and at least to sense the unity of Being. Everything becomes merged in that unity: "it was impossible to tell where ship ended and sailor began or, for that matter, to clearly distinguish what was ship, what sailor, and what sea, for in this chaosmos of roily water and fire, formless mist and men flying everywhere, the sea and all within it seemed a churning field that threw out forms indistinctly" (183). Like the god and the sea, this chaos of unity is infinitely energetic and endlessly creative. Like characters, their rooms, and their odors, individuals and their surroundings become indistinguishable, as individuals become inseparable from unity.

In *Oxherding Tale*, Johnson similarly privileges an ontological unity in which conventional boundaries disappear. The focus begins with attention to the interiors of objects and people. Ezekiel is said to be able to "perceive the interior of objects" (9), and opium temporarily affords Andrew the same power (63). The offbeat veterinarian, Hiram Groll, reports the theory "that all creatures have their own heaven—or harmony—within them, which corresponds to the harmony of the universe" (70). Although the enigmatic Groll is not clearly Johnson's spokesperson, Andrew's progress toward enlightenment corresponds to this theory. As a youth he is confused by Ezekiel's claim that "everything was

son, to absorb enough different perspectives to reach middle-class normality and respectability.

But before this process can occur, the existing order and the individual psyche must be subverted. As in the carnivalesque mode, the old, inflexible order must be shaken, and transformations must be allowed, so that a new, much more tolerant and enlightened order can be established. In *Oxherding Tale,* the subversion begins with Andrew's conception, continues with his visit to Flo, moves into high gear when he successfully passes for white, climaxes when Reb overthrows Bannon, and culminates in Andrew's permanent place in the new order of Spartansburg. In *Middle Passage* the subversion is more thorough, when the predatory leader of the *Republic* is overthrown and dies, allowing a communal fellowship to replace the former destructive hierarchy on the ship. Following this carnivalesque interregnum, the old order literally sinks, and a new, benevolent order is established on the *Juno* and, correspondingly, in Illinois.[12]

For Johnson's vision of African-American acceptance in American society to be complete, the questing heros must also subvert their former selves and re-create new identities. Like African-American history, each hero is exiled and alienated from his past, undergoes an open-ended journey to find a new place, and creates his future out of his adventures. Andrew and Rutherford each must pass beyond his conventional but narrow self, a self bound to the wheel of desire and conflict. Each must mediate that self with the selves of others to gain a sense of intersubjectivity, and each must assimilate enough of the Allmuseri philosophy to appreciate the unity of self and Other and therefore to recognize his ontological relation to his father, the past, and the community. Only then can the two pilgrims reenter American society as accepted, normal, and loving citizens. Only then can they, in Andrew's words, "turn to the business of rebuilding . . . the world" (*Oxherding* 176). Only then can they become, in Rutherford's words, "a cultural mongrel" (*Middle* 187) aligned with Johnson's philosophy, with community, and with American society.

5

"LISTENING BELOW THE SURFACE"

Beyond the Boundaries in Gloria Naylor's Fiction

Compared to the fiction of Wideman, Bambara, Johnson, and Gaines, in Gloria Naylor's novels the intersubjective web of mental connections among individuals is the most elusive. Neither family nor community provides consistent mechanisms for characters to reconstruct the past or to rediscover personal meaning through integration of self and group. No apocalyptic changes appear likely to regenerate characters or communities, and characters' journeys rarely move them significantly toward enlightenment. Typically, the external forces of life—particularly the pressures of race, gender, and class—are overwhelming, and such forces usually skew the characters' identities so that even when change is possible, the characters cannot take advantage of the opportunity. What little individual and community progress is made seems fragile and momentary. In *Mama Day* (1989) and *Bailey's Cafe* (1992), such progress occurs only in nonworldly, magical settings, never in realistic ones. Despite this relative skepticism, Naylor's novels are enriched by her ability to carry readers into the bittersweet conditions of contemporary life. By depicting the complex and paradoxical mixtures of tragedy and joy in African-American characters' lives, Naylor leads her characters and readers into the ambiguous but strangely satisfying realm of the *différance,* into life at the edge of the abyss, fully conscious of the abyss but willing and able to accept its inevitable tragedy and still endure.

The symbol for this theme in Naylor's fiction is well-like images such as basements, alleys, and walls. These physical images suggest both the psychological dead ends into which some characters are driven and the social and psychological forces that pressure them into such conditions. Concurrently, Naylor's fiction places other characters symbolically on the rims of wells, in intimate proximity to the unforgiving conditions of modern life, aware of such conditions but not overwhelmed by them and therefore able to survive them. The surviving characters intuitively model the Derridean stance of accepting play, open-endedness, and plurality. Not locked into insistence on a unitary self, on bipolar opposites, or on the well as a death trap, they are able to return to the well, to defer and to differ, in short to accept the *différance*.

Jacques Derrida, meditating on the ontology of books, describes "the unnameable bottomless well" (*Writing* 297) as "the abyss" (296), an image of the center that is "the absence of play and difference, another name for death" (297). Any book, as a completed, enclosed entity, "was to have insinuated itself into the dangerous hole, was to have furtively penetrated into the menacing dwelling place" (297–98). For Derrida, only by repetition does one escape from this well/trap. If we return to the book, to the hole, we attain a "strange serenity" and we are "fulfilled . . . by remaining open, by pronouncing nonclosure" (298). The well for Derrida is a potentially dangerous opening but at the same time an opportunity for discovery, peace, and self-development. The well is destructive if taken as a fixed, monologic entity; but it is beneficial if taken as part of a fluid and multivalent orientation toward the open-endedness of being.

The well and ordinary space thus constitute a traditional binary opposition, but, as with all other binaries such as presence/absence and self/other, Derrida argues that the relationship is infinitely complex rather than one-dimensional. Taken singly, the well represents the forces that drive characters into closed, monologic reliance on originary selves as well as the condition of an illusionary self-presence. In this sense, the well is the absence of play, repetition, and life; but simultaneously, the well, including its rim, is the unspeakable *différance* that allows for life. As long as we return to it, as long as we incorporate it into a larger and more complex multiplicity, the well—a womb as well as a tomb—is that which allows us to live. The well symbolizes the shift from a monologic, either/or perspective to an open, both/ and stance in which attention is focused not on fixed entities but on the endless flux within and between entities. Presence and absence, self and other, ordinary space and the well are equally acknowledged. Such thinking thus shifts from the traditional Western emphasis on fixed entities and the irreconcilable separations between binary opposites to a blurring of boundaries and an embracing of inclusiveness.[1]

Naylor's only literal image of a well occurs in the revealing scene in *Mama Day* in which Miranda Day overcomes her fears and opens the well where her sister, Peace, killed herself. As Gary Storhoff asserts, Miranda had "evaded the symbolic truth of the well" (42), fearing to face her family's tragedy. She had only sensed the loss felt by Peace's mother, ignoring the loss and grief also borne by her father. Opening the well enables Miranda, like Violet Trace in Morrison's *Jazz*, to reconnect with the past, in her case to identify with her father's pain: "looking past the losing was to feel for the man who built this house and the one who nailed this well shut" (285). This opening at the edge of the well gives Miranda access to her paternal ancestry, which heretofore had been overshadowed by her reliance on her female ancestors, especially her legendary foremother, Sapphira Wade. Miranda, the ancestor figure in the novel and the griot for her niece, Cocoa, thus discovers the well as the site for contact with her forgotten male ancestor. For Naylor, such connections to the familial, communal, and cultural past and therefore to neglected dimensions of the intersubjective web are rare, and, as this incident reveals, often fraught with pain and fear. Nevertheless, the effects of such breakthroughs are powerful—in this case, Miranda's opening herself to her father's grief not only contributes to the community's ongoing reinterpretations of its history and its identity but also leads her to an understanding of George's strength of will and to her discovery of the means of saving Cocoa.[2]

For Miranda, as for Violet, the well symbolizes the tragic familial past and the grief that cannot be borne or even admitted but must be acknowledged. To prevent future family tragedy, she must return to and accept the past tragedy. She must "look past the pain" (283)—hers as well as her father's. To do so constitutes a reawakening: "She sleeps within her sleep. To wake from one is to be given back ears as the steady heart tells her—look past the pain; to wake from the other is to stare up at the ceiling from the mahogany bed and to know that she must go out and uncover the well where Peace died" (283). The well itself is an image of death and decay: "a bottomless pit," full of "foul air," the surface of the water "slimy and covered with floating pools of fungus" (284). At first Miranda feels nothing, but, "refusing to let go of the edge," she closes her eyes and then viscerally feels the repressed pain: "And when it comes, it comes with a force that almost knocks her on her knees. She wants to run from all that screaming" (284). Inhabiting the position at the side of the well is essential, for there one comes into significant relationship with the unimaginable.

In such proximity, that Other is no longer a fixed or originary entity inflated out of proportion because of its inaccessibility; instead, one can learn to know it by returning to it, consumed neither by its presence nor by a futile attempt to decree its absence. At the rim of the well, Miranda experiences the *différance,* since her act is both a spatial differentiation and a temporal deferral. By entering another space and another time, she returns to the site of her father's—and the family's—deepest pain and innermost being. This essential truth had been repressed, buried in Miranda's and the family's unconsciousness, because the entire family had privileged consciousness and presence in their acceptance of the ancestry of Sapphira Wade and their denial of the family's tragedies.[3] Miranda cannot return fully to her father's grief, but at the well she encounters its trace, another form of the *différance,* a substitute for the absent present, a "simulacrum of a presence that dislocates, displaces, refers itself" (Derrida, *Margins* 24). The well and Miranda's epiphany there are also analogous to Derrida's concept of the breach, which is yet another way of conceiving of the gap between oppositions. The breach is a potentially disruptive break in ordinary perception or consciousness, but it is a break that "opens up a conducting path" (Derrida, *Writing* 200) by allowing for a reconceptualization; it is a deconstruction that is simultaneously a reconstruction. Like Derrida's breach, Miranda's encounter with the previously unacknowledged and inconceivable Other stuns her but also creates new dimensions of consciousness.

Although Naylor's first two novels have no actual wells, their settings are based on well-like images. Brewster Place and Linden Hills are physically shaped like wells: the former is an urban block, closed off from the bustling city by a high brick wall, whose "hallways" become "blind holes" (191); the latter is a V-shaped hill whose circular drives wend downward to the Nedeed house. As Barbara Christian argues, both communities are "self-enclosed," cut off from the rest of American society, much like African Americans throughout American history ("Gloria" 352). Also like African-American culture, characters in both communities are linked to white society as the radically disprivileged terms of an inflexible binary opposition. For most of the characters, life in these well/traps is hellish, in Brewster Place primarily because of the impositions of white power, and in Linden Hills primarily because of the greed, envy, and social ambitions of the residents.

In *The Women of Brewster Place*, the external exigencies of racial discrimination, gender exploitation, and poverty are implacable, creating a present that is nearly unendurable. At the same time, the past does not provide a curing perspective, no alternative future is projected, and no better place is offered. There are no accommodations, no play, no unraveling of binaries, only dead ends. As Maxine Lavon Montgomery puts it, Brewster Place "is itself an inverted world" ("Fathomless" 42), a "bottomless night world" (47). The street and the African Americans who inhabit it are representative of African Americans' historic position in the United States. Plans for developing the neighborhood are "conceived" (1) in the promise of the end of World War I; just as many African Americans hoped that their participation in the war would integrate them into American society, "it seemed as if Brewster Place was to become part of the main artery of the town" (2). But in the political infighting of the city, "there was no one to fight for Brewster Place," and so, like disempowered African Americans, the street is cut off from the mainstream and develops its own "personality," "language," "music," and "codes" (2).[4]

As a result of this segregation, the neighborhood community is fragile at best. In addition to alienation from white society, many of the women feel alienated from the neighborhood: for example, Etta Mae Johnson, always addressed as "Mrs. Johnson," lives with a sense of the "alien undercurrents" among her neighbors (57), and Lorraine and Theresa are excluded from the community because of their lesbianism. Because so many residents are transient and impoverished, the community is unstable: "People often came and went on Brewster Place like a restless night's dream, moving in and out in the dark to avoid eviction notices or neighborhood bulletins about the dilapidated condition of their furnishings" (129). When Kiswana Browne tries to hold a meeting to form a tenants' association, the meeting breaks up in eruptions of anger and suspicion (144–46).

That the street and the community as a whole are dead ends is reiterated by the lives of the women depicted in the novel. Mattie Michael's well is the impotence she feels in being unable to help her son overcome his own helpless condition, the "void in his being" (52).[5] Etta Mae Johnson has survived by denying a true self, living through "carefully erected decoys" (58), with the result that she is trapped in a nongenuine life, as she is trapped by the wall at the end of Brewster Place that threatens to devour her "like a pulsating mouth awaiting her arrival" (73). Lucielia Louise Turner ("Ciel") is trapped in the "poison of reality" of her failed relationship with Eugene and then in the black hole of her daughter's death: "Ciel's whole universe existed in the seven feet of space between herself and her child's narrow coffin" (101). Cora Lee is locked into an impasse of endless childbirths because her only comfort comes from pampering her infants and her life is dominated by her inability to control her children, her life, and "the shadows" who father her children (113). Lorraine and Theresa cannot escape the well into which the community places them,[6] and then Lorraine, who had futilely sought accommodation between her lesbianism and the community of heterosexual women, mistakenly enters the alley, another well-like image, a dead end within the dead end of Brewster Place. The domain of C. C. Baker's macho gang, young males also trapped in a figurative well of pseudo-identity, the alley becomes her figurative tomb (Fraser 101) and Ben's literal one.[7] Ground down by the social and economic bleakness of their lives, the residents of Brewster Place remain in the well, unable to know themselves, to understand the world around them, or to effect significant change.[8]

The exception is Mattie. Despite the debacle of her son's jumping bail, she emerges as the first of Naylor's privileged characters. Like such later women as Mama Day, Eve, and Nadine, she has a practical orientation to life's exigencies, knowing that "we gotta face what happened so we can see our way clear from this" (48). Uncritically, she provides "light," "love," and "comfort" for the otherwise alienated Etta Mae, and Cora appreciates her non-judgmental attitude (123). Prefiguring Mama Day's nursing of Cocoa and Eve's nurturing of Jesse and Mariam, Mattie rescues Lucielia from her nearly suicidal grief for her dead child.

But unlike Naylor's subsequent heroines, Mattie has no transcendent or mythic powers and thus is powerless to prevent Lorraine's death or the demise of the neighborhood. Restricted to the implacable harshness of reality, Mattie and the other women in this novel can only dream of better conditions and more viable selves. Knowing that it will not work, Etta Mae yields to the fantasy that sexual intercourse with Reverend Woods will change her plight; Kiswana Browne fantasizes that she will soar like the bird she identifies with (75); Cora Lee, caught up in the atmosphere of *A Midsummer Night's Dream,* imagines that her children will succeed in school and then in "good jobs" (126). The women's only recourse to oppression is Mattie's dream of trying to obliterate the opposite term, to tear down the obstructing wall, to annihilate the well. In the carnivalesque atmosphere of Mattie's dream, the normal rules are suspended as the women of Brewster Place try to destroy the symbol of their oppression. Like carnival, this fantasy brings momentary relief and the "miracle" (188) of returning sunshine, but the inversion is brief, bringing no lasting reform or satisfaction. As Brewster Place "still waits to die" (192), the women who formerly lived there seem merely to wait for death, preserving only their dreams: "the colored daughters of Brewster Place, spread over the canvas of time, still wake up with their dreams misted on the edge of a yawn" (192).

In *Linden Hills,* most members of the community have failed even more completely, since their failure results from their own social ambition and material success. Each house in Linden Hills becomes a well/tomb for its African-American inmates, who have given up their souls to gain supposed status and "have turned away from their past and from their deepest sense of who they are" (Ward 182). Laurel Dumont's empty swimming pool is literally her death trap when she dives into it, but the house as tomb is most graphic for the generations of Nedeed women, each of whom is trapped in the house and the obsessions of her husband. The series comes to its macabre conclusion with Willa Prescott Nedeed, who, locked in the basement, a former morgue, is "entombed in 'otherness' " like all black women (Werner 51). In that well, however, Willa reconnects with her ancestors and with a few threads of her lost community when she discovers literal traces of the myriad sufferings of the former Mrs. Nedeeds—in their journals, their recipes, their photograph albums. What she finds is not full representations but fragments, suggestive of the fragmented lives to which the women and Willa herself were reduced. According to Margaret Homans, Willa finds "a record simply of effacement and silencing" (159), not presence but presence of absence, a pattern repeated once again in Willa's own life

(Homans 160). Through her research in the well, reading the "books" of her predecessors, Willa vicariously reimagines their tragic lives, places her own tragedy in perspective, and thereby rediscovers her lost self. She exemplifies Derrida's idea of the return to the book, experiences the spatial difference and the temporal deferral of the *différance*, and thereby achieves "the strange serenity of such a return" (Derrida, *Writing* 298). Forced in her captivity to confront herself, her history, and the histories of her predecessors, Willa awakens to her responsibilities for her own life (Ward 192). Willa is like most women in Naylor's fiction— displaced, isolated, needing to (re)connect with their feminine community, past and present. Like Mattie Michaels, Willa cannot transcend the narrow restrictions of reality. Her rebirth comes too late, so she can return to life only momentarily, only long enough to reorder her life—symbolized by her cleaning the kitchen and settling accounts with her husband. Despite the brevity of her return, the self-awareness she achieves in her agony indicates the power of such confrontation with the past and the hidden self, power that Miranda Day is able to marshal after she opens the well.

In this novel, Willie and the Andersons provide a constructive alternative to the enclosed community. For them, generosity, empathy, and love outweigh status and economic success; their perspectives, outside Linden Hills and symbolically on the rim of the well, allow them to nurture their own and others' souls rather than to lose them.[9] Linked to Willa by their names and by his empathy for her, Willie holds the promise of a deferred fruition, a fruition achieved in Miranda's extension of the preliminary work accomplished by Mattie, Willa, and Willie.

In *Mama Day* and *Bailey's Cafe,* the settings are again isolated communities, but the emphasis shifts from narrow failures to partial successes. Settings shift from the realistic Brewster Place and Linden Hills to the magical Willow Springs and the surreal neighborhood of *Bailey's Cafe.* Since they are out of the real world, these latter sites function as entrances into the *différance,* as alternative places and times, in myth rather than everyday existence, where miracles can occur. Willow Springs, a place out-side history and geography, allows for a new perspective, not limited to the racial stereotypes and cultural restrictions of ordinary places. Through the islanders' spiritual power and especially Miranda's reconciliation of mainstream American and island values, Naylor suggests that the island is simultaneously present and absent, existing and not existing, in a geographic limbo: "Willow Springs ain't in no state. Georgia and South Carolina done tried, though—been trying since right after the Civil War to prove that Willow Springs belong to one or the other of them" (4–5). Located "on the edge of things" (Christol 349), adjacent to but not in the United States, the island is on the rim of the well.

Although such an advantageous placement does not create utopian conditions, life in Willow Springs has many valued qualities. There is a strong sense of community, replete with local heros like Sapphira Wade, indigenous myths like the 18 and 23 (3–5), unique traditions such as Candle Walk and "standing forth" at funerals (268), and a local system of deeding land ownership to the second generation (219). Not needing any elected officials (249), the community practices an unselfish socialism in which "the folks here take care of their own" (79). The closeness of the community is further suggested by members' ability to intuit everything that is happening on the island, for example that Bernice is driving her dead son up the road (257) or that it is time for her son's funeral (268).

The community's strength is based on several factors that suggest its African as opposed to Western orientation. Human beings here are intimately connected with nature, accepting the damage a hurricane can cause, reading the signs of the seasons and the approaching storm, and understanding the soil ("Walking with Ambush through his fields was to watch the hand of a virtuoso stroke the instrument of his craft" [200]). Residents are also "resonant with the ever-present past" (Juhasz 134): they revere their founding ancestor, Sapphira Wade, and have turned the year of her emancipation, 1823, into a myth of her and their mystical ways of knowing. But the island's inhabitants are not locked in a limiting preoccupation with the past because "time, for its own sake, [is] never a factor [t]here" (281), so the residents can "forget about time" (160) because they have transcended it in their acceptance of it. Having acquired the wisdom that "Some things stay the same," "Some things change," "And some things are yet to be" (312), they have moved beyond linear time into the Great Time of myth. The residents' African holism is also conveyed by their transcendence of the barrier between the living and the dead, which is explicitly suggested when everyone who stands forth at Little Caesar's funeral is confident that he or she will see the dead boy again. For Hélène Christol, the journey to Willow Springs is a reverse Middle Passage that allows for "the exploration of the interface between life and death" (356).

Unlike Naylor's first two novels, in which external objects and events overwhelm the characters, in *Mama Day* the balance shifts to the powers of the characters' minds to overcome external reality. Part of this enhanced mental power derives from the ability of the inhabitants of Willow Springs to tap into their suprarational dimensions. Such dimensions are evident, for example, when the collective voice of the community asserts that Sapphira Wade retains mythic power because she "don't live in the part of our memory we can use to form words" (4), when Cocoa understands George's deepest anxieties about not knowing his mother by making "the connection . . . in the realm just beneath thought" (201), and when Miranda and Abigail understand that "some things can be known without words" (267). For the island residents, the power of their own belief translates into spiritual harmony. They are content because they "see" a holistic world in which human and nonhuman are integral, living and dead are inseparable, and the "magical" is as valid as the nonmagical. Lacking that transforming power of the mind, the outsider George cannot comprehend the island and the magical events that occur there. He can describe "what [he] saw" but is at a loss to "describe air that thickens so that it seems as solid as the water" (175). For this "quintessential rationalist" (Hayes 184), the evidence of Cocoa's near-fatal conjuring cannot be processed: "it was one of those moments when your mind simply freezes to protect itself from the devastation of a thousand contradictions" (257). Since George lacks the nonrational powers of the islanders, the magic of Willow Springs would either drive him "insane" or must be relegated to "the stuff of dreams" (258).

The novel's emphasis on mental power is manifested in the motif of interpretation. All the characters engage actively in it: they interpret the weather, each other, nature, illnesses, and deaths. The main plot hinges on Miranda's interpretation of Ruby's conjuring of Cocoa and on Miranda's understanding of her own need for George's help. The novel begins with a lesson in interpretation for the reader, when Reema's boy, fresh with his anthropological ideas and methods, is mocked for completely misinterpreting the meaning of the local myth of 18 and 23 (7–9).[10] Cocoa and George's relationship shifts from their initial failures to interpret each other correctly, and to some degree their mutual rejections of their interpretations of each other, to a shared ability to interpret each other accurately and to accept their interpretations. As each encounters the evil side of Willow Springs after Ruby casts her spell on Cocoa, neither is able to fathom what is happening: Cocoa cannot understand the voices saying that she will break George's heart (223–24) and in her delirium is lost in "a whirl of confusing echoes—visual, emotional, verbal" (259), and George is at a loss to comprehend Dr. Buzzard (187), islanders' nonverbal communication (198, 205), the whole way of life on Willow Springs (256), Cocoa's illness (282), and, most significantly, the riddle of what Miranda wants him to bring back from the chicken coop (300–301).

The most able interpreter, and the exemplar of the strengths of Willow Springs, is of course Miranda. She is the acknowledged leader of the community, able to prevent vacation development on the island, " 'cause if Mama Day say no, everybody say no" (6). She is the leader because she has greater mental powers than anyone else: she can read nature's signs, foresee events, outconjure the other conjurers, and transcend the barrier between life and death. She knows that "the mind is a funny thing . . . and a powerful thing at that" (96) and, more emphatically, that "the mind is everything" (90). She is privileged by Naylor because she respects her limits, honors her own gifts, and listens deeply. Although never a literal mother, she is associated with life and with giving birth through her care for hens and their eggs and through her talents as a midwife, talents that have earned her the nickname of Little Mama. As Storhoff puts it, "it is as if life emanates from her" (37). Naylor also privileges Miranda by giving her the same kind of tough love that she gives to the privileged proprietors in *Bailey's Cafe*. Like Eve, Nadine, Bailey, and Gabriel, Miranda does not coddle those she loves but instead teases and confronts them. Along with her "intuitive thinking" (Hayes 179), she is a hardheaded realist who knows that "getting at the truth" is often painful (230) and that often the best course is to "leave things be, let 'em go their natural course" (138).

Much of Miranda's power derives from her connections to her ancestral past. Throughout the novel she is troubled by the deaths of her sister, Peace, and her nieces, Peace and Grace, and she seeks to restore "peace" to her family by somehow redeeming their deaths. This spiritual need to reverse the tragic maternal lineage of the Day family sharpens her desperation to save Cocoa's life. Miranda is equally mindful of her male ancestry, particularly her grandfather, Jonah Day, and her father, John-Paul Day. She repeatedly recalls her father's advice (169, 170, 255, 261) and even hears him whispering advice from beyond the grave (78, 88). Miranda's links with her ancestral past are conveyed by her preservation of "the other place," the original family home on the island, and her predilection to tend the family graves, where she is able to hear her ancestors as she moves "down into time" (150).

Despite Miranda's extraordinary powers and her privileging by Naylor, she struggles to interpret with complete accuracy. At first, she can only sense "something in the air" (86, 173) without realizing that it is the approaching hurricane. Similarly, she vaguely senses that someone or something is going to die but cannot determine who or what (226), and later she "can't get rid of the heaviness way down in her center, holding there for a reason she can't put her finger on" (249). Such uncertainties and limitations imply that, although her powers are unmatched, she is missing a dimension or quality that would complete her.

That dimension is her connections with her male ancestors, and her growth in the novel is to add empathy for them to her empathy for her female relatives. She gains the realization that the light in the Candle Walk myth and its ritualized words, "Lead on with light," refer not to the death of her mother but to her father's need for light to find her mother's body: "Oh, precious Jesus, the light wasn't for her—it was for him" (118). That revelation anticipates her climactic revelation when, armed with her male ancestors' legacies—Bascombe Wade's ledger and John-Paul's cane—she opens the well her father had sealed after Peace's suicide. By opening the well, Miranda opens herself to her male ancestors' heritage, their pain, and their knowledge. By so doing she unites the female and male sides of her family, and she realizes that George, like the men in her family, "*believed*—in the power of themselves, in what they were feeling" (285), and therefore she knows that Cocoa can be saved only by the combination of her own female power and George's male power: "together they could be the bridge for Baby Girl to walk over" (285).

Miranda's position at the rim of the well replicates Willow Springs's position at the edge of the mainland. In both cases, the sorrows, the pain, and the brutality of the well are not ignored, and obsession with the well does not entrap one within it. Instead, she transcends the well as she embraces a position in the interstices, a postmodern position that allows for the play between binaries and for a liberating multiplicity rather than a confining singularity. Miranda's "nonhierarchical multiplicity" (Hayes 185) is evident in her fascination with Chicago and New York City as well as Willow Springs, as she deconstructs "the facile binarism of 'Civilization vs Primitivism' " (Storhoff 38). Miranda's move into the *différance*—her opening of the well—is echoed in the motif of her opening "an unknown door . . . to help Baby Girl" (280), "door upon door upon door" (283). Her props for such opening are significant. Much as Willa Nedeed used her ancestors' documents to redeem her life, Miranda uses Bascombe Wade's ancient ledger, with its family history, names, and records, whose only remaining legible words constitute the legacy Miranda is thus able to transmit to Cocoa: "Law . . . knowledge . . . witness . . . inflicted . . . nurse" and "Conditions . . . tender . . . kind" (280; Christol 355). With the ledger and her father's cane, Miranda needs only her hands, hands that also transmit her father's legacy for they "look like John-Paul's hands" (285). With those hands, she had to "reach back to the beginning for us to find the chains to pull [Cocoa] out of this here trouble," and now Miranda tells George that she wants to "reach out with the other hand and take yours" (294). Miranda's hands thus would constitute a human chain, a bridge, to connect the genders and the generations past, present, and future. They are the hands of unquestioning "trust" (294, 295), the hands and gestures of the extreme act of love, empathy, and spiritual union. George nearly intuits the truth when he wonders if the answer to Miranda's riddle—what he is supposed to bring back from the chicken coop—is his own empty hands, his part of the mystical chain.[11]

Like Naylor's first two novels, *Mama Day* is replete with examples of characters' harmful fixations on narrow objectives, obsessions that limit them metaphorically to the closed unity of the well. For example, the Day family history is marked by suicides, Frances and Ruby exhaust themselves in their single-minded pursuit of Junior Lee, and George kills himself in his determination to save Cocoa. As Meisenhelder argues, characters who try to achieve their purposes in isolation always fail, but success comes to those who perceive the quiltlike pattern of life in which everything and everyone is independent—a distinct piece of the fabric—but joined in harmony with all the other pieces. Cocoa moves in this direction, relinquishing her urban chippiness and her propensity to reduce other women to gaudy metaphors usually related to food, such as "cherry vanilla" (20) and "kumquat" (21). Her recovery from her near-fatal illness constitutes a purging and rebirth experience that brings her much more fully into the community of the island and her extended family. Despite his very rule-bound, rationalistic, and limiting personality, George also moves toward integration within the holistic environment of Willow Springs. It is he, not Cocoa, who suggests that they reside there, and he longs for the rich heritage and the emotional depth that Cocoa, Abigail, Miranda, and the other islanders enjoy. But his progress is cut short by Cocoa's crisis, and, confronted with that crisis, he can only rely on what he knows—that is, his old self and a world governed by reason. He is thus unable to escape from his well even as he sacrifices his life to save Cocoa's.

Compared to the relatively straightforward narrative forms of Naylor's first two novels, the narration of *Mama Day* is complex and subtle. Since the story focuses on the characters' mental powers, on the interweavings of voices and perspectives, and on the privileging of a holistic, flexible, and multiple perspective, the narration is not confined to the predictable or the univocal. As Christol notes, Naylor uses many narrators, including George and Cocoa's dialogues across the grave; first-person narrations from Miranda, John-Paul, and Jonah, and a "first introductory narrator"; and the compete narration includes the three introductory "texts": the stylized map of the island, the genealogic chart of the Day family, and the bill of sale for Sapphira Wade (354). Just as Miranda and later Cocoa are empowered to hear the voices of the living and the dead, so Naylor allows the reader to do so.

Although line breaks make clear when Cocoa and George are narrating to each other, the boundaries are blurred between the first-person plural narrator speaking as the voice of the community, the conventional third-person omniscient narrator, and Miranda's point of view. Sometimes these voices are distinct. The voice of the community is folksy and oral: it opens the novel's text with "Willow Springs. Everybody knows but nobody talks about the legend of Sapphira Wade. A true conjure woman: satin black, biscuit cream, red as Georgia clay: depending on which of us takes a mind to her" (3). The third-person narrator is more neutral and sounds more like written English, as in "Abigail is sweeping her front porch when Miranda crosses the main road between their places, loaded down with two foil-wrapped cakes and a paper bag of eggs" (44). Usually it is clear when the narration comes directly from Miranda's consciousness, as in "Start the morning with your nerves sticking out all over the place and you're bound to be upsetting whatever you touch all day. Them cakes took one look at her evil face and refused to rise" (169). But frequently it is not clear where the voice of the community ends and the omniscient narrator or Miranda's point of view begins. For example, in successive sentences the narration may slide between a third-person rendition of Miranda's thoughts and a first-person one: "Miranda lifts up the foil and sniffs at the aroma of shrimp fried in onions and tomatoes over a pile of seasoned rice. Bless you, Abigail, but I'm too tired to swallow my own spit. Sitting down and stretching out her aching legs, she lets her hand drop over the letter tucked into the flap of the envelope" (91).[12]

Besides creating a polyvocal narration and blurring the boundaries among its multiple voices and perspectives, Naylor also pushes the narration beyond the usual, a technique that Bailey calls going "one key down" (*Bailey's* 34). In such odd moments, the narration may shift to the distant past, as when Miranda suddenly becomes her five-year-old self seeing "Peace breathing too, at the bottom of the open well" (36). Or Miranda's consciousness may abruptly shift to her father's voice: "Little Mama, these woods been here before you and me, so why should they get out your way—learn to move around 'em" (78).[13] Such shifts in narration not only reinforce the novel's emphasis on polyvocalism both for its characters and for itself but also create for the reader an elusive text. Readers, like the characters, are thereby required to extend themselves beyond their normal limits, to open up their minds to different forms of experience, to listen with every part of their minds. As the voice of the community tells readers, "ain't nobody really talking to you. We're sitting here in Willow Springs, and you're God-knows-where. It's August 1999—ain't but a slim chance it's the same season where you are" (10). Since the characters must use all parts of their minds, even the nonverbal, readers are reminded of the fictionality of the fiction. As they read the words on the page, they are asked to imagine that they are hearing the community voice, Cocoa's voice talking to the dead George, the dead George's voice talking to Cocoa, or Miranda's ruminations on all levels of consciousness. Naylor wants readers to listen and hopes that by really listening they will hear not her or her narrators but themselves: "Really listen this time: the only voice is your own" (10). Such total immersion has the potential to keep readers and characters out of the fatal confinement of the well.

In *Bailey's Cafe* Naylor pursues further many of the themes and techniques she uses in *Mama Day*. In this book, her fourth novel, she creates a complex dynamic between the crushing stories of the characters who have drifted into the mystical neighborhood and the neighborhood itself, presided over by the four proprietors—"Bailey," Nadine, Eve, and Gabriel. The lives of the visitors have been destroyed by their horrific encounters with racial and gender discrimination, a monologic power that has been inflicted implacably, brutally, without question or hesitation, transforming the visitors into radically disprivileged terms of traditional binaries. Psychologically, they are in the well, unable to imagine any alternative to their victimhood. Their personalities crushed, they have lost all connections with their families, communities, and society.

Sadie, never desired or loved, fell "through the cracks of the upswings and downswings" (41). Innately possessing a sense of "class" (68), she is driven deeper and deeper into her private sorrow, forced into a debilitating absorption of defeated self-presence. She tries to make a home with Daniel, but his drinking and the thunderous trains drive her further inward.[14] All her dreams must be infinitely deferred, as in Langston Hughes's poem, "What Happens to a Dream Deferred?" which Naylor uses as the epigraph to *The Women of Brewster Place*. Liquor bottles become Sadie's personal well, as she finds solace only in the

"stars" printed on them (65). After years of psychological depriva-
tion, she internalizes the well, "the endless space of the black
hole waiting to open in her heart" (64). She dreams of a normal
place within a community, replete with a house, a picket fence,
geraniums, laughter, Waterford crystal, and a good meal (72–77),
but such a vision of normality is so disconnected from her reality
that she cannot accept Iceman Jones's offer of a shared life. She
cannot escape the well/trap of her preoccupying struggle and her
victimized self; hence, she cannot form an attachment to anyone,
cannot return to the intersubjective web of community.

Esther is driven even farther into the psychological well, even
farther apart from the threads that bind people together. Directed at age twelve by her older brother to have sex in the dark
basement with a man he calls her husband, she develops a psy-
chosis that allows her to exist only in the dark basement of Eve's
boardinghouse and the symbolic well of her mind. Aside from
the johns who must bring her white roses and call her "little
sister," her only companions are the spiders and a radio hero
called The Shadow. She herself lives as a shadow, in dark, silent
exile from the human community. Because her "husband" cau-
tioned her, "We won't speak about this, Esther," silence becomes
her mode, as she can never find "a word for what happens between us in the cellar" (97). Lacking language, she cannot communicate, cannot connect with others. Unable to sense the
différance, she has no play, only absolutes. She is at the bottom
of the well, isolated in the dark like Willa Nedeed but lacking
Willa's contacts with her ancestors, barely able to survive spiritually and unable to reclaim her life.

For other lost souls, the well of isolation takes other forms. For
Mary/Peaches it starts as the wall her father builds around their
house to keep boys out and becomes the internal wall she builds
between her repressed self and her whore self that she sees reflected in every man's lustful eyes. The external and internal
walls become barriers blocking her from meaningful interaction
with others, so she disfigures her face in a futile attempt to eliminate that lust and integrate her two selves. For Jesse Bell, the

well is the alcohol and the heroin that she uses to blot out her history of mistreatment and loss, to repress her memories of alienation and separation from her parents, her husband, and her child. Her only sustaining hope is to return to her childhood bedroom, which becomes the image of which she dreams.

Between these unfortunate visitors to the neighborhood and the four proprietors is Miss Maple. At Stanford, in prison, and in his unsuccessful job search, he experiences society's monologic insistence on an absolute white-black polarity. But he is spared the extreme brutality that the women experience and, perhaps as a result, develops a more integrated and multiple response characterized by his female persona, his job as Eve's bouncer and janitor, his success in jingle contests, and his plans for his own company. His balance also emanates from his diverse genealogy that includes African-American, Native American, and Mexican ancestors. That mixed ethnicity translates into his nonbinary mixing of genders, when he sensibly yields to sexual aggression in prison and later chooses comfortable female clothing. These accommodations allow Miss Maple to find his own integrated identity (to "be my own man" [173]), to be free (according to Bailey, he is "one of the freest men I know" [216]), and to find harmony between his individuality and his social position.

Miss Maple thus shares many of the characteristics of the four proprietors. Like Mattie, Miranda, and Abigail, they offer acceptance and solace based on a hard-nosed acknowledgment of life's brutalities, on a relativistic incorporation of multiplicity, on a gritty compromise at the rim of the well. They have learned the futility of endorsing any fixed or originary value; in short, they are comfortable with the *différance*. Together, despite overwhelming odds, they have formed a viable community, a true neighborhood.

The neighborhood, in particular the cafe, is a metaphysical crossroads. Existing nowhere and everywhere, it is in the *différance*. Like Derrida's writing, which "is always explicitly inscribed in the margins of some preexisting text" (B. Johnson x), it is "right on the margin between the edge of the world and infinite possibility" (*Bailey's* 76). Like Willow Springs, it is not on any map, and yet "you can find [it] in any town" (112). It is a spiritual "way station" (221), a place "to take a breather for a while" (28), a place you cannot find unless you already know about in your soul: "If they can't figure out we're only here when they need us, they don't need to figure it out" (28). In a world wracked by the vicious oppression that nearly destroys each of the female visitors to the neighborhood, the proprietors have created a miraculous haven, an alternative place and time where those rejected by and alienated from American society are offered a respite, compassion, and healing. As the epigraph and the musical terminology in the chapter titles suggest ("The Jam," "Mary [Take One]," "Miss Maple's Blues," "The Wrap"), it is an incarnation of the blues (Montgomery, "Authority" 30).[15] Like the blues, the neighborhood simultaneously accepts hardship and mourns the associated loss. As Derrida advocates, it returns—infinitely—to the past, not in a futile attempt to erase the past but to rerealize it, to retrace it, to unravel the oppositions.[16] The philosophy is tough love—you are neither hassled nor coddled; you follow the "routine" at the cafe or you do not eat; you play by Eve's "house rules" or you do not play (92).

Behind the cafe is the well. It is a "void" (76), an "endless plunge" (76), a "black empty space" (137), where many visitors come to commit suicide (162). But, like Naylor's other wells, it is double edged. Once the well is accepted—that is, once the unyielding harshness of life, including death, is accepted, and once one frees oneself from the narrow constraints of binary oppposites—out back is where deferred dreams come true. Sadie and Jones "dance under the stars" (40), Jesse Bell sees her dream of "the simple bedroom she'd had as a girl" (137), Mariam finds "exactly what her childlike mind called up: endless water" (228), and Miss Maple "steps off boldly into the midst of nothing and is suspended midair by a gentle wind that starts to swirl his cape around his knees" (216). These idyllic images imply that the miracle of the neighborhood consists of its power to allow its residents to create in the imagination the love, security, and human bonds that American life has denied them. Out back, the inter-subjective web can flourish in the mind even if it cannot exist in material reality.

The abyss is not threatening to Miss Maple or the four proprietors because they have accepted it and all it represents. At the edge of the well, they perpetually return to it and hence are not bound by it; it is absorbed into their stoic acceptance of life. Privileged by Naylor, the four proprietors are clear-sighted, straightforward, and direct. Bailey claims, "I call 'em the way I see 'em" (32), and he praises Nadine for the same quality: "like me, she calls 'em as she sees 'em" (116). Like Miranda and Abigail in *Mama Day,* they are realists, trying to be honest but not necessarily nice. Despite their sometimes rough exteriors, they are compassionate and tolerant, helping others endure the pain of the real world or pass beyond it. They are as well adjusted as anyone can hope for in Naylor's grim world, and, like her, they have no illusions about life, expecting little from it: Gabe knows that "the world, it still waits to commit suicide," and Bailey accepts that "life is [not] supposed to make you feel good, or to make you feel miserable either. Life is just supposed to make you feel" (219).

Like Miranda and Abigail, these four proprietors have extraordinary strength of character, which has helped them avoid becoming or remaining victims. All were relegated to the margins, like Eve having no place and nowhere to go: "it seemed there was nowhere on earth for a woman like me" (91). Nadine escapes victimization by believing wholeheartedly in herself: she confines her letters to Bailey to "short short" ones, but with "perfect timing" (13), and unlike most people "doesn't bother" to "translate [her] feelings for the general population" (19). When confronted by her tyrannical father, Eve escapes, treks through the delta, and eventually establishes her rigidly run boardinghouse and her beloved garden (92). Together, the four proprietors are able to build a community because of their individual strengths.

These characters are larger than life, possessing almost super-human powers. Gabe is able to rescue Mariam; Bailey "can get inside a lot of heads around here" (165); and Nadine looks "like an African goddess" (13). Eve is the most mythical, becoming one with the delta dust (86) and walking across the delta for "a thousand years" (82). She knows the cafe routine before she arrives (80), "already knew" Esther's story (99), and "sets up" Mariam's dreamscape (224). Reminiscent in name and personality of the biblical Eve and of Eva Peace in Toni Morrison's *Sula*, she is a dream maker, a griot, who forces those she helps to help themselves, to face their inner selves, and to work harder than they have ever worked. Eve is thus similar to the healers in Bambara's *The Salt Eaters*, who know that the future will ask more of everyone than they can imagine. She and Nadine are the kind of women Naylor admires, women who have "turned their backs on the world" and who have "been selfish to some degree" (Naylor, "Gloria" 572). They, like Miranda, Abigail, Bailey, Gabriel, and Naylor, have said, "*I am here*. That *I* contains myriad realities— not all of them pretty, but not all of them ugly, either" (Naylor, "Love" 31).

Through her four presiding figures, and often through Bailey as their principal spokesperson, Naylor creates a worldview that privileges tolerance, open-endedness, and complexity, all of which become possible when one has acknowledged and accepted the abyss, when, like Miranda, one has been bold enough to open the well. Given the individual courage and strength of the four proprietors and given such ennobling values, the broken threads of the damaged community web can be reconnected. Through the power of love and imagination, the proprietors create an alternate reality that allows for individual rebirth and fulfillment within the new community. For Naylor, this can only happen outside the parameters of the real world, but it can happen through the combined mental powers of the inhabitants of Willow Springs or Bailey's neighborhood, just as it happens in the imaginations of Naylor and her readers.

The neighborhood accepts all comers, all who have suffered and who need relief. Customs from all over the world are welcomed: Miss Maple admires the loose-fitting business clothes of non-Westerners (201), and Bailey enjoys the music of many cultures (162). At the end of the novel, the ritual performance of George's circumcision brings the community together in a celebration of cross-cultural harmony. This valuing of tolerance contrasts sharply with the novel's refrain of intolerance and bigotry, as the book's "abundance plays against the particular pains contained in the various characters' stories" (K. Fowler 27).

The neighborhood's ethos of tolerance is reinforced by the belief that everything always remains open. Emancipated from the constraints of monologism, the neighborhood has no beginning, no end, no fixed points; it exists in the pure play of the nontemporal and nonspatial. Bailey expresses the apparently shared views that life has "more questions than answers" (229) and that "no life is perfect" (228). Instead of desiring answers or perfection, Bailey relishes endless flux: "If life is truly a song, then what we have here is just snatches of a few melodies. All these folks are in transition; they come midway in their stories and go on" (219). Everything remains open partly because everything is more complex than it may appear: Iceman Jones knows "that most things aren't what they seem" (70), and Bailey warns readers, "if you're expecting to get the answer in a few notes, you're mistaken" (4).

This insistence on complexity is expressed in the metaphor of going under the surface. Bailey, listening closely to the stereotyped opinions of Sister Carrie and Sugar Man, warns readers not to oversimplify: "If you don't listen below the surface, they're both one-note players" (33). Hearing only that one note is insufficient, for everyone in this novel—and, Naylor implies, every human being—has a complex story: "But nobody comes in here with a simple story. Every one-liner's got a life underneath it. Every point's got a counterpoint" (34). Bailey advises readers that "Anything really worth hearing in this greasy spoon happens under the surface. You need to know that if you plan to stick around here and listen while we play it all out" (35). To participate in this community—to read the novel—readers must learn what the four proprietors have learned and what the victimized visitors are struggling to learn—how to go below the surface, to "take 'em one key down" (34). Readers, proprietors, and visitors must learn not only tolerance for others but also tolerance and understanding of the multiple layers of meanings. All must move beyond monologism into multiplicity.

The form of the novel itself exhibits these values of openness and depth. The musical metaphors around which the narrative is structured push the written medium toward a nondiscursive, nonprescriptive mode, a mode that suggests rather than defines, that opens rather than narrows. For this reason, the point of view is not restricted to one voice or one perspective. Although Bailey is the principal narrator, usually introducing and concluding each character's story, his voice is not sufficient. Montgomery argues that this multiplicity is necessary because "the male voice is severely limited in its ability to decode the very private experiences the women relate" ("Authority" 28). But the larger point is that no single voice is adequate to convey the characters' experiences. A single voice would metaphorically place the text in the well, in a confining monologism; therefore, a multiplicity of voices is necessary to convey the multiplicity of life, to ensure that life and the novel keep their play, and to enact the principle of the mutual creation of the communal web. For this reason, when Bailey's voice is insufficient to narrate Mariam's story, two additional voices—Nadine's and Eve's—are required.

To avoid the constrictions of a single perspective, Naylor includes the voices of nearly every character: direct transcription of Sadie's thoughts alternate with Bailey's narration (72–78); Eve (81–91), Mary/Peaches (102–12), Esther (95–99), and Miss Maple (165–213) take over the telling of their stories; Jesse Bell's first-person narration is interpolated into Bailey's narration (137–41); and Nadine and Eve narrate Mariam's life story (143–60). Naylor even quotes minor characters, such as the anonymous soldiers and their officer, who shout their determination to "kill Japs" (21), the unnamed customers with whom Bailey argues (31), the religious zealot Sister Carrie and the hipster Sugar Man (e.g., 32–34), Esther's miscellaneous customers (95), Esther's "husband" (e.g., 95), and Miss Maple's father (185). Through these extremes of multiple narration, Naylor's narrative form literally creates a participatory community.

Naylor underscores and extends the plural and oral-like narration by unexpectedly shifting between one character's indirect discourse and another character's words. For example, Miss Maple's narration is interrupted by a direct transcription of the Gatlin boys' thought: "What they couldn't tear apart, they stomped—*My God, look, it ain't got a tail after all*" (180, emphasis added). Similarly, Bailey's narration is interrupted by Gabe's thought: "And banging down old radios and flinging used overcoats into boxes and sweeping up a dust storm. *Puppy, cover your ears, a goy shouldn't be hearing these things*" (221, emphasis added). With this doubling of free indirect discourse, Naylor implies that, even within a single sentence, no single voice suffices.

In addition to creating a communal narration, Naylor's narrative technique transforms the written text into oral performance. On one level, the entire text carries the sense of being spoken directly to the reader. From beginning to end, Bailey's language sounds more spoken than written, with its contractions, its informality, its casualness: the novel starts with "I can't say I've had much education. Book education" (3) and ends with "And that's how we wrap it, folks" (229). As in the latter sentence, Bailey frequently addresses readers directly: they are customers at his cafe ("And if you've got a problem with how I feel, well, there are other cafes" [12]); they are recipients of his lessons ("If you don't listen below the surface, they're both one-note players" [33]); they are taken under his wing ("But I think you've got the drift" [35]); they hear his complaints ("I want you to know right off that Nadine lied on me" [161]); and we receive his hints ("And what I heard is too ignorant to believe. And just guess who I heard it from? [Sister Carrie and Sugar Man, in case you need a hint]" [223]). The sense that readers are listening directly to the novel is sustained when both Nadine and Miss Maple also address them. Nadine begins her narration with "You already know that my name is Nadine" (143), and Miss Maple interjects a "dialogue" with readers in which he poses and then answers their presumed questions: "And now I'm going to hold a conversation with what I assume are some of your more troubling thoughts about this whole endeavor" (203). The entire novel functions as a multivoiced, multilayered conversation among characters, character-narrators, author, and readers, thus enacting the re-creation of the communal web that has been denied its characters in the world outside Bailey's neighborhood.

On another level, the language of the text is addressed to and heard by the other characters. Several times Bailey directs asides to Nadine, implying that she is listening to his narration, for example, "Nadine, nobody asked you" (4). Nadine acknowledges that she has heard Bailey's long address to the reader: "You already know that my name is Nadine, and my husband's told you that I don't like to talk" (143). This mutual participation in the narrative peaks during the circumcision of the new infant, George, the ritual that inducts the infant into the social and religious communities. Everyone is there, even Esther, who "wonder of wonders . . . smiled" (225). Peaches begins to sing a spiritual, and soon everyone is singing: "One voice joined in. Another voice joined. And another" (225). They sing of their assertions of identity ("Anybody ask you who you are? Tell him— you're the child of God") and of the harmony of human beings and God, of "Peace on earth" (226). The three men share the male roles appropriate for the ritual: Gabriel is the father and rabbi, Bailey is the godfather, and Miss Maple "took the role of the other male guests to help [Bailey] respond to the blessing" (226). Their song, their participation in the communal ritual, and even their combined presence as a functioning community demonstrate the power of this reweaving of the hitherto damaged social fabric.

Just as Bailey is impressed with the Jewish communal ritual ("And that's what I like the most about Gabe's faith; nothing important can happen unless they're all in it together as a community" [227]), Naylor structures her novel so that this most important event—the first birth on the block—brings this community together. Individuals may—and will—be trapped in their well-like tragedies, but communities, as in the brick-throwing demonstration in *The Women of Brewster Place* and in the annual candle walk in *Mama Day,* can gain at least momentary relief by singing, by performing time-honored rituals, by telling and hearing each other's stories, and by embracing each other and each other's cultures. Multiple voices can create communities and thereby help characters avoid the isolation of the well. But for Naylor such re-creations in the real world are fleeting and perhaps illusory, like the brick-throwing demonstration, or they occur only in alternate realities like Willow Springs and Bailey's neighborhood where the imaginations of mythlike characters can overcome the brutal conditions of American life.

As the multiple narrations and orality in *Bailey's Cafe* weave the connections among characters and readers, the shifts in point of view often enact the principle of going beneath the surface. Bailey uses the metaphor of going "one key down" (34) to indicate the deeper layer(s) of meaning beneath the surface. He illustrates this strategy in his transcriptions of Sister Carrie's and Sugar Man's actual words and then in his translations of what the two really mean (33–35). After presenting their spoken words, he tells us what they are really saying "one key down" and on "even a lower key" (34). Through Bailey, Naylor thus creates an explicit model for the reader: the stories of Naylor's characters must be read as Bailey reads the words of Sister Carrie and Sugar Man, not merely for their surface meaning but for the layers of deeper meanings. When characters and their readers accomplish this multiple layering, they become participants in the mutual construction of the intersubjective web. Naylor structures her stories of the novel's characters to encourage such participatory reading strategies. In "Mood: Indigo," the narration of Sadie's story goes one key down when it shifts from Bailey's point of view to the italicized paragraphs directly depicting Sadie's dream of middle-class comfort (72–77). Similarly, the narration goes beneath the surface when it shifts from Bailey's voice to the voices of Eve (81–91), Esther (95–99), Mary/Peaches (102–12), Jesse Bell (117–32), and Miss Maple (165–213).

In the Jesse Bell chapter, the narration descends even lower when Sister Carrie and Eve duel with contrasting biblical passages as commentaries on Jesse (134–36). During this exchange Eve sarcastically signifies on Carrie when she calls out, "somebody in here likes Ezekiel. Somebody even likes the *sixteenth chapter* of Ezekiel" (135). Eve subdues Carrie with this and similar counterpassages that emphasize divine love for the fallen. Naylor invites the reader to play the biblical game and thus to join in the novel's communal construction when she quotes Ezekiel 16:6 without identifying it, letting it stand as a concluding, and tolerating, comment on Jesse: "And when I passed by thee, and saw polluted in thine own blood, I said unto thee when thou wast in thy blood, Live; yea, I said unto thee when thou was in thy blood, Live" (136).

The narration also goes one key down to stress the interconnections among its participants when Jesse's indirect discourse is interpolated, without warnings or transitions, into Bailey's narration. For example, when Bailey narrates, "Jesse didn't quite know what it meant, but this weird mama-jama was beginning to scare her" (137), "weird mama-jama" is Jesse's term for Eve, not Bailey's. The technique is most obvious in the following complete paragraph, in which the first person shifts abruptly from Bailey to Jesse: "Jesse has never tried to describe for me what it was like that second time around. She says there are no words for the experience. I can only tell you this, Bailey, I sincerely prayed to die" (142).

As it draws characters and readers closer together, the multiple, shifting, and oral narration of this novel reinforces the mental connections among the participants and all human beings. Since the point of view can flow back and forth among the characters, and since the characters can overhear each other's narrations to the reader, the physical and psychological distances among them are metaphorically eliminated. All can join in each other's dream fantasies; all can participate in the celebration of George's birth. One passage in particular, a one-key-down passage, suggests such metaphysical interconnections. As Bailey recalls his experiences in World War II, his identity expands to incorporate all American soldiers in the Pacific. This merger begins cryptically with the refrain, "We weren't getting into Tokyo" (21–23), and develops into a full-blown monologue within Bailey's narration. As the universal soldier, Bailey has been present at every Pacific battle, imagines that "the end of the world is blue" (e.g., 23), feels the horror of Japanese civilians caught in the war, participates in the atomic bombings of Hiroshima and Nagasaki, and worries about the "unborn children" and the "new age" (26) to follow. Bailey encompasses not only every soldier but also every victim and even unborn victims because he transcends the barriers that usually isolate individuals. Entering the *différance,* he floats free of any limiting self-presence, just as the novel's narration allows the characters and its readers to escape theirs. He merges his consciousness with the consciousnesses of all others just as the novel reenacts similar mergers among its participants.

Characters in this book are able to cross such boundaries because, unlike Naylor's first three novels, here the characters are not enmeshed in limiting stereotypes. The residents of Linden Hills are trapped by their own conformity to white values of economic success and social status, and George and Cocoa in *Mama Day* must struggle with their preconceived absolutes, in particular, white values of love, courtship, and life.[17] But *Bailey's Cafe* culminates with the multicultural, communal celebration of the birth of Mariam's son. This birth is the occasion for the neighborhood's coming together, but, in keeping with Naylor's and the privileged characters' tough realism, it is only one local event that will not change the world: "Life will go on. Still, I do understand the point this little fella is making as he wakes up in the basket: When you have to face it with more questions than answers, it can be a crying shame" (229).

For Naylor to end this novel with a birth is particularly significant because births are rare throughout her fiction and, when they do occur, are associated with extreme hardship. In *The Women of Brewster Place,* Lucielia's first child is electrocuted and her second one aborted; in *Linden Hills,* Willa Nedeed must watch the corpse of her son as she struggles toward her own psychic rebirth and physical death; and in *Mama Day,* Berenice Duvall first develops cysts instead of a baby and then her baby dies, and pregnancy for Cocoa Day almost kills her. In Naylor's fictional world, the difficulty of entering life is a metaphor for the difficulty of joining the community and for the problems of creating and maintaining viable communities. Given this context of difficult pregnancies and births, George's birth at the end of *Bailey's Cafe* is especially miraculous. Not only is he the first child born in this neighborhood, but he is born to a woman whose vagina had been ritually sewn shut. His conception is thus a mystery and a miracle, which suggests his Christlike status in this novel. Mariam's sealed vagina is another well image, in this case a closed well, a well like a tomb, but a double-edged well, a well of life closed into an image of death but then retransformed into a source of life. From this paradoxical source, George arrives as the catalyst for the coming together of this very fragile community and for the celebration of that union.

Parallel to the hardships of birth in Naylor's novels, deaths are also traumatic. Many characters meet violent deaths: Serena, Lorraine, and Ben in *The Women of Brewster Place;* Laurel Dumont and the three Nedeeds in *Linden Hills;* Little Caesar and George in *Mama Day;* and numerous, unnamed suicides in *Bailey's Cafe.*

That birth and death should be so difficult is predicted by the doubled womb/tomb image of the well. Well, birth, and death are mysterious and unavoidable. As Derrida and Naylor intimate, the temptation to ignore such abysses must be resisted and their inevitability must be acknowledged. In *Bailey's Cafe,* Naylor establishes a community of privileged characters—the proprietors plus Miss Maple—who have done just that, who are comfortable with the abysses of a devastating world and therefore are secure in their identities and their communal roles. They endure because they have acquired the traditional West African harmony among self, society, and cosmos; because they have accepted the brutality of African-American life in a racialized, patriarchal, and class-dominated society; because they have transformed their double consciousness into an advantage; because they have embraced the *différance;* because, excluded from the larger society, they have created their own community web.

In one sense the occasion of George's birth restores a sense of cosmic harmony in the novel's characters, establishes for them a living and livable African-American space and thereby confirms a sense of the past and provides hope for the present if not the future. The event also strengthens the secure identities of the four privileged characters and offers the hope of positive identity formation for some of the others. All these things can happen because all the characters, as well as the participating reader, have learned to accept the abyss. Like the inhabitants of the Bottom in Morrison's *Sula,* they have learned that "the presence of evil was something to be first recognized, then dealt with, survived, outwitted, triumphed over" (118).

In another sense, however, such positive implications of George's birth are called into question. In *Mama Day,* the male protagonist is the same George, born to a fifteen-year-old mother across the street from Bailey's Cafe and raised in an orphanage (130–31). In that novel, George is far from a Christ figure, bound up in his rigid self-presence and insisting on his narrowly rationalistic point of view. Although his birth unites the community in *Bailey's Cafe,* that miraculous moment is only a moment, and it is only a moment in a mystical place and time removed from material reality. This suggests that for Naylor, as for Derrida, there can be no ultimate solutions; instead, life is a continuous process of difference and deferral. Beginning with the notion of deferral in Hughes's "What Happens to a Dream Deferred?" Naylor's novels exhibit ongoing deferral in the explicit links among their settings and characters, for example, in the geographic, economic, and social connections between Linden Hills and Brewster Place and in the implicit developmental progressions from Willa to Willie and from Mattie and Willa to Miranda and Eve. Reading *Bailey's Cafe* and *Mama Day* in reverse order, the bright promise of George's birth at the end of *Bailey's Cafe* is deferred to the birth of George and Cocoa's son, also named George, at the end of *Mama Day*. With that repetition, Naylor returns to the symbolic event of the first George's birth, defers its promise, and leaves open and alive the potential of the second George.

Naylor's exploration of the *différance* and the repair of shattered communal bonds reflects broad cultural concerns. The synthesis of cultures, individuals, genders, and generations at the end of *Bailey's Cafe* projects the cosmic harmony that characterizes West African religions and philosophies. This worldview, in contrast to the Euro-American emphasis on differences and "dissent," as Miss Maple calls it (192), stresses the integration of individual, community, nature, and the supernatural.[18] The supportive community created by the four proprietors and Miss Maple reflects their balancing of all such dimensions of their lives. This novel and the celebration in which it culminates also depict Naylor's imaginary creation of an alternative African-American place and time. American reality for these characters is overwhelmingly hostile, rending individual psyches and dislocating all previous attempts at establishing meaningful bonds. For these characters, as for many African Americans, the assigned places have been in the well at the bottom of American society. The refugees in *Bailey's Cafe* have been denied not only a place in the real America but any meaningful past, just as African Americans have historically been denied a past. Since their identities have been defined by the totalizing powers that dominate American society, the characters, like many African Americans and many Euro-Americans, have trouble establishing and maintaining viable identities. Pursuing a sense of identity in the face of such displacements, Naylor's characters attempt "to define and express [their] totality rather than being defined by others," as Barbara Christian urges all African-American women to do (*Black* 159). In that process, they are forced to confront the false illusions of traditional binaries and instead adopt the survival strategies of deferral, flexibility, and multiplicity. Some—like Sadie and Mariam—cannot overcome their devastating pasts. Others—

such as Mary/Peaches, Jesse Bell, and even Esther—gain the possibility of emerging into stable identities. The four proprietors and Miss Maple model the creation of healthy personalities and a cohesive community in the face of a brutalizing reality. They, like Naylor and then her readers, can reconnect personal and interpersonal threads through the imagination—through spiritual, collective, and artistic productions of alternative places, times, identities, and therefore communities.

6

"You Don't See What I Don't See"

Communal Construction of Meaning in Ernest Gaines's Fiction

The times and places in the fiction of Ernest Gaines are strictly in this world: there are no alternative realities as in *Mama Day* and *Bailey's Cafe*, no fantastic voyages through history as in *Oxherding Tale* and *Middle Passage*, no apocalyptic thundering as in *The Salt Eaters*. Gaines's fictional world is realistic, similar to that of John Edgar Wideman, but Gaines's verbal style is much more grounded in ordinary conversation and description than is Wideman's. Gaines's milieu is the plantations and towns of southern Louisiana, inhabited by an interracial mixture of Cajuns, Anglos, and African Americans. As in the United States itself, there is a sense of a multicultural community in these parishes, as the characters share knowledge of each other's habits and personalities. That community, however, is heavily marked by tensions, tensions emanating from the severe imbalances in social, economic, and political power among the three groups.

Particularly in *In My Father's House*, *A Gathering of Old Men*, and *A Lesson before Dying*, Gaines focuses on a seemingly small event that temporarily disturbs the established status quo of this fragile multicultural community. The event may be the return of a man's illegitimate son (*House*), the murder of a Cajun overseer (*Gathering*), or a young African American's need for counseling before being executed (*Lesson*). The disturbing event(s) in each of Gaines's novels sends shock waves throughout the interracial community, temporarily disrupting it and opening up the possibilities of change within it and especially within the identities of the characters directly involved in the event. Like the other authors discussed in this book, Gaines is unwilling to describe such possible futures in any detail—it is enough to suggest that the events he does describe have the potential to induce change.[1]

In two earlier novels, events seem to have no continuing effect, and the community reestablishes its former status quo. In *Catherine Carmier*, after the potential love affair between Jackson and Catherine is thwarted, the community returns to normal, and after the failure of Marcus and Louise's planned escape in *Of Love and Dust*, the dust settles and nothing has changed. In Gaines's subsequent novels, when change does occur or at least when the disturbing event seems likely to induce lasting change, the changes are local and subtle, not sweeping or revolutionary. The return of Phillip Martin's son in *House* radically alters Martin's life, realigning his sense of himself, his relationship to his wife, his role in the community, and therefore the community itself. In *Gathering*, the murder of Beau Boutan and the gathering of the old African-American men shock the entire community, and the old men's action and mutual testimony, as well as subtle changes in the relations among all three ethnic groups, suggests that lasting changes are occurring throughout the community and even in the wider American society. In *A Lesson before Dying*, there are many lessons. Most obviously, Jefferson, the condemned young man, grows into manhood, a small but significant progression not just for him but for his grandmother and for the African-American community. At the same time, Grant Wiggins learns the more complex lesson that he can and does make a difference, not just to Jefferson but also to his students, and therefore that he should stay in the community. Suzanne Jones argues that both Jefferson and Grant, like Gil Boutan in *Gathering*, must learn the lessons of the new masculine order—"to express emotion other than anger," "to articulate one's feelings," "to empathize with black people," and "to resolve conflict in non-aggressive ways" (49, 56). The community is enriched because both men do learn these lessons, because Jefferson gains a true self, and because Wiggins gains self-respect and maturity. All these changes may seem like small steps, but in Gaines's fictional world small steps are the ones that matter.

In each case the relatively static status quo is shaken by an unexpected event. The event causes one or more male characters to question the system and his place in it, as the emphasis shifts from relatively secure knowledge to uncertainty and doubt. The character(s) must act, but they do not know how, and in their uncertainty they are forced to rethink relationships between self and community. In each novel the event leads to a redemptive death: Martin's estranged son, Etienne; Charlie Biggs; and Jefferson. But those sacrifices are preconditions for the protagonists' potential rededication to the community and for the community's renewed vitality: "the achievement of a communal vision occurs in the works of Gaines only after some act of martyrdom" (Papa 188).

In all three novels, members of the community share a high degree of community knowledge. In *House,* Virginia Colar knows not only that Fletcher Zeno is "at home" but that he is "drinking hot coffee" (11). In *Gathering,* Miss Merle knows "most of the history of that river and of that parish in the past fifty years" (25), "everybody on the bayou know" that Ding Lejeune cannot shoot straight (53), and Snookum knows that Rufe will be working and singing in his garden (6). *Lesson* begins with Grant Wiggins's assertion that he knows everything in the community, whether or not he is physically present: "I was not there, yet I was there. No, I did not go to the trial, I did not hear the verdict, because I knew all the time what it would be" (3). Later, he states the general rule for life in Gaines's parish: "Living and teaching on a plantation, you got to know the occupants of every house . . . and I could tell the lives that went on in each one of them" (37–38).

Characters know each other and their community so intimately that ordinarily they can accurately interpret each other. Even though he is not her close friend, Grant knows in detail what Thelma's *here* means:

It was the kind of "here" your mother or your big sister or your great-aunt or your grandmother would have said. It was the kind of "here" that let you know this was hard-earned money but, also, that you needed it more than she did, and the kind of "here" that said she wished you had it and didn't have to borrow it from her, but since you did not have it, and she did, then "here" it was, with a kind of love. It was the kind of "here" that asked the question, When will all this end? When will a man not have to struggle to have the money to get what he needs "here"? When will a man be able to live without having to kill another man "here"? (*Lesson* 174)

Besides knowing what other characters' words mean, characters can usually understand each other's looks: merely by her appearance, Shepherd "could see [Virginia] was scared" (*House* 23), Griffin knows by Candy's "slow and hard" look that she isn't going to back down" (*Gathering* 95), and throughout *Lesson* Grant and other characters are adept at reading each other's eyes and looks.[2]

Such community knowledge extends to characters' abilities to understand each other's deepest feelings and motivations. Phillip Martin's godmother, Angelina (*House* 107–15), his wife, Alma (136), and his friend, Beverly (211–13) know him better than he knows himself. The old men in *Gathering* enjoy a near unanimity of mind as they instantly respond to Candy's call, each sharing in the deeper, historical meanings of the occasion. Not only do Mat and Chimley know each other's thoughts (28–32), but Cherry senses "why we was all there" (46) and Clatoo "could see how proud they was to be there" (51). Grant Wiggins's lover, Vivian, and Reverend Ambrose are able to help Grant discover his true values because they know that he has those values before he does (*Lesson* 94, 105, 141, 213–16).[3]

Against this background of community knowledge and mutual interpretation, the crisis in each novel is couched in terms of the characters' sudden and unusual inability to interpret events and behavior. No one can understand Etienne—who calls himself Robert X—when he appears at the beginning of *House,* and then his presence leads to equally inexplicable behavior by his father.

The plot of *Gathering* revolves around the characters' inabilities to interpret Beau Boutan's death, the old men's confessions of the murder, and the possible retaliation by the Boutan family. In *Lesson*, Grant's forced role in Jefferson's case requires him to address his hitherto unaddressed and uninterpreted questions about his own life.

The unusual inability to interpret people and events leads characters into a proclivity to ask unanswerable questions. Before Etienne's arrival, Phillip Martin seemed to have all the answers, but his son's presence entangles him in a virtually endless series of unanswered questions about his son, his past, his identity ("Who really was Phillip Martin, and what, if anything, had he really done?" [72]), and God ("How come He let this happen?" [209]). As in *The Salt Eaters*, the characters in *Gathering* are deeply confused about the present and anxious about the unknown future; hence, most of the questions are external, most often taking the form of "what's wrong?" or "what's happening?"[4] In *Lesson*, Grant Wiggins's attempts to convince Jefferson of the latter's humanity embark Grant on a quest for his own inner self that encompasses his asking the unanswerable about himself: "Who am I? God?" (31) and "Why wasn't I there? Why wasn't I standing beside him? Why wasn't my arm around him? Why?" (250). Correspondingly, Grant effects change in Jefferson by posing unanswerable questions to him, such as "Are you trying to make me feel guilty for your being here?" (84), "What do you want?" (84), and "Jefferson, do you know what 'moral' means?" (139).

In *In My Father's House* and *A Lesson before Dying*, Gaines uses a similar strategy of doubling his two leading male characters: Phillip's problems come to resemble Etienne's, and Grant learns the same lessons he imparts to Jefferson. But the movement of the paired characters is essentially opposite, for Phillip follows Etienne toward psychic confusion and concomitant isolation from the community, whereas Grant and Jefferson rediscover their identities and simultaneously recommit themselves to communal values.

When Etienne arrives in St. Adrienne at the beginning of *House,* he is, as his pseudonym, Robert X, suggests, the epitome of an alienated individual.[5] His characteristic mode is antisocial, and he refuses repeatedly to answer Virginia, Elijah, Shepherd, and Phillip and does not bother to answer knocks on his door. For him life is hopeless, because "Nobody can do nothing" (25), so he drinks because "it kills the pain" (25). His malaise is profound, leading him to feel that his "soul is sick" (27) and to suspect that life is like a rubbish-strewn alley (26). At the heart of his problems is not only his sense of abandonment by his father but his questioning of his own manhood since his younger brother, Antoine, rather than Etienne himself, had avenged their sister's rape and thereby become the man of the house: Antoine "had even forgiven Etienne for not taking the gun. But now he was the man, and he let Etienne know it. When he pulled that trigger, then he was the man. His sister, the way she looked at him, let him know that he was the man. Even Johanna [their mother]. Even Etienne himself let him know that he was the man now" (198).

Starting from the opposite position as the community's leader, Phillip Martin becomes remarkably like Etienne. He too begins to refuse to answer people, such as his wife (51, 73) and Elijah (58, 60). After abandoning his responsibilities to his community when he unilaterally agrees not to lead a protest against the store owner, Albert Chenal, Phillip becomes increasingly isolated from the community. By the end of the novel he, like his son, no longer cares (208) and only has faith in alcohol: "Be like that boy there. Don't put no faith in nothing. Not in God. Not in work. Not in love. In nothing. Put it in the bottle" (210). Just as Etienne's soul is sick, Phillip asserts, "I'm at war with myself, Adeline. I'm at war with my soul" (178). Like his son, Phillip's problems stem from doubts about his manhood, which his fainting at the party causes him to question: "Men supposed to clamb up off the floor" (57). Then, while trying to explain why he abandoned Johanna and her children, Phillip argues that at that time he "wasn't a man" (102) but since then has become one. The return of

Etienne, however, erodes that conviction, sending Phillip back into the loss of manhood and consequent loss of identity that he thought he had escaped.

Both Etienne and Phillip attempt to atone for the past, Etienne by finding Phillip and Phillip by accepting Etienne's claims on him. Neither is successful, however, because each attempts to do so by himself, against rather than with the community. Etienne's hatred and despair cut him off from everyone, and Phillip sacrifices the community's cause against Chenal in favor of his individual need. In Phillip's subsequent quest for help, he encounters many individuals who might aid him—such as his wife, his church deacons, and his godmother—but he does not tell them the truth about Etienne, thus isolating himself further. He then crosses the river to Baton Rouge and again encounters people who might help him but who fail to alleviate his isolation: "Reverend" Peters, Billy, and Adeline Toussaint. Even after he hears the story of Johanna's family from his old friend, Chippo, Phillip remains "lost" (214). As Keith Byerman concludes, Phillip fails to understand himself or his community because he thinks that the past is "an account book" (97) that he can balance by replacing Robert X with Etienne. In Gaines's fiction, individuals can help the community only when they act within it, and the community's past is redeemed only when an individual's needs and actions coincide with the community's. By trying to isolate the individual and the communal and thereby unconsciously violating West African principles of harmony, Phillip only manages to isolate and confuse himself (Plant 15). Although Phillip's path largely parallels Etienne's, Gaines, creating a fictional landscape that is "an evolutionary space" in which change is possible rather than "a polemical space" where situations are fixed (Beavers 101), leaves the door open for Phillip to recover. As Herman Beavers argues, Phillip does listen to Chippo and then to his friend Beverly, and the "ability to recover an understanding of the importance of listening" (Beavers 94) may help him realize the necessity of working within the community to regain his own integrity. Heretofore, Phillip has not heeded the advice of those close to him, but the novel closes with his wife's willingness to give him another chance—"We just go'n have to start again" (214).[6]

In many ways the situation of Grant Wiggins and Jefferson in *Lesson* resembles that of Phillip Martin and Etienne. Condemned to die for a murder he did not commit, Jefferson is as alienated, hateful, and indifferent to life as Etienne. Even more sharply than for Etienne, manhood is the issue for Jefferson, since he has internalized his white lawyer's conclusion that he is more like a hog than a human. Grant, like Phillip, starts from a position of leadership and respect within the community and similarly attempts to restore the younger character's integrity, identity, and manhood. Also like Phillip, Grant's position within the community is not as secure as it first appears, for he chafes under what he feels are the community's inability to change and its undying legacy of slavery and consequent emasculation of its African-American men: "What [Miss Emma] wants is for him, Jefferson, and me to change everything that has been going on for three hundred years" (167). Grant's spiritual position on the edge of the community causes him, like Phillip, to be internally divided, "unable to accept what used to be my life, unable to leave it" (102), and to ask unanswerable questions about such crucial topics as himself ("Who am I?" [31]), his relationship to Jefferson ("What do I say to him?" [31]), his manhood ("Do I know what a man is?" [31]), his effectiveness as a teacher ("What am I doing? Am I reaching them at all?" [62]), and the legal system ("Who made them God?" [157]). He is in danger of becoming as cynical as his former teacher, Matthew Antoine, who became completely alienated in his "hatred for himself as well as contempt for us" (62) and whose only advice was to flee.

Just as Phillip's efforts to reach Etienne bring him closer to his son's alienation, so Grant's counseling of Jefferson reveals the parallels between their positions. As Philip Auger attests, Grant is a prisoner within the schoolhouse, subject to the racial inequities of the county and supervised by his "warden," the superintendent, Dr. Joseph Morgan (76). But the essential difference between Phillip and Grant is that Grant, despite his discomfort, works within the community, listening to the supporting people around him and becoming their agent for reconciliation and redemption as well as the agent for his own personal growth. In direct contrast to Phillip, Grant sacrifices his personal desire—his hope of escaping the parish—to help his aunt, Miss Emma, and the community. Unlike Phillip, who refuses to answer his wife and his would-be counselor, Elijah, Grant listens fully to his fiancée, Vivian; Reverend Ambrose; and his aunt, Tante Lou, allowing them to function as his conscience.[7] When for example Ambrose tells him, "You're just lost," he agrees (217) and then repeats the admission to Jefferson (222). Vivian understands Grant's values better than he will admit, knowing that "you love [Tante Lou and Miss Emma] more than you hate this place" (94), that he believes in God ("You don't want to, but I know you do" [105]), and that, even if he is not changing Jefferson, he himself is "changing" (141). Even though he asserts to Ambrose (101) and his aunt that "I don't know a thing about the soul" (182), he finds his own way of reaching Jefferson and thus himself, whereas Phillip and Etienne languish in soul sickness.

As Grant convinces Jefferson of the latter's humanity, he convinces himself of the same lessons as he voices the values that his aunt, his fiancée, and Reverend Ambrose know he believes in. Grant's first argument to Jefferson applies equally well to Grant himself: they have obligations to their friends. Both Grant and Jefferson need to learn not to hurt people who love them (129) and to "do anything to please a friend" (190). Grant pushes harder with Jefferson, arguing that the latter has the rare opportunity of becoming a hero, someone who can give something meaningful to his community and who can alter the slave-based myth of racial relations (191–92), but again Grant's lesson applies equally well to himself. He comes to realize that he, and perhaps everyone, is "a slave" (251), and he as well as Jefferson become heroes, as the white deputy Paul Bonin beams, "You're one great teacher, Grant Wiggins" (254). Grant's third lesson for Jefferson is that love—human love and God's love—cannot be underestimated: "there is something greater than possessions—and that is love" (222). Grant becomes increasingly aware of the developing connection between himself and Jefferson when he says that he needs Jefferson to clarify his own life: "I need you much more than you could ever need me. I need to know what to do with my life" (193). By recognizing Jefferson as his teacher, by thereby respecting Jefferson as a human being, and later by shifting the focus from himself to Jefferson (S. Jones 57), Grant establishes new bases for both Jefferson's and his own integrity and manhood. As Grant reflects to Jefferson, both of them are pieces "of drifting wood, until we—each one of us, individually—decided to become something else. I am still that piece of drifting wood, and those out there are no better. But you can be better. Because we need you to be and want you to be" (193). Grant's future, like Phillip Martin's, remains open, because Gaines, like the other writers considered here, refuses to define his characters' futures; but Grant, unlike Phillip, has clearly found himself while helping Jefferson find himself and while showing the community a testimony of its potential.

Since Grant's primary purpose in counseling Jefferson is to convince the other man of his humanity, his manliness, it is significant that Grant's own behavior parallels that lesson. He wants Jefferson to stand up and walk like a man, not to go to his execution like an animal, but also not to go merely in acquiescence to the white-controlled system. Similarly, while helping Jefferson, Grant must retain his own independence, his pride, his resistance to that system. Thus, he obeys the summons to Henry Pichot's house and enters by the back door as he must, but he retains his dignity by refusing to sit or to eat any of Pichot's food. He also accepts the white-imposed regimen of the jail, but he finds ways within that regimen to allow both himself and Jefferson to maintain their dignity and manhood. Although he will not accept Pichot's food, he demonstrates to Jefferson that eating his godmother's food reciprocates her love and therefore reasserts his humanity and his membership in the community. Grant knows that he has succeeded with Jefferson when the boy asks

Grant to "tell the chirren thank you for the pe-pecans" (186), indicating not only that Jefferson has accepted their offer of food but also that he rejoins the community and humanity by thanking them.

The narrative forms of *House* and *Lesson* mirror these thematic differences. The narrator of the former is third person, distant from Phillip Martin, because, as Gaines says, "You cannot tell that story from the minister's point of view because the minister keeps too much inside him. He does not reveal it—he won't reveal it to anybody" (Rowell, "This" 89). Moreover, that narration does not include direct transcription of the community members' voices, for the emphasis in this novel is on the isolation of Phillip and Etienne from the community. Conversely, in *Lesson,* most of the narration is from Grant's first-person perspective, since Grant does reveal what is inside him. And when Grant is not physically present he can still narrate events because he is integrated within the community; he knows what everyone else in the community knows, he is "there" even when he is not "there" (3). To demonstrate the impact of Grant's communal integration, Gaines expands the narration late in the novel to include Jefferson's diary entries (220, 226–34), which allow him a voice and which reassert his identity by giving him the power of the written word (Auger 83; Babb, "Old-Fashioned" 262). From that initial movement outward from Grant's narration, Gaines then depicts the day of Jefferson's execution in third-person narration from the perspectives of Reverend Ambrose, Sheriff Sam Guidry, Deputy Paul Bonin, and several other townspeople. This multiple perspective formally places Jefferson's fate, as well as Grant's heroic transformation of Jefferson, into the community, both African American and white. As Valerie Babb puts it, "The novel's final events are not rendered directly but are quilted together through the stories and reminiscences of a variety of characters" ("Old-Fashioned" 263).

In *A Gathering of Old Men,* Gaines employs a multiple, communal narrative form, using fifteen characters to narrate twenty chapters. Like William Faulkner's *As I Lay Dying,* the chapters are titled by the narrating characters' names, and the narrators include a central core of characters (the old men and the Bundrens) as well as "outsiders" who provide continuity and corroboration.[8] Just as the lack of an omniscient, authorial narrator in Faulkner's novel replicates the Bundrens' loss of Addie (Sundquist, *Faulkner* 39–40), the multiple narrators in Gaines's novel revolve around an absent center—the soul of the black community on the Marshall plantation. In both novels the multiple narrations become joint efforts to restore what has been lost.

The narrative form of *Gathering* empowers the old men, enabling them to redeem many past failings. They gain power by their words and actions, both of which force other characters to come to terms with the men even more than with Beau Boutan's death. At the same time, the narration focuses attention on them by allowing them to narrate eight of the fifteen chapters and by pointedly not allowing other major characters in the plot— Charlie, Mathu, Mapes, Candy, Gil, and Fix—to be narrators. The old men are further empowered by Gaines's assertion in the novel's title that they are "men" and by his inclusion of their full names in the chapter titles.[9] Collectively, the "choral litany" (Rowell, "Quarters" 747) of the old men's narrations is their declaration of manhood. By finally standing up to the illegal authority of the Cajuns and the legal power of the white-controlled social system, the men insist on their individual integrity as they reestablish their community. No single narrator—whether Lou Dimes, as Gaines originally planned (Lowe 188, 243), or one of the old men—could perform this communal function. The group must narrate because only through the group, not through any individual, can the infinite threads of the community be reconnected. Moreover, the men's narrations and stories effectively document the necessity of remembering the past. Without a shared past, the community will be obliterated, just as the Cajuns' tractors threaten gradually to plow under the African-American cemetery. As the old men insist on the relevance of the past, they also enact their redemption of it. Through their actions and words, they attempt to atone for their past failures, and thus, by rewriting the past, they create a new present on which to build a newly envisioned future.

Several features of the novel's narrative form underscore its significance. One such feature is that oral communication is frequently problematic. Despite the orality of the first-person narrations and the reported interchanges of dialogue that dominate the novel, communication is often lacking. For example, Lou tries to talk with Candy, but "she wouldn't listen" (73) and "she just sat there all tight-lipped" (184). When the coroner, Herman, arrives, he does "not speak" (74) in response to Mapes's greeting, and Mapes returns the favor by not providing Herman and his assistant an explanation of the situation: "They thought Mapes owed them some kind of explanation about what was going on. Mapes didn't say anything" (75). During the Boutan family council, communication does occur, but it does so slowly and haltingly, for example, when Fix must wait for Gil to explain his feelings, twice pressing him with "Well?" (135, 136) and asking him for clarification ("What are you trying to say, Gi-Bear?" [137]).

By using multiple narrators, Gaines underscores the acts of witnessing and testifying. In a literal sense, Mapes is the interrogator, demanding pseudo-legal testimony from the old men. They and Candy falsely testify that they killed Beau and therefore witnessed the murder. Candy warns Mapes that she has "a lot of witnesses" (68) of his abuse of the old men, and later Mapes threatens Luke that he has witnesses to the fact that Luke's gang shot Mapes. Ironically, Mathu, who witnessed the murder and whom everyone believes committed it, is not asked to testify. And then the irony is doubled when Charlie, whom everyone thought the most incapable of killing Beau, returns and, unasked, testifies. This scene of repeated pseudo-legal testimony and pseudo-legal judgment is echoed first in the Boutan house, where Fix presides much like a judge and interrogator, asking for testimony from his sons and brothers, and again in the courtroom scene, where a legally constituted judge presides and hears legal testimony.

But in the African-American oral tradition, to *witness* is to share empathetically in another person's experience or feeling and to *testify* is to express orally that shared experience (Smitherman 58). In this sense, Beavers claims that "Gaines's characters are 'articulate witnesses' whose voices rupture their respective forms of confinement by breaking the connection between experience and unspeakability while insisting on the value of kinship ties" (x). The old men, having experienced directly and indirectly the abuses of racism—in other words, having witnessed such abuses—had previously failed in their corresponding obligation to testify. Now, before they die, they are finally standing up to do so. They are testifying not really about the murder of Beau but about generations of mistreatment, to protect not just Mathu but also their heritage, their community, and their integrity and to insure the survival of what has been almost lost, what cannot be seen, what has been relegated to absence by the white-dominated system. They insist that what has been left to them is not enough, that the status quo is too demeaning and limiting, and that larger issues of identity, humanity, and integrity are at stake.

These two forms of testifying are related to a common feature of *In My Father's House*, *A Gathering of Old Men*, and *A Lesson before Dying:* questions and responses. As characters encounter the bizarre situation at Mathu's cabin, they seek information about it. The novel starts with a barrage of questions from characters on the plantation: Gram Mon (4), Snookum (5, 6), Janey (7–9, 21–25), and Miss Merle (12–19). Since the respondents to these questions know very little about the situation, are unwilling to say very much about it, or are extremely upset about it, they either do not answer the questions or answer in mystifying fragments. For example, Miss Merle cannot understand why Candy has summoned the old men, repeatedly asking, "Candy?" (18–19), a vague question that Candy ignores. The pattern of informational questions followed by nonreplies continues when each outsider arrives at Mathu's cabin: Lou (59–62), Mapes (65–73), Herman (75–77), and Gil (119–22). Paralleling the scene at Mathu's, Fix Boutan conducts his family council primarily by asking questions of his brothers and sons about what has happened and what they should do about it (131–48). In these exchanges, even though the characters assume that they know who killed Beau, responses to questions still tend to avoid direct answers. In Irving Goffman's terms, the characters tend to respond but not to reply, for they repeatedly "break frame" by not aligning their response with the previous question (35, 43). For example, when Gil's brother, Jean, asks Fix, "What will we do when we go to Bayonne, Papa? Who will go to Bayonne?" Fix responds without replying, "You don't want to go to Bayonne?" (139). Then Jean says, "I live in Bayonne, Papa," which implies his reluctance to seek vengeance on Mathu but which does not reply directly to the question.

The pattern of questions and responses is quite different for the old men. After the initial flurry of questions in the chapters narrated by Snookum, Janey, and Miss Merle (3–26), the fishing scene with Chimley and Mat is markedly serene. When they hear about Beau's death, the two men remain quiet, not even looking "at each other for a while" (28). The questions they do ask are noticeably gentle, such as "He works in mysterious ways, don't He?" (29). Unlike the other characters, they do not press each other for answers: "You don't have to answer this 'less you want to, Chimley" (29). They are serene because the literal details of Beau's murder do not matter to them; instead, for them the murder is a symbolic event, calling up all the persecutions they have suffered. They do not need to question each other because they know what the other is thinking: "We was thinking about what happened to us after something like this did happen. . . . This what I was thinking, and I was sure Mat was doing the same" (28–29). In contrast to the rest of the community, the murder of Beau sends the old men not into shock but into the deeper reserves of their community, their mutual understanding, their love for each other. While the murder threatens the stability of the larger community, it instantly restores the hitherto damaged intersubjective web of the old men.

As the men gather in Clatoo's truck and at the cemetery, they are synchronized with each other in the nonquestioning, tranquil mode of Chimley and Mat—"all there, to do something for the others" (46). When questions are asked, responses are gentle: whether they will have to fight Fix is up to him (47); what they are supposed to do with their empty shotgun shells will be explained later (48). As with Chimley and Mat's unspoken agreement, questions such as "Anybody feel like turning around?" (49) do not require an answer because the men already agree on the deepest levels. Throughout the novel the old men retain this communality, each one sticking to the group's plan of testifying that he is the person who killed Beau.

Gaines's rhetorical technique of nonanswered questions has a number of implications. As with the unanswered questions in *The Salt Eaters, In My Father's House,* and *A Lesson before Dying,* Gaines creates, in Paul Grice's terms, a conversational implicature violating the maxims of Quantity, Relation, and Manner (26–27).[10] By structuring the dialogue in *Gathering* around unanswered questions, Gaines creates a social texture marked by noncooperation, which reflects the community's shock over the strange events of this day. The ever-present gaps in oral communication between blacks and whites, men and women, adults and children, and insiders and outsiders reflect the deeper fissures, especially racial ones, in the novel's society and in the United States. In contrast, the easy give-and-take of questions and answers among the old men and, even more noticeably, their lack of need for questions of each other reflect the contrasting strength of their spiritual community.

The pattern of question/nonanswer also has temporal implications. Most of the characters' questions seek information about what has happened (for example, who killed Beau and what brought the old men to Mathu's) or about what is going to happen (what is Fix going to do). Other than the old black men, the characters are in a curious temporal limbo: the present is confusing, yet they have insufficient information about the immediate past that might help explain the causes of the present mystery, and they have considerable dread, but again no reliable information, about the possible consequences in the immediate future. Both the past and the future concern them yet are essentially unknowable. Goffman proposes that questions are directed toward the future, toward an anticipated answer—"questioners are oriented to what lies just ahead, and depend on what is to come"—and that, conversely, "answerers are oriented to what has just been said, and look backward, not forward" (5). But if neither the past nor the present is sufficiently known, as in this novel, then both questioners and would-be answerers are in the dark. Questioners keep asking questions in their desperation to pass beyond the unknown and dangerous present into a presumably more known and therefore secure future, but respondents cannot or will not answer because they cannot or will not look back to the past.

The persistent lack of answers naturally has the effect of leaving questions up in the air, open-ended, lacking closure. While this often frustrates questioning characters, it also forces them to wrestle with their lack of information, allowing them opportunities to answer their own questions and/or to realize on their own that no answer is possible or sufficient. The characters are thus forced to witness, think, participate, and in their own turn testify about the mysterious past, present, and future. At the same time, readers are also confronting the unanswered questions and, like the characters, are thereby forced to wonder and to participate. Like the other novels discussed in this book, this novel consistently opens, and leaves open, spaces for characters and readers to enter, inviting them to think about the possible answers that have not been provided, to interpret what has not been said, to focus on what is absent at least as much as what is present.[11]

This process is especially evident near the end of the novel when one of the old men, Dirty Red, awed by Charlie's transformation, asks, "What you seen back there, Charlie?" (208). As predicted by the question/nonanswer pattern, Charlie responds ambiguously, "You seen it too, Dirty. . . . All of y'all seen it" (208). Charlie has previously described his afternoon in the weeds and cane fields and his realization that he can no longer run away from manhood, so in a sense he has no more to say. But his nonanswer, intensified by his assertions that Dirty Red has had the same experience and should know the answer to his own question, redirects the question back to the questioner and the reader, both of whom must then try to fill in the exposed gap.

Throughout the novel the old men fill in that gap. For them, Beau's murder is not merely what it appears to be, is not an isolated incident, but is inextricably linked to the many hardships the old men have endured. They are not worried about the immediate questions of what happened, what is the matter, or what is going to happen because the incident opens up their entire pasts. For them, the murder and Candy's call for help offer, finally, a chance to redeem their pasts, to stand up to oppression, to become men, and they move immediately and communally through the space opened by the unanswered questions into a mutual epiphany about the meaning of their lives and their community.

After his wife's repeated questioning, "what's the matter with you?" (35–37), Mat finally reveals the symbolic and historical level on which he and the other old men react to the murder:

What's the matter with me? Woman, what's the matter with me? All these years we been living together, woman, you still don't know what's the matter with me? The years we done struggled in George Medlow's field, making him richer and richer and us getting poorer and poorer—and you still don't know what's the matter with me? The years I done stood out in that back yard and cussed at God, the years I done stood out on that front garry and cussed the world, the times I done come home drunk and beat you for no reason at all—and, woman, you still don't know what's the matter with me? Oliver, woman! . . . Oliver. How they let him die in the hospital just 'cause he was black. No doctor to serve him, let him bleed to death, 'cause he was black. And you ask me what's the matter with me? (37–38)

Mat's leap from the immediate import of Ella's question to its far-reaching and past meanings constitutes an obvious conversational implicature. This instance is a synecdoche for the novel, which similarly passes from the specifics of the day Beau is killed to the broadest implications of those events.

As in Mat's impassioned plea, the implications of Beau's murder extend within the old men's minds over their entire lives and therefore over the remembered history of life in the parish. In other words, the novel is about what one "sees" inside one's head, what one remembers and imagines, what is physically absent but emotionally and spiritually present. This kind of vision occurs when characters gaze absently over the landscape, not seeing literally but seeing inwardly beyond the literal scene; for example, when Rufe describes Johnny Paul's reverie: "He wasn't looking at Mapes, he was looking toward the tractor and the trailers of cane out there in the road. But I could tell he wasn't seeing any of that. I couldn't tell what he was thinking until I saw his eyes shifting up the quarters where his mama and papa used to stay" (88). A striking instance of such inner vision is Charlie's epiphany during his escape. While he agonizes over his responsibility and his manhood, he runs in each direction but cannot leave Marshall property because he is stopped by a wall he cannot see: "Something like a wall, a wall I couldn't see, but it stopped me every time" (192).[12]

The most powerful exploration of the unseen but inwardly envisioned past occurs in Johnny Paul's debate with Mapes (87–92). In polite but superficial response to Jacob Aguillard's memory of a white crowd's abuse of his sister, Mapes responds, "I see" (87). Johnny Paul takes offense at Mapes's innocent remark, making the leap from its ordinary meaning to its symbolic possibilities: "You see what?" (87) and "No, you don't see" (88). When Johnny asks Mapes what he sees, Mapes responds on the literal level—"I see nothing but weeds" (88). Johnny then delivers a sermonlike, interactive discourse with Mapes and the rest of the crowd about what he and the African Americans do not see—that is, what they remember from the old days when there were flowers, heroic individuals like Jack and Red Rider, and, in short, a true community in the quarters. What Johnny Paul and the others literally do not see is what they still remember and imagine inwardly and what they now realize that they have missed and desperately need. Mapes and the other whites cannot "see" any of that because they were not part of that community: "You had to be here then to be able to don't see it and don't hear it now" (92). Because Johnny and the other blacks were there then, they can testify—taking *testify* in the sense of the Black English oral tradition—about their former community and about the white power that everyone in that community endured, as Tucker, Yank, Gable, Coot, Corinne, and Beulah proceed to do. Since Gaines wants all participants in his novel to envision the absent Other, "What you don't see" is like the gaps left by the novel's unanswered questions. Both strategies open up spaces beyond what can be said, written, heard, or seen—spaces of a lost past, lost meaning, lost community—and opening up these spaces and retrieving that past begins to forge new community bonds.

As the novel probes what is absent, time is a crucial factor. The murder of Beau Boutan breaks the traditional Euro-American continuity of time, opening up the past for therapeutic re-evaluation and creating a new future for constructive speculation. Past, present, and future are conflated in a symbolic passage to the synchronicity of Great Time. Gaines raises questions about the future, but, rather than trying to specify that unknown, the novel, like the other novels discussed in this book, marks a moment of release from time. In that release, the present is so heightened that social and psychological norms are thrown out of kilter; the past is recalled in a new way that atones for previous errors and that transforms the testifiers and the new witnesses; and a new future, before inconceivable, is made possible. This day is in the *différance*, a present that has been indefinitely deferred, a time that is out of time, a day when the future, the present, and the past coalesce.

Confronted by Johnny Paul's daring contradiction, Mapes, an authority figure acting under a linear sense of time, at first tries to bully his way with the argument that "I don't have time for people telling me what they can't or don't see" (88), but Johnny Paul corrects Mapes with a circular sense of time: "You ain't got nothing but time, Sheriff" (88). Moving into the simultaneity of all times, the old men feel that this is the Judgment Day—it is "the day of reckonding" when they will "speak the truth" (81), a day they never thought they would see (181). Especially for Charlie it is the day of radical change, of transformation into manhood and beyond manhood into myth. This is the coming of *the* day—"they comes a day!" (189). This is when his, and the old men's, shameful pasts are transcended and the long-deferred future arrives.

Although the plot focuses attention on the immediate past—the temporarily unknown events surrounding Beau's death—the attention on that brief gap in time leads to deeper speculations and memories about the characters' entire lives. Miss Merle (15–16) and Lou (129) recall how she and Mathu raised Candy. Miss Merle's strategy for mobilizing the old men is to make Janey recall the black community's animosity toward Fix—"Who do you know don't like Fix?" (23)—and, because of her vast communal knowledge, she remembers that Fix's brother tried to rape one of Clatoo's sisters. The old men gather first at the African-American cemetery, where they reenter their personal and communal pasts by recalling their ancestors: "the very same land we had worked, our people had worked, our people's people had worked since the time of slavery" (43). Their memories ignited, the old men recall not merely personal persecution, such as the death of Jacob Aguillard's sister (45) and the execution of Gable Rauand's son (100–102), but a way of life, as in Tucker's memory of his brother's John Henry–like battle against Felix Boutan's tractor (93–97) and Corinne's rhapsody on the former community life on the river (107).

For the old people in the quarters, recalling their past, like brushing back the weeds from the family burial plots, is an attempt to reconstitute their nearly erased community. To a stranger like Sully, the quarters already look "like a western ghost town" (117), and empty cane fields remind Cherry of the absence of friends and the community's vitality: "The rows looked so naked and gray and lonely—like an old house where the people have moved from. Where good friends have moved from, leaving the house empty and bare, with nothing but ghosts now to keep it company" (43). The quarters are full of ghosts, remembered traces of the lost past, and the old people have been reduced to markers of absence. On this day they collectively stand up for themselves to redeem their past failures, to reestablish the meaningfulness of their lives, and therefore to prevent the erasure of their community and their heritage. As Byerman puts it, the old men's stories "attempt, for the only time in their lives, to get recognition of their own definitions of reality" (99).

Whereas the old African-American men reenter the past to transform it and the future, the old white men are unable and unwilling to readdress the past. Fix Boutan presides over his family council just as in the old days, with unquestioned patriarchal authority. For him there should be no change: vigilante retribution, what he calls "family responsibility" (143), should be as swift and as overwhelming as in the past. But his refusal to alter the past requires his commitment to family loyalty, so when his family does not unite behind him, his power ironically evaporates. Fixed, as his name suggests, in the past, he is bypassed and becomes spiritually dead: "They say my ideas are all past. . . . No, there's only one place left to go now, to the cemetery there in Bayonne" (146). While the old black men are gathering at their families' cemetery to resurrect their pasts and reimagine their futures, Fix insists that the past cannot be changed and worries that he has no future. Another old white man, Jack Marshall, the owner of the Marshall plantation, remains stuck in a past to which he was never reconciled. He has refused, and still refuses, the burden of ownership: "I have no niggers. . . . Never had any niggers. Never wanted any niggers. Never will have any niggers" (159). Instead of being liberated by that refusal, Jack drinks himself into paralysis, an alienating denial of self, responsibility, past, present, and future.

Like the old white men, Candy and Mapes are deeply committed to the status quo of the past, but they are flexible enough to be affected by the old men's stand. For all her well-meaning love for Mathu and her protectiveness of the African Americans on the Marshall plantation, Candy reenacts historical white superiority, and her possessiveness becomes clear when she does not get her way.[13] But as Lou explains to her, Mathu's independence has freed her from her need to protect him and the others, and her probable liberation and emerging maturity are implied when she takes Lou's hand at the trial and waves goodby to Mathu and thereby, as John Callahan suggests, to her evasions and controlling behavior (259). The old men's claim for integrity and solidarity is the catalyst for Candy to move beyond her well-meaning but condescending maternalism toward a healthier relationship with Mathu and Lou and toward a more grown-up identity. When Mapes initially tries to beat the truth out of the old men, he is stuck in the past, not liking it but knowing no alternative: "He did not like what he was doing, but he didn't know any other way to get what he wanted" (69). At the same time, he places no value on the past, dismissing Beulah's argument because she is "talking about thirty-five, forty, fifty years ago" (108). But during the wait for the vigilantes, Mapes learns to respect the old men, later listening attentively to Charlie's testimony and agreeing to call him Mr. Biggs. Although they do not have the same memories and hence the communal inner vision, Candy and Mapes are affected by the old men's and women's testimonials: Mapes becomes "quiet," "starting to feel what was going on" and, in contrast to his previous haste, knowing "he had to wait" (93); and Candy, even though she cannot testify, looks "over the yard, down the quarters, toward the fields. She knowed Tucker was telling the truth" (94). The old people's increased sense of their own community allows Candy and Mapes to understand their perspective and, empathizing with them, to adopt a more accepting relationship to the African-American community.

While the novel's plot forces broader recapitulations of the past, it even more pointedly raises questions about the future. As characters repeatedly ask what is going to happen, their refrain of questions not only carries the literal meaning of the characters' immediate future but also suggests what in general their future lives will entail. Some—such as Jack, Bea, and Fix—appear to have no future; others, such as Mapes and Candy, seem to be changing their perspectives toward the future; and the old men, having atoned for the past and thereby regained their integrity and identity, acquire a viable future. This day has so shaken up the foundations of the mixed society in the parish that Tee Jack worries, "What in the world is this world coming to?" (163). While Gaines will not specify the future, he suggests that the world, at least in southern Louisiana, is changing from Fix's vigilantism to Gil's collaboration with his white teammate, Cal;[14] from Mapes's police brutality to his respect for human dignity; from Candy's possessive protectionism to her acceptance of African Americans as equals; and from the gradual erasure of African-American heritage to its celebration.

On this day, events transcend the ordinary, and characters are transformed. The legendary Fix and his vigilante retribution are vanquished, metamorphosed into the ritual of racial cooperation on the football field. As Beavers argues, Gil's and Cal's integrated efforts mark a rebirth of the land on the new "pastoral site" of the football field where the "community is renewed" and where "African American participation is synonymous with African American citizenship" (169). In his relief that Fix is not coming, Mapes recognizes the effects of change—"Something happened the last ten, fifteen years. Salt [Cal] and Pepper [Gil] got together" (170). Candy and perhaps Mapes are released from their imprisonment in the worn-out practices of racial prejudice; for Candy, the release means "there's going to be a big change in [her] life" (184). The old men emerge from the weeds of their shame and regret to claim their manhood, to become men instead of boys, soldiers instead of tramps (49). The men's stand also changes Mathu from "a mean, bitter old man" who "put [him]self above all" to a true man who loves and respects his fellows: "I been changed by y'all" (182).

The most radical change is reserved for Charlie, who is transformed from a fifty-year-old boy through manhood to transcendent hero. His experience epitomizes the old men's. Like them, he is at first cowardly, then makes his stand, and therefore gains self-respect and a man's name: "A nigger boy run and run and run. But a man come back. I'm a man" (187). His retreat from Mathu's after the murder becomes his mythic quest into the discovery of himself, just as the men's journeys from their homes to the graveyard and then to Mathu's cabin constitute their mythic quests. Charlie becomes Mr. Biggs in the eyes of the others, including Mapes, just as the men gain the respect of each other, Mathu, Mapes, and the other whites.

But Charlie's transformation extends deeper than the old men's: while theirs is a human change, his goes beyond human. He is so changed that he nearly becomes a new person: "Mathu . . . wasn't sure that it was Charlie doing this talking" (191). His change is like a religious conversion, an epiphany: "there was something in his face that you see in faces of people who have just found religion. It was a look of having been freed of this world" (193). Appropriately, he addresses the meeting "like some overcome preacher behind the pulpit" (189), and then he comes "out of a trance" (190). Freed from this world, Charlie becomes the men's unofficial leader, praising their stand and commanding them: "For a bunch of old men, y'all did all right today. Now go on home. Let a man through" (193). In the battle with Luke Will's gang, Charlie continues his heroic and transcendent role by asserting his lack of fear of Luke, by leading the men's charge out of Mathu's cabin, and by personally going after Luke.

As Charlie nears his suicidal standoff with Luke, Charlie becomes larger than human, three times described as "like a big bear" (207–9). He passes beyond human time and place, possessing a hero's secret knowledge of the Other—what he "saw" during his quest but cannot explain to a mere mortal like Dirty Red (208). Charlie no longer listens to humans—"Charlie wasn't listening to anybody" (209)—as he completes his mythic journey by taking his revenge on all his white persecutors as he kills Luke in exchange for his own, now superfluous, human life. His body becomes instantly sacred, as the rest of the black community recognizes his apotheosis: "I leaned over and touched him, hoping that some of that stuff he had found back there in the swamps might rub off on me. After I touched him, the rest of the men did the same. Then the women, even Candy. Then Glo told her grandchildren they must touch him, too" (209–10).[15]

Charlie's ascendance and the other characters' transformations are possible because this day reenacts the carnivalesque pattern.[16] As in carnival, the normal system of rules and authority is questioned and temporarily overturned, and the upheaval releases repressed energies that regenerate individuals, the African-American community, and the larger society. According to Angelita Reyes, carnival is "a very important event of rejuvenation, a ritual passage of *communitas,* and a symbolic 'takeover' by the people who have been most negated by colonialism" (187). As the old men, the weakest members of the society, overturn white-controlled legal and illegal power, they enjoy themselves throughout the day and at the trial, in contrast to the whites' pervasive discomfort.

Carnival festivals typically perform the ritual of deposing ordinary rulers, replacing them with mock rulers, and then in turn deposing them and restoring the real ones: "the primary carnival performance is the *mock crowning* and subsequent *discrowning of the king of carnival*" (Bakhtin, *Problems* 102). Echoing this ritual, Beau Boutan and the Cajuns, the normal rulers, are deposed when Charlie kills Beau. This inversion exposes hitherto repressed changes in the Cajun power structure, leading to Gil's and his brother's abdications and Fix's loss of power. Charlie, backed by the collective action of the newly empowered old men, is the temporary carnival king. During his brief but significant reign, he removes Luke Will, a mock surrogate for the Boutans, further demonstrating that social change is possible. After the day of carnival, normal order is restored as the scene shifts to a courtroom, the model of order in American society, presided over by Judge Reynolds, the new normal ruler, who dispenses justice fairly and amicably. The joyful outcome of the trial completes the comic pattern of the novel, which, like the carnivalesque mode, proceeds from normality through inversion to restoration of a more tenable normality.[17]

The novel reinforces the carnivalesque mode by inverting established authorities, most notably by disempowering Sheriff Mapes, the symbol of established law and order. Even though Mapes's height and weight fit the stereotype of the white, southern sheriff, his power is already slightly undermined when he arrives looking "very tired" (63) and sweating heavily. His authority is further reduced by the weakness of his deputy, Griffin, who is obviously "scared" (63), "sticking as close [to Mapes] as a small frightened child would stick to his father" (64). Candy and the old men further undermine Mapes's authority by lying to him about the murder, by refusing to obey his orders, and by failing to yield to his slaps. The unraveling of Mapes's authority becomes clearer when he has no answers for the coroner's questions about the situation, when Dirty Red interrupts him (" 'You trying to cut in on me when I'm talking to you?' Mapes asked him" [87]), and when Johnny Paul directly contradicts him: " 'You ain't got nothing but time, Sheriff' " (88). A few pages later, Mapes is reduced to a bystander—"So now he just stood there, a big fat red hulk, looking down at the ground" (93)—whom the old men feel free to ignore: "Yank didn't pay him any mind" (98).

When Mapes hears that Fix is not coming, he is triumphant (170–72), and during Charlie's confession Mapes temporarily regains control, which he wields with new respect for everyone. Converted to an empathetic understanding of the positions of the old men, he no longer thinks of slapping or bullying them but is now sympathetic to their cause. But when the fight with Luke's gang breaks out, the comic usurpation is completed. Mapes is wounded, comically in the buttocks, and Charlie and Clatoo, not Mapes or his deputy, lead the old men against Luke. Mapes tries to transfer his authority legally by placing Lou in charge (201), but, as Luke realizes, Charlie is really in command: "We got to deal with Charlie now" (206). Normal law and order are eventually restored, but Mapes's humiliating testimony at the trial comically recalls his fall from power: "The whole fight, I was sitting on my ass in the middle of the walk" (213).

Other authority figures are also undermined. The inversions begin with the total overthrow of Beau's power when Charlie kills him. Like his son, Fix Boutan is also the victim of a power reversal when two sons and one brother do not agree with his desire to retaliate. Deputy Griffin, whose skinniness, fear, and haughtiness render him nearly powerless to begin with, is even more undermined than Mapes. Tucker calls him a "little no-butt nothing" (94) and "boy" (95), the crowd laughs at him (95), and Mapes dismisses him (95). Later, Griffin refuses to obey Mapes (175) and eventually quits, actions that reduce both his authority and Mapes's. Candy's authority as the representative of the Marshall family is also undermined when the old men, including Mathu, exclude her from their meeting and when Lou ignominiously carries her to her car. Reverend Jameson is reduced to a weak sniveler who is not allowed to speak and is afraid to fight even a woman (105–6). Like Candy (173), he tries to maintain his authority by asserting, "This is my place" (106), but on this day of inversions, neither character has any power.

Besides these losses of authority by normally powerful characters, the novel includes numerous other examples of disobedience and inversion. Mat disobeys his wife, Ella, when she demands to know what is going on, a scene repeated in many of the old men's houses. Gil and Cal's interracial friendship is temporarily inverted when Gil is rude to Cal after hearing of Beau's murder (113). The normal order at the Boutan family meeting, in which, as Fix repeatedly asserts, outsiders do not speak, is violated when Luke and then Russ do speak. On this carnivalesque day, even the Bible is not followed: "'Sometimes you just has to go against your Bible, Sheriff,' Uncle Billy told Mapes" (81). And the expected order of serving food is abrogated when Miss Merle distributes her sandwiches without regard to anyone's status (125, Rickels and Rickels 218). Since carnival is associated with food and specifically with the eating of food before Lent (Bakhtin, *Rabelais* 5–10), this violation of normal order marks a particularly significant moment of inversion.

The carnivalesque day of the old men's revolt ends with the return to normalcy of the trial. As David Estes argues, for the white judge and journalists the trial is simply humorous, as they miss the more serious implications of the old men's victory (246–47). That the trial is comic is crucial, for severity at this point would undermine the novel's comic structure and its effectiveness. As when they made their stand, the old men are still triumphant, enjoying themselves, relishing their wounds and the public spotlight. Their joy suggests the deeper meaning of their revolt—like Charlie, they have become men, have redeemed the past, and have saved their community from erasure. They are heros returned from their quest, holy grail in hand. But the white establishment cannot see the meaning of their stand, for to acknowledge it would be to revolutionize the division of power between blacks and whites. The trial reveals both the return to normalcy after the aberrations of carnival and the differences, especially for the African-American characters, that the carnival period has created.

The liberating energy of carnival brings about changes not only in individual characters but also in the African-American community and the broader interracial community. Before this day, the African-American community did exist, as reinforced by characters' use of "the people" (e.g., 13) to refer to the African Americans on the Marshall plantation. The cemetery is a synecdoche for this community, a record of the families and individuals in the quarters: "each family had a little plot, and everybody knowed where that little plot was" (44). But this community is at risk. Reduced to old people and children, it is no longer economically viable, it is choked by weeds that have replaced the flowers that everyone remembers, and, like the cemetery, it is threatened with extinction. In spiritual and economic decay, the threads of connection within it are nearly broken, as many of the old men had not even seen each other in years. By finally standing up for themselves against white oppression, and in the process remembering the strengths of their past—that is, by welding the present with the absent—the old men and women regenerate and thus re-create their community and their identities.

At the same time, the events of this day unleash energies that bind the broader community closer together. The tradition of white vigilantism is weakened if not broken when the Boutans, for the first time, do not retaliate, and when their parodic surrogate, Luke Will's gang, is reduced to fear and tears and Luke is killed. Along with Luke, the old way of doing things, the "little civic duties" (159) that reinforced white terror, may also be dead. Simultaneously, new models for interracial cooperation have come to the fore, primarily on the football field and in the social celebration related to it. Russ expresses this optimism when he urges Gil to play in the big game: "Sometimes you have to plow under one thing in order for something else to grow. You can help Tee Beau [Gil's nephew] tomorrow. You can help this country tomorrow. You can help yourself" (151). The football game, like the old men's stand, is collective action that makes new communal meaning.

As the novel depicts the making of this new meaning, it focuses on forces that profoundly affect people but can be neither seen nor spoken: What makes a man a man? What connects people? What ensures the life of a community? Of what value are memories? What is integrity? pride? respect? truth? The novel suggests that an all-inclusive approach is needed for such questions. Mapes tries direct confrontation, based on established power and white authority, but his effectiveness is steadily diminished until he becomes a buffoon. The old men's course is the reverse, going from buffoons to newly empowered authorities. Univocal and repressive authority is replaced by multivocal and empathetic community.

Gaines reinforces this movement by opening, and leaving open, gaps in the text that allow characters and readers to supply meaning derived from what has previously been unprivileged, unacknowledged, and absent. The absent dominates the novel's plot and its meanings. Charlie's absence from the quarters makes possible the gathering of the old men and the related tension, Beau's absence in death generates the predictions of Fix's revenge, and the absence of that revenge further astonishes everyone. The old men's testimonials reassert the significance of the absent past, which has been forgotten and unprivileged. Absent images remind them, and their auditors and readers, of what is missing, as when Clatoo recalls that "Candy met us at the gate, where the gate used to be; you didn't have a fence or a gate there now" (50). Although physically the gate is now absent, for the old people it is still very much there; like the nearly erased past, it exists as powerfully as any real object, and the novel insists on the value of its presence/absence. In the characters', and now the readers', minds, the gate is as real as the flowers that Johnny Paul and the other African Americans do not literally see but now do remember, as real as the church bell that Johnny, Beulah, and the other African Americans hear ringing but Mapes does not (90), as real as the ghosts Jack Marshall still hears at Tee Jack's bar (153–54), and as real as whatever Charlie sees in the swamps that makes him a man. Even though Dirty Red claims not to have seen anything, Charlie, speaking now for Gaines, knows that Dirty and all the men "already got it" (208). Charlie, the old men, nearly all the African-American characters, the reader, and even some of the white characters, Gaines would hope, have gotten it.

7

PERFORMING CULTURAL WORK

"Incontestably mulatto" (Murray, *Omni-Americans* 22), America
has always been suspended in a delicate balance between unity
and division. Albert Murray's metaphor not only implies the
unity within division of a mixed-race country but also identifies
race as the primary division within the multiply fractured American cultural body. The five contemporary African-American writers considered in this volume are poised at the interstices of this
endemic split in American culture. With Ralph Ellison's "special
perspective" (*Shadow* 131), they are well positioned to perceive
and depict the divisions in American culture and the individual
and societal displacements that have resulted from such divisions, including the misremembering, the repression, and the ro-
manticization of the American past; the flaws and failures in the
visions of an idealistic American future; and the skewing of identities—both black and white—that results from pervasive raciali-
zation. These writers also project beyond such divisions and
beyond the present to the possibilities of alternative futures not
restricted by the confining oppositions of the past; to prospects
of reconstituted, healthier, and more integrated identities; and to
the creation of more connected, empathetic, and viable communities. Seeing the tangled threads of the American community, as
well as the African-American one within it, and seeing how those
threads have become frayed and disconnected as well as how
they might be reinvigorated and reconnected, these writers offer
much-needed analyses of America's past, present, and future, its
weaknesses and its strengths, and its failings and its promise.
Simply depicting the issues that have hindered America's fullest
development is valuable. Even more valuable is to depict them

so that readers can share the authors' wider vision, not only to see the problems but to help Americans imagine better selves and a better nation; to move beyond confining absolutes into a more tolerant, open-ended, and flexible communality; and, in short, to revitalize the process of remaking American identities and the American community.

For John Edgar Wideman, the crucial issue in this process is the ongoing struggle between alienation and narrow individualism on the one hand and nurturing community on the other. In that struggle, it is essential—and always difficult—to keep creating the community through telling and hearing the stories by which human beings reconnect with the past and thereby create a future together:

One day neither in the past nor future and not this moment either, all the people gathered on a high ridge that overlooked the rolling plain of earth, its forests, deserts, rivers unscrolling below them like a painting on papyrus. Then the people began speaking one by one, telling the story of a life, everything seen, heard, and felt by each soul. As the voices dreamed, a vast, bluish mist enveloped the land and seas below them. Nothing was visible. It was as if the solid earth had evaporated. Now there was nothing but the voices and the stories and the cloud of mist and the people were afraid to stop the storytelling and afraid not to stop because no one knew where the earth had gone.

Finally, when only a few storytellers remained to take a turn, someone shouted: Stop. Enough, enough of this talk. Enough of us have spoken. We must find the earth again.

Suddenly the mist cleared. Below the people the earth had changed. It had grown into the shape of the stories they'd told, a shape wondrous and new and real as the words they'd spoken. But a world also unfinished because all the stories had not been told.

Some say death and evil entered the world because some of the people had no chance to speak. Some say the world would be worse than it is if all the stories had been told. Some say there are no more stories to tell. Some believe untold stories are the only ones of value and we are lost when they are lost. Some are certain the storytelling never stops and this is one more story and the earth always lies under its blanket of mist being born. (*Fatheralong* 177–78)

For Toni Cade Bambara, there is a crisis at all levels of human existence and therefore an urgent and continuing need for healing. Healing must come from all imaginable sources—no bound-aries, limitations, or assumptions must be allowed to limit the eclecticism. In particular, Americans must reexamine the past to find the energy sources and the healing powers that might enable them to move ahead together toward an unknown, challenging, but invigorating future:

> One would tap the brain for any knowledge of initiation rites lying dor-mant there, recognizing that life depended on it, that initiation was the beginning of transformation and that the ecology of the self, the tribe, the species, the earth depended on just that. In the dark of the woods, the ground shaking underfoot, the ancient covenants remembered in fragments, one would stand there, fists pummeling the temples, trying to remember the whole in time and make things whole again. (*Salt Eaters* 247–48)

For Charles Johnson, America, like Andrew Hawkins and Rutherford Calhoun, must retravel the difficult journeys of the past, such as the Middle Passage and the slaves' flight to freedom. By doing so, individuals can expand their own limited perspec-tives by experiencing the perspectives of other individuals. To move toward their own enlightenment and therefore toward a healthier community, human beings must engage in such acts of empathy, must become the Other to achieve communal cohesion and to participate in the unity of all Being. In his epiphany as he gazes at Bannon, Andrew experiences that unity:

> I lost his figure in this field of energy, where the profound mystery of the One and the Many gave me back my father again and again, his love, in every being from grubworms to giant sumacs, for these too were my father and, in the final face I saw in the Soulcatcher, which shook tears from me—my own face, for he had duplicated portions of me during the early days of the hunt—I was my father's father, and he my child. (*Oxherding* 176)

For Gloria Naylor, American life is characterized by selfish-ness, repression, and violence, usually based on race, gender, and class. Physical survival is difficult, and spiritual survival is even more problematic. The most effective recourse is to imagine alternative realities that provide sanctuary, that offer love, that allow individuals to flourish, and that create meaningful communities outside the damaged communal space of ordinary life. Having found and helped create such a sanctuary, Miss Maple is in harmony with the cosmos:

He takes his full champagne glass to the rear of the cafe. As I watch from the doorway, he steps off boldly into the midst of nothing and is suspended midair by a gentle wind that starts to swirl his cape around his knees. It's a hot, dry wind that could easily have been born in a desert, but it's bringing, of all things, snow. Soft and silent it falls, coating his shoulders, his upturned face. Snow. He holds his glass up and turns to me as a single flake catches on the rim before melting down the side into an amber world where bubbles burst and are born, burst and are born. (*Bailey's* 216)

For Ernest Gaines, the rural parishes of southern Louisiana constitute a microcosm of the racially diverse nation. Communal ties are strong but are fraught with tensions based on the inequalities of power among Cajuns, Anglos, and African Americans. When events disturb this oppressive status quo, the past is made newly available, individuals see themselves in new ways, and the force fields within the community are realigned. While not apparently revolutionary, such subtle changes are significant and necessary; as Russ advises Gil Boutan:

Sometimes you got to hurt something to help something. Sometimes you have to plow under one thing in order for something else to grow. You can help Tee Beau tomorrow. You can help this country tomorrow. You can help yourself. (*Gathering* 151)

The recent fiction by the five novelists I have considered has the potential to help America imagine itself anew. Multiple characters in each novel engage in spiritual and psychological quests toward greater self-knowledge, increased awareness of their relationship to their community, and therefore more enduring harmony. In that process, they must reconnect with their personal, familial, communal, and cultural pasts, and they do so, or at least attempt to do so, through individual memory, the collective memory of storytelling and listening, and association with influential culture bearers. To the extent that they realize the importance of the past and their relationship to it, the characters are perforce more fully integrated into the community—past, present, and future. The more successful characters, having (re)discovered their communal connections, then find appropriate roles for themselves in the continuing and mutual creation of community. Part of that creation is ongoing reenvisionings of possible futures, futures that are open-ended, not necessarily idyllic, and at least partially redemptive of the past.

As the characters weave their lives, their voices, and their minds more fully into the tangled threads that constitute their communities, the novels reproduce that productive entanglement through their own complex discourses. The language of these texts allows multiple voices to be heard and multiple perspectives to be seen, so that the novels themselves become paradigms of the open and polyvocal communities that the characters rediscover and re-create. Just as many voices must be heard, so many times must be recorded; just as no single voice is allowed to become authoritative, so past, present, and future are intermingled in nonlinear abundance. The engagement of authors, narrators, and characters in these efforts requires the readers' full participation, not only in the novels but also by extension in the novels' projected revalidations of individual identities and their implied reconstructing of African-American, American, and global communities.

NOTES

Chapter 1

1. Fisher argues that this country was founded on the principles of an open, transparent grid on which each individual was assumed to be free to move to any node: in addition to "representation," the "essential features" of a "continuous and democratic social space" were "the absence of limits, openness to immigration and expatriation, [and] internal mobility" (74).

2. Like physical movements, the possibility of passing for white, with its implications of social and economic movement into white society, is another version of the image of passage. For perceptive analyses of passing, see Ginsberg.

3. Ironically, even as movement was highly valued, mobility for African Americans was often restricted by Jim Crow laws and practice (F. Griffin 20).

4. Quilts and quilt making constitute a similar image of the intersubjective web. Susan Meisenhelder applies this image to Gloria Naylor's *Mama Day*, and Margot Anne Kelley associates it with the identities constructed by African-American women ("Sisters'" 62–66). For Houston Baker, Jr., and Charlotte Baker-Pierce, "A patchwork quilt, laboriously and affectionately crafted from bits of worn overalls, shredded uniforms, tattered petticoats, and outgrown dresses stands as a signal instance of a patterned wholeness in the African diaspora" (149, 156).

5. This list is meant not to be inclusive but to be manageable. Other contemporary African-American novelists and novels that could readily be considered in such terms include David Bradley's *The Chaneysville Incident*, Paule Marshall's works (especially *Praisesong for the Widow*), Ntozake Shange's *Sassafras, Cypress, and Indigo*, and Sherley Anne Williams' *Dessa Rose*. I have previously commented on the novels of Toni Morrison, all of whose fiction I would add to this list.

6. Farah Jasmine Griffin makes the similar point that recent Afri-

can-American novels "show the possibility of constructing an alterative black self through the use of migrant-defined spaces but warn us against any utopian notions of complete resistance and survival" (140).

7. Gerald Early eloquently expresses this duality: Black History Month "is nothing more than a monumental confession that the African-American plays out as a national ritual, a painful drama of psychic exile, identity confusion, double-consciousness that is forced to stand apart from the double-consciousness, the psychic exile, and the identity confusion that afflicts this nation" (9).

8. Shlomith Rimmon-Kenan broadens these claims by contending that such temporal vulnerability affects all ethnic and feminine literatures, which must emphasize reinstatement, rehumanization, and reengagement because they are "motivated by the desire to rescue a history from the oblivion to which the majority group has consigned it" (5).

9. F. Griffin asserts that the basic contradiction of the South is its combination of physical beauty and horror (16).

10. As Barthold explains, time in traditional West African cultures was equivalent to duration: "each moment embodied a recurrence of a past moment, and implied was a potential future recurrence" (10). In Great Time, time is circular or synchronous, not linear, as past, present, and future are equally available.

11. Whereas Awkward limits this quest and this goal to women writers, the novels of Gaines, Johnson, and Wideman demonstrate that male authors and male characters share these needs. Other analyses of black women writers, such as those by Karla F. C. Holloway (*Moorings*) and Margot Anne Kelley ("Sisters' Choices"), may also be usefully extended to these and other male writers.

12. For discussions of the inseparability of the sacred and the profane in West African cultures, see Mbiti 2; Smitherman 91–93.

13. Angelita Reyes reads Marshall's *Praisesong for the Widow* and *The Chosen Place, the Timeless People* in terms of the carnivalesque spirit and pattern. See chapter 6 for a discussion of the carnivalesque in Gaines's *A Gathering of Old Men.*

14. *Différance* is a neologism coined by Jacques Derrida that means both the spatial gap, the difference, between any two ideas or entities and the temporal gap or displacement in the act of deferral between any two moments. The ever-present but unrealizable principle that creates difference and hence meaning, it is "the non-full, non-simple, structured and differentiating origin of differences" (*Margins* 11).

15. I am indebted to Yvonne Atkinson for my awareness of the oral tradition.

16. *Character-narrator* is to me an easier term than Gerard Genette's "homodiegetic narrator" (245–46).

17. By this logic, readers have the obligation to testify about their experience with the text; informal conversations, classroom discussions, conference presentations, and written publications thus continue the process.

Chapter 2

1. James Coleman notes that "trains signify danger in all of Wideman's fiction about the Homewood experience" (*Blackness* 106).

2. For the Wilkes-Brother-Doot connection, see Coleman, *Blackness* 107; Gysin; Rushdy 336; and Wilson 257. For the circular tradition, see Coleman, *Blackness* 99; Mbalia 104.

3. Between 1938 and 1941, the song was recorded four times—by Count Basie, Benny Goodman, Les Brown, and Nat Gonella and their orchestras. For recording information, see Rushdy 321 n.6.

4. Wideman states that "music is a dominant, organizing metaphor" in the Homewood trilogy (Preface v).

5. Francis King and Mbalia (140) note this parallel; Coleman posits that in the novel, "stories are entangled in stories" ("Going" 338); and Bennion argues that "the shape of the novel . . . is the shape of Doot's memory" (145).

6. Prior to this reference to Zasetsky, Wideman quotes at length from this volume (107), in which Luria describes the effects of a head wound on Zasetsky's mental condition and records the victim's descriptions of his inability to remember, read, write, locate parts of his body, or perceive stability in external objects.

7. Robert Stepto associates African-American culture with what he calls the "modal," or both/and, perspective (xiii).

Chapter 3

1. For assertions about the novel's direction toward wholeness, see Dance 182; Hull 225; Kelley, "Damballah" 484; Rosenberg 174–75; and Melissa Walker 181, 186. For form-content parallels, see Butler-Evans 176; Byerman 123; Hargrove 40; Kelley, "Damballah" 488; and Willis 130–31, 139. For the novel's nonlinearity, see Dance 481; Hull 221–22; Kelley, "Damballah" 488; and Traylor 65. And for the open ending, see Byerman 128; Shipley 126–27; and M. Walker 188–89.

2. Hargrove (40) compares the novel to T. S. Eliot's poem.

3. I am indebted to Kasmira Finch for attention to the war motif.

4. As Kelley explains, the novel illustrates chaos theory by depicting "bifurcation points" at which a system can settle into one of a number of possible states ("Damballah" 489).

5. In analyzing the symbolic implications of the characters' names, Rosenberg points out that both of Fred's names have four letters (168).

6. As I discuss in chapter 6, the same motif is evident in Ernest Gaines's *A Gathering of Old Men.*

7. See, e.g., pp. 66–67.

8. The fourth healer is Cleotus Brown, the hermit, but he remains entirely in the background.

9. Throughout the novel Velma is haunted by the mud mothers, who resemble prehistoric women with their mud-caked hair, "serrated teeth" (259), and "hairy hides" (255). Carrying babies, they emerge from caves (8, 19, 38, 255) and then from the mirror (259) to tell Velma "what must be done all over again" (255). They seem to embody the ancient, nurturing, female past with which modern women must reconnect to assure a viable future. Noting that Bambara "never fully describes" them, Willis associates the mud mothers with "the child's repressed fear of the mother" and with women's need to express themselves in modes not dominated by men (155).

10. In West African and Egyptian mythologies, the deities Legba and Isis are the primary intermediaries between human beings and other deities.

Chapter 4

1. Jennifer Hayward argues that the novel both glorifies the Eternal Feminine and depicts the opposite, the male terror of the powerful female.

2. Elizabeth Muther contends that Rutherford and Isadora are parallel, each in a position of social subservience, trying to control the other (655–56).

3. Similarly, Johnson admires American society because it "struggled mightily" to deal with the problems associated with discrimination. In America, as in Johnson's novels, "The self [is] a verb, not a noun—a process, not a product" (Boccia 617).

4. In contrast to my view, Fagel sees Rutherford's middle position as an ultimately limiting one, allowing him "no constancy" (629) and causing him to remain "all anger and frustration" (630).

5. Vincent O'Keefe, conversely, regards the seriality in which these

images are conveyed as an indication of the "residual calcification" in Rutherford's potential enlightenment (643).

6. In contrast, O'Keefe is concerned that these metanarrative interruptions merely separate the reader from the text.

7. Muther disagrees, finding that Rutherford's writing is "informed with too much knowledge," knowledge that "erupts in the creation of a fictive self who cannot quite believe the terms of his own story and who offers it therefore with a parodic doubleness, glibness and unease" (654).

8. For additional examples see *Oxherding* 169, 175.

9. O'Keefe agrees that *Middle Passage* attempts to send readers on a "perceptual middle passage" (635) but then argues that, unlike Morrison's *Beloved, Middle Passage* fails to do so (643–45).

10. Johnson claims that he "spent six years reading every book and rereading every book I could on that subject, anything relating to sea adventure" (Little 165).

11. It is interesting how often Johnson alludes to Herman Melville. For example, in *Oxherding Tale*, Andrew alleges that Melville "is an old family acquaintance" (124), the text refers directly to the Dead Letter Office in "Bartleby, the Scrivener" (123) and to *Pierre* (124), and Andrew's description of his job as a teacher is reminiscent of *The Confidence Man* (128). *Middle Passage* abounds with parallels to both "Benito Cereno" and *Moby-Dick*. The slaves' takeover of the ship but then their homelessness doubles the situation of the slaves in "Benito," and the parallel is made explicit by Johnson's reference to Amaso Delano (173), his naming one slave Babo and another Atufal, and his echo of Melville's hatchet sharpening (132). There are also parallels between Falcon and Ahab, the Allmuseri god and Fedallah, Tommy and Pip, Cringle and Starbuck, and Rutherford and Ishmael.

12. Muther asserts instead that Rutherford and Isadora's future remains indeterminate, as suggested by their failure to consummate their marriage.

Chapter 5

1. Elsewhere, I have speculated on the significance of wells in Toni Morrison's *Jazz* ("Traces"; *Dangerous Freedom* 159–77).

2. Susan Meisenhelder points out that Miranda contributes to the community's quiltlike interpretations of itself by appreciating the male perspective of Sapphira's owner, Bascombe Wade (415).

3. Following Freud, Derrida argues that humans tend to privilege

the conscious over the unconscious and that recognition of the *différance* and the consequent unraveling of the binary opposition between consciousness and unconsciousness allows for the recovery of what has been repressed (*Margins* 16–22).

4. Celeste Fraser analyzes the novel in the context of the myth of the African-American matriarchy created by such public documents as the 1964 Moynihan report.

5. As Virginia Fowler puts it, Mattie "continues to define herself completely through Basil" (29), thus entrapping herself in her personal well.

6. Naylor asserts that "just like the world had put a wall in Brewster Place, [the community] had put a wall between themselves and Lorraine and Theresa" (Carabi 41).

7. For a detailed discussion of the implications of the rape, see Tanner 82–88.

8. Alternatively, Montgomery finds that although the women descend physically, they ascend spiritually because they "establish a new cosmology, an underground world in which they are agents of their own destiny" ("Fathomless" 44).

9. Catherine C. Ward emphasizes that Ruth Anderson represents a perspective characterized by pure human love (186).

10. As Karah Stokes puts it, the story of Reema's boy "teaches us how to read the novel by following the narrator's shifts from literal to figurative and back" (208), and V. Fowler asserts that his story cautions readers not to bring the perspective of the mainland to the novel (96).

11. Meisenhelder likewise asserts that George should return with his empty hands (412), whereas Storhoff argues that Miranda sends him to gather eggs (41). V. Fowler comments on the significance of hands throughout the novel (106, 112, 119).

12. Lindsey Tucker contends that this blurring of narratorial boundaries further links Miranda with the community (175), Helen Fiddyment Levy conflates Miranda's voice with the voice of the community (278) and insists that the communal voice is female (280), and V. Fowler claims that the third-person narrator is limited to Miranda's consciousness (98).

13. For other examples of unusual narrative moments, see the unassigned quotations of Cocoa's friends' criticisms of George (121) or the shifts of perspective into Miranda's innermost consciousness (138, 249).

14. The almost demonic power of trains in Sadie's life resembles their similar force in Wideman's *Sent for You Yesterday*.

15. The epigraph is as follows:

hush now can you hear it can't be far away
needing the blues to get there
look and you can hear it
look and you can hear
the blues open
a place never
closing
Bailey's
Cafe

16. As Derrida puts it, "Thus one could reconsider all the pairs of opposites on which philosophy is constructed and on which our discourse lives, not in order to see opposition erase itself but to see what indicates that each of the terms must appear as the *différance* of the other" (*Margins* 17).

17. Meisenhelder demonstrates that George and Cocoa try unsuccessfully to understand each other and Willow Springs in terms of white myths (405–12).

18. For commentaries on traditional West African worldviews, see Jahn; Mbiti.

Chapter 6

1. As Jeffrey Folks puts it, "Gaines's fiction implies an acceptance of, even an insistence on, change" (37).

2. Charles Heglar and Annye Refoe note that Grant "'reads' rather than hears" his aunt (60) and that "this silent rhetoric demonstrates the characters' intimate knowledge of each other" (61).

3. Heglar and Refoe comment that Vivian "can even explain things that Grant does not know how to express about himself" (63).

4. Alice F. Freed distinguishes four general categories of question functions: external (questions seeking information external to the conversation), talk (questions asking about the conversation), relational (open-ended questions about the relationship between the participants), and expressive (questions reflecting the speaker's style, the answers to which are usually already known by the speaker) (632–33).

5. Karla F. C. Holloway notes that Etienne's adopted name "signifies the loneliness and isolation he has experienced" ("Image" 181).

6. Critics differ in their assessments of Phillip Martin. Beavers sees his potential for "transcendence" (96), and Valerie Babb asserts that he is revising himself constructively (*Ernest* 97–109). Conversely, Byerman, Folks, Holloway ("Image"), and Shelton see him continuing to be

enmeshed in his own egotism and consequent isolation. Taking a middle position, Plant concludes that "when he is lost," he "begins to find himself" (16).

7. Similarly, S. Jones demonstrates that Jefferson, Vivian, and Ambrose become Grant's teachers (62–63).

8. In several interviews Gaines cites being influenced by *As I Lay Dying* (Lowe 44, 64, 133), but he claims that he "was not particularly thinking of Faulkner" when he decided on multiple narrators for this novel (Lowe 188).

9. Exploring the significance of nicknames and formal names in the novel, Joseph Griffin asserts that characters' names imply the novel's theme of the "coming of age of persons and the concomitant maturing of the society" (92).

10. See chapter 3 for my discussion of implicature in *The Salt Eaters*.

11. Gaines admires Hemingway's ability to "leave out every other line and still get [his] message over. That's what I try to do" (Lowe 315).

12. For other characters' moments of inner vision, see Bea (21); Candy (94); Gil (116); and Jack Marshall (152).

13. Babb discusses Candy's imperiousness (*Ernest* 124–26), Harper comments on Candy's failure to understand changes in the quarters (306), and Shannon comments on Candy's ineffectiveness as a white liberal (207–8).

14. For Beavers, Gil is an all-American in the broadest sense, representing integration, upward mobility, and the New South (170), and Daniel White agrees that "Gil Boutan represents the future of the white man of Louisiana" (177).

15. For additional commentary on Charlie's mythic adventure, see Bourque 35; Harper 304–5. For commentary on his ritualized death, see Beavers 171–72.

16. Beavers sees the carnivalesque in the collapse of ordinary time and space in the novel. For him, the suspension of the ordinary in that moment allows for the creation of new conditions, new reflections, and even a paradigm shift in the race relations of the parish and in the black people's consciousnesses (166, 171–73). See chapter 1 for a discussion of the carnivalesque pattern.

17. For S. Jones, the novel's first ending—the shootout—suggests the old masculine order in which violence is the only way to end an argument, and the second—the trial—implies a new order in which "talking can produce results" (58). In terms of the carnivalesque, the first ending is an antisocial resolution within the inverted time and space of carnival, whereas the second ending terminates the violence and the inversions in the normal time and space outside carnival.

WORKS CITED

Allen, Ray. "Back Home: Southern Identity and African-American Gospel Quartet Performance." *Mapping American Culture*. Ed. Wayne Franklin and Michael Steiner. Iowa City: U of Iowa P, 1992. 112–35.

Applebome, Peter. *Dixie Rising: How the South Is Shaping American Values, Politics, and Culture*. New York: Random House, 1996.

Atwood, Margaret. *Survival: A Thematic Guide to Canadian Literature*. Toronto: Anansi, 1972.

Auger, Philip. "A Lesson about Manhood: Appropriating 'The Word' in Ernest Gaines's *A Lesson before Dying*." *Southern Literary Journal* 27.2 (1995): 74–85.

Awkward, Michael. *Inspiriting Influences: Tradition, Revision, and Afro-American Women's Novels*. New York: Columbia UP, 1989.

Babb, Valerie Melissa. *Ernest Gaines*. Boston: Twayne, 1991.

————. "Old-Fashioned Modernism: 'The Changing Same' in *A Lesson before Dying*." *Critical Reflections on the Fiction of Ernest J. Gaines*. Ed. David C. Estes. Athens: U of Georgia P, 1994. 250–64.

Baker, Houston A., Jr. *Afro-American Poetics: Revisions of Harlem and the Black Aesthetic*. Madison: U of Wisconsin P, 1988.

————. *Workings of the Spirit: The Poetics of Afro-American Women's Writing*. Chicago: U of Chicago P, 1991.

Baker, Houston A., Jr., and Charlotte Pierce-Baker. "Patches: Quilts and Community in Alice Walker's 'Everyday Use.'" *"Everyday Use": Alice Walker*. Ed. Barbara Christian. New Brunswick, NJ: Rutgers UP, 1994. 149–66.

Bakhtin, Mikhail. *The Dialogic Imagination*. Trans. Caryl Emerson and Michael Holquist. Ed. Michael Holquist. Austin: U of Texas P, 1981.

————. *Problems of Dostoevsky's Poetics*. Trans. R. W. Rotsel. N.p.: Ardis, 1973.

————. *Rabelais and His World*. Trans. Helene Iswolsky. Cambridge: MIT P, 1968.

Bambara, Toni Cade. *The Salt Eaters*. New York: Vintage, 1980.

Barthes, Roland. "From Work to Text." *Textual Strategies: Perspectives in Post-Structuralist Criticism*. Ed. Josue V. Harari. Ithaca: Cornell UP, 1979. 73–82.

Barthold, Bonnie. *Black Time: Fiction of Africa, the Caribbean, and the United States*. New Haven: Yale UP, 1981.

Beavers, Herman. *Wrestling Angels into Song: The Fictions of Ernest J. Gaines and James Alan McPherson*. Philadelphia: U of Pennsylvania P, 1995.

Bell, Bernard. *The Afro-American Novel and Its Tradition*. Amherst: U of Massachusetts P, 1987.

Bennion, John. "The Shape of Memory in John Edgar Wideman's *Sent for You Yesterday*." *Black American Literature Forum* 20 (1986): 143–50.

Bentson, Kimberly W. "I Yam What I Am: The Topos of (Un)naming in Afro-American Literature." *Black Literature and Literary Theory*. Ed. Henry Louis Gates, Jr. New York: Methuen, 1984. 151–72.

Bercovitch, Sacvan. *The Rites of Ascent*. New York: Routledge, 1993.

Bhabha, Homi. *The Location of Culture*. London: Routledge, 1994.

Boccia, Michael. "An Interview with Charles Johnson." *African American Review* 30 (1996): 611–18.

Bourque, Darrell. "Looking for My Own People: The Hero in Ernest Gaines's *The Autobiography of Miss Jane Pittman* and *A Gathering of Old Men*." *Griot* 4.1–2 (1985): 29–36.

Bradley, David. *The Chaneysville Incident*. New York: Harper and Row, 1981.

Butler-Evans, Elliott. *Race, Gender, and Desire: Narrative Strategies in the Fiction of Toni Cade Bambara, Toni Morrison, and Alice Walker*. Philadelphia: Temple UP, 1989.

Byerman, Keith. *Fingering the Jagged Grain: Tradition and Form in Recent Black Fiction*. Athens: U of Georgia P, 1985.

Byrd, Rudolph P. "*Oxherding Tale* and *Siddhartha*: Philosophy, Fiction, and the Emergence of a Hidden Tradition." *African American Review* 30 (1996): 549–58.

Callahan, John F. *In the African-American Grain: Call-and-Response in Twentieth-Century Black Fiction*. 2d ed. Middletown, CT: Wesleyan UP, 1988.

Carabi, Angels. Interview with Gloria Naylor. *Belles Lettres* 7.1 (1992): 36–42.

Christian, Barbara. *Black Feminist Criticism: Perspectives on Black Women Writers*. New York: Pergamon, 1985.

———. "Gloria Naylor's Geography: Community, Class, and Patriarchy in *The Women of Brewster Place* and *Linden Hills.*" *Reading Black, Reading Feminist: A Critical Anthology.* Ed. Henry Louis Gates, Jr. New York: Penguin, 1990. 348–73.

Christol, Hélène. "Reconstructing American History: Land and Genealogy in Gloria Naylor's *Mama Day.*" *The Black Columbiad: Defining Moments in African American Literature and Culture.* Ed. Werner Sollors and Maria Diedrich. Cambridge: Harvard UP, 1994. 347–56.

Coleman, James W. *Blackness and Modernism: The Literary Career of John Edgar Wideman.* Jackson: UP of Mississippi, 1989.

———. "Charles Johnson's Quest for Black Freedom in *Oxherding Tale.*" *African American Review* 29 (1995): 631–44.

———. "Going Back Home: The Literary Development of John Edgar Wideman." *College Language Association Journal* 28 (1985): 326–43.

Cooper-Lewter, Nicholas C., and Henry H. Mitchell. *Soul Theology: The Heart of American Black Culture.* Nashville: Abingdon P, 1986.

Dance, Daryl Cumber. "Go Eena Kumbla: A Comparison of Erna Brodber's *Jane and Louisa Will Soon Come Home* and Toni Cade Bambara's *The Salt Eaters.*" *Caribbean Women Writers: Essays from the First International Conference.* Ed. Selwyn R. Cudjoe. Wellesley, MA: Calaloux, 1990. 169–84.

Derrida, Jacques. *Margins of Philosophy.* Trans. Alan Bass. Chicago: U of Chicago P, 1982.

———. *Memories for Paul DeMan.* Trans. Cecile Lindsay, Jonathan Culler, and Eduardo Cadava. New York: Columbia UP, 1986.

———. *Writing and Difference.* Trans. Alan Bass. Chicago: U of Chicago P, 1978.

Dixon, Melvin. *Ride out the Wilderness: Geography and Identity in Afro-American Literature.* Urbana: U of Illinois P, 1987.

———. "Singing Swords: The Literary Legacy of Slavery." *The Slave's Narrative.* Ed. Charles T. Davis and Henry Louis Gates, Jr. Oxford: Oxford UP, 1985. 298–318.

Du Bois, W. E. B. *The Souls of Black Folk.* New York: Penguin, 1989.

Early, Gerald. "The American Mysticism of Remembrance." *Race: An Anthology in the First Person.* Ed. Bart Schneider. New York: Crown, 1997. 4–17.

Ellison, Ralph. *Invisible Man.* New York: Random House, 1952.

———. *Shadow and Act.* New York: Vintage, 1972.

Estes, David C. "Gaines's Humor: Race and Laughter." *Critical Reflections on the Fiction of Ernest J. Gaines.* Ed. David C. Estes. Athens: U of Georgia P, 1994. 228–49.

Fabre, Genevieve. "African-American Commemorative Celebrations in the Nineteenth Century." *History and Memory in African-American*

Culture. Ed. Genevieve Fabre and Robert O'Meally. New York: Oxford UP, 1994. 72–91.

Fagel, Brian. "Passages from the Middle: Coloniality and Postcoloniality in Charles Johnson's *Middle Passage*." *African American Review* 30 (1996): 625–34.

Faulkner, William. *As I Lay Dying*. New York: Vintage, 1990.

Fisher, Philip. "Democratic Social Space: Whitman, Melville, and the Promise of American Transparency." *The New American Studies: Essays from* Representations. Ed. Philip Fisher. Berkeley: U of California P, 1991.

Folks, Jeffrey J. "Ernest Gaines and the New South." *Southern Literary Journal* 24.1 (1991): 32–46.

Foucault, Michel. *The Order of Things: An Archeology of the Human Sciences*. New York: Pantheon, 1970.

Fowler, Karen Joy. Rev. of *Bailey's Cafe*, by Gloria Naylor. *Chicago Tribune* 4 October 1992. Reprinted in *Gloria Naylor: Critical Perspectives Past and Present*. Ed. Henry Louis Gates, Jr., and K. A. Appiah. New York: Amistad, 1993. 26–28.

Fowler, Virginia C. *Gloria Naylor: In Search of Sanctuary*. New York: Twayne, 1996.

Fraser, Celeste. "Stealing B(l)ack Voices: The Myth of the Black Matriarchy and *The Women of Brewster Place*." *Gloria Naylor: Critical Perspectives Past and Present*. Ed. Henry Louis Gates, Jr., and K. A. Appiah. New York: Amistad, 1993. 90–105.

Freed, Alice F. "The Form and Function of Questions in Informal Dyadic Conversation." *Journal of Pragmatics* 21 (1994): 621–44.

Gaines, Ernest J. *Catherine Carmier*. New York: Vintage, 1993.

———. *A Gathering of Old Men*. New York: Vintage, 1983.

———. *In My Father's House*. New York: Vintage, 1992.

———. *A Lesson before Dying*. New York: Vintage, 1994.

———. *Of Love and Dust*. New York: Vintage, 1994.

Gates, Henry Louis, Jr. "Thirteen Ways of Looking at a Blackbird." *Race: An Anthology in the First Person*. Ed. Bart Schneider. New York: Crown, 1997. 143–62.

Genette, Gerard. *Narrative Discourse: An Essay in Method*. Trans. Jane E. Lewin. Ithaca: Cornell UP, 1980.

Ginsberg, Elaine K., ed. *Passing and the Fictions of Identity*. Durham, NC: Duke UP, 1996.

Goffman, Irving. *Forms of Talk*. Philadelphia: U of Pennsylvania P, 1981.

Grice, Paul. *Studies in the Way of Words*. Cambridge: Harvard UP, 1989.

Griffin, Farah Jasmine. *"Who Set You Flowin'?": The African-American Migration Narrative.* New York: Oxford UP, 1995.

Griffin, Joseph. "Calling, Naming, and Coming of Age in Ernest Gaines's *A Gathering of Old Men.*" *Names* 40 (1992): 89–97.

Gysin, Fritz. "Predicaments of Skin: Boundaries in Recent African American Fiction." *The Black Columbiad: Defining Moments in African American Literature and Culture.* Ed. Werner Sollors and Maria Diedrich. Cambridge: Harvard UP, 1994. 286–97.

Hargrove, Nancy D. "Toni Cade Bambara." *Contemporary Fiction Writers of the South: A Bio-Bibliographic Sourcebook.* Ed. Joseph M. Flora and Robert Bain. Westport, CT: Greenwood, 1993. 32–45.

Harper, Mary. "From Sons to Fathers: Ernest Gaines's *A Gathering of Old Men.*" *College Language Association Journal* 31 (1988). 299–308.

Haverkamp, Anselm. "Introduction: Deconstruction Is/as Neopragmatism? Preliminary Remarks on Deconstruction in America." *Deconstruction Is/in America: A New Sense of the Political.* Ed. Anselm Haverkamp. New York: New York UP, 1995.

Hayes, Elizabeth T. "Gloria Naylor's *Mama Day* as Magic Realism." *The Critical Response to Gloria Naylor.* Ed. Sharon Felton and Michelle C. Loris. Westport, CT: Greenwood, 1997. 177–86.

Hayward, Jennifer. "Something to Serve: Constructs of the Feminine in Charles Johnson's *Oxherding Tale.*" *African American Review* 25 (1991): 689–703.

Heglar, Charles J., and Annye L. Refoe. " 'Survival with Dignity': The Elderly African American in the Novels of Ernest Gaines." *Crossroads: A Journal of Southern Culture* 3.1 (1994–95): 57–68.

Hogue, W. Lawrence. "Problematizing History: David Bradley's *The Chaneysville Incident.*" *College Language Association Journal* 38 (1995): 441–60.

Holloway, Karla F. C. "Image, Act, and Identity in *In My Father's House.*" *Critical Reflections on the Fiction of Ernest J. Gaines.* Ed. David C. Estes. Athens: U of Georgia P, 1994. 180–94.

———. *Moorings and Metaphors: Figures of Culture and Gender in Black Women's Literature.* New Brunswick, NJ: Rutgers UP, 1992.

Homans, Margaret. "The Woman in the Cave." *Gloria Naylor: Critical Perspectives Past and Present.* Ed. Henry Louis Gates, Jr., and K. A. Appiah. New York: Amistad, 1993. 152–81.

Hubbard, Dolan. *The Sermon and the African-American Literary Imagination.* Columbia: U of Missouri P, 1994.

Hull, Gloria T. " 'What It Is I Think She's Doing Anyhow': A Reading of Toni Cade Bambara's *The Salt Eaters.*" *Conjuring: Black Women,*

Fiction, and Literary Tradition. Ed. Marjorie Pryse and Hortense J. Spillers. Bloomington: Indiana UP, 1985. 216–32.

Jahn, Janheinz. *Muntu: An Outline of the New African Culture.* Trans. Marjorie Grene. New York: Grove, 1961.

Johnson, Barbara. Translator's Introduction. *Dissemination.* By Jacques Derrida. Chicago: U of Chicago P, 1981. v–xv.

Johnson, Charles. *Being and Race: Black Writing since 1970.* Bloomington: Indiana UP, 1990.

———. *Middle Passage.* New York: Plume, 1991.

———. *Oxherding Tale.* New York: Grove Weidenfeld, 1982.

———. "A Phenomenology of *On Moral Fiction.*" *Thor's Hammer: Essays on John Gardner.* Ed. Jeff Henderson. Conway: U of Central Arkansas P, 1985. 147–56.

———. "Philosophy and Black Fiction." *Obsidian* 6 (1980): 55–61.

Johnson, Joseph A. "Jesus the Liberator." *The Black Experience in Religion.* Ed. C. Eric Lincoln. Garden City, NY: Anchor, 1974. 127–38.

Jones, Lawrence A. "They Sought a City." *The Black Experience in Religion.* Ed. C. Eric Lincoln. Garden City, NY: Anchor, 1974. 7–23.

Jones, Suzanne W. "Reconstructing Manhood: Race, Masculinity, and Narrative Closure in Ernest Gaines's *A Gathering of Old Men* and *A Lesson before Dying.*" *Masculinities* 3.2 (1995): 43–66.

Juhasz, Suzanne. "The Magic Circle: Fictions of the Good Mother in Gloria Naylor's *Mama Day. Critical Response to Gloria Naylor.* Eds. Sharon Selton and Michelle C. Loris. Westport, CT: Greenwood, 1997. 129–42.

Kelley, Margot Anne. " 'Damballah is the First Law of Thermodynamics': Modes of Access to Toni Cade Bambara's *The Salt Eaters.*" *African American Review* 27 (1993): 479–93.

———. "Sisters' Choices: Quilting Aesthetics in Contemporary African-American Women's Fiction." *Quilt Culture: Tracing the Pattern.* Ed. Cheryl B. Torsney and Judy Elsley. Columbia: U of Missouri P, 1994. 49–67.

King, Francis. "Close Circles." Rev. of *Damballah, Hiding Place,* and *Sent for You Yesterday,* by John Edgar Wideman. *Spectator* 22 December 1984: 46.

King, Martin Luther, Jr. *A Testament of Hope: The Essential Writings and Speeches of Martin Luther King, Jr.* Ed. James Melvin Washington. San Francisco: HarperCollins, 1991.

Levine, Lawrence. *Black Culture and Black Consciousness: Afro-American Folk Thought from Slavery to Freedom.* New York: Oxford UP, 1977.

Levy, Helen Fiddyment. "Lead on with Light." *Gloria Naylor: Critical*

Perspectives Past and Present. Ed. Henry Louis Gates, Jr., and K. A. Appiah. New York: Amistad, 1993. 263–84.

Lincoln, C. Eric. "The Black Church since Frazier." *The Negro Church in America and the Black Church since Frazier*. E. Franklin Frazier and C. Eric Lincoln. New York: Schocken, 1963.

Little, Jonathan. "An Interview with Charles Johnson." *Contemporary Literature* 34 (1993): 159–81.

Lowe, John, ed. *Conversations with Ernest Gaines*. Jackson: UP of Mississippi, 1995.

Luria, A. R. *The Man with a Shattered World*. Trans. Lynn Sclotoroff. New York: Basic, 1972.

Marcus, James. "The Pain of Being Two." Rev. of *A Glance Away*, *Hurry Home*, *The Lynchers*, and *The Homewood Trilogy*, by John Edgar Wideman. *Nation* 4 (October 1986): 321–23.

Marshall, Paule. *The Chosen Place, the Timeless People*. New York: Vintage, 1984.

———. *Praisesong for the Widow*. New York: Plume, 1983.

Mbalia, Dorothea Drummond. *John Edgar Wideman: Reclaiming the African Personality*. Selinsgrove, PA: Susquehanna UP, 1995.

Mbiti, John. *African Religions and Philosophy*. 2d ed. Oxford: Heinemann, 1989.

McHale, Brian. *Postmodernist Fiction*. New York: Methuen, 1987.

Meisenhelder, Susan. "'The Whole Picture' in Gloria Naylor's *Mama Day*." *African American Review* 27 (1993): 405–19.

Miller, J. Hillis. *The Form of Victorian Fiction: Thackeray, Dickens, Trollope, George Eliot, Meredith, and Hardy*. Cleveland: Arete, 1979. Notre Dame, IN: U of Notre Dame P, 1968.

Montgomery, Maxine Lavon. *The Apocalypse in African-American Fiction*. Gainesville: UP of Florida, 1996.

———. "Authority, Multivocality, and the New World Order in Gloria Naylor's *Bailey's Cafe*." *African American Review* 29 (1995): 27–33.

———. "The Fathomless Dream: Gloria Naylor's Use of the Descent Motif in *The Women of Brewster Place*." *The Critical Response to Gloria Naylor*. Ed. Sharon Felton and Michelle C. Loris. Westport, CT: Greenwood, 1997. 42–48.

Morrison, Toni. *Beloved*. New York: Knopf, 1992.

———. *Jazz*. New York: Knopf, 1992.

———. "Rootedness: The Ancestor as Foundation." *Black Women Writers (1950–1980): A Critical Evaluation*. Ed. Mari Evans. Garden City, NY: Anchor/Doubleday, 1984. 339–45.

———. *Song of Solomon*. New York: Signet, 1978.

———. *Sula*. New York: Bantam, 1975.

————. *Tar Baby*. New York: Signet, 1981.

Murray, Albert. *The Hero and the Blues*. New York: Vintage, 1973.

————. *The Omni-Americans: New Perspectives on Black Experience and American Culture*. New York: Outerbridge and Dienstfrey, 1970.

Muther, Elizabeth. "Isadora at Sea: Misogyny as Comic Capital in Charles Johnson's *Middle Passage*." *African American Review* 30 (1996): 649–58.

Naylor, Gloria. *Bailey's Cafe*. New York: Vintage, 1992.

————. "Gloria Naylor and Toni Morrison: A Conversation." *Southern Review* n.s. 21 (1985): 567–93.

————. *Linden Hills*. New York: Penguin, 1985.

————. "Love and Sex in the Afro-American Novel." *Yale Review* 78 (1988–89): 19–31.

————. *Mama Day*. New York: Vintage, 1989.

————. *The Women of Brewster Place*. New York: Penguin, 1983.

O'Keefe, Vincent A. "Reading Rigor Mortis: Offstage Violence and Excluded Middles 'in' Johnson's *Middle Passage* and Morrison's *Beloved*." *African American Review* 30 (1996): 635–47.

O'Meally, Robert, and Genevieve Fabre. Introduction. *History and Memory in African-American Culture*. Ed. Genevieve Fabre and Robert O'Meally. New York: Oxford UP, 1994. 3–17.

Page, Philip. *Dangerous Freedom: Fusion and Fragmentation in Toni Morrison's Novels*. Jackson: UP of Mississippi, 1996.

————. "Traces of Derrida in Toni Morrison's *Jazz*." *African American Review* 29 (1995): 55–66.

Papa, Lee. "'His Feet on Your Neck': The New Religion in the Works of Ernest J. Gaines." *African American Review* 27 (1993): 187–93.

Pederson, Carl. "Middle Passages." *Massachusetts Review* 34 (1993): 225–39.

Plant, Deborah G. "Cultural Collision, Africanity, and the Black Baptist Preacher in *Jonah's Gourd Vine* and *In My Father's House*." *Griot* 14 (1995): 10–17.

Reyes, Angelita. "Reading Carnival as an Archaeological Site for Memory in Paule Marshall's *The Chosen Place, The Timeless People*, and *Praisesong for the Widow*." *Memory, Narrative, and Identity: New Essays in Ethnic American Literatures*. Ed. Amritjit Singh, Joseph T. Skerrett, Jr., and Robert E. Hogan. Boston: Northeastern UP, 1994. 179–97.

Rickels, Milton, and Patricia Rickels. "'The Sound of My People Talking': Folk Humor in *A Gathering of Old Men*." *Critical Reflections on the Fiction of Ernest J. Gaines*. Ed. David C. Estes. Athens: U of Georgia P, 1994. 215–27.

Rimmon-Kenan, Shlomith. *A Glance beyond Doubt: Narration, Representation, Subjectivity*. Columbus: Ohio State UP, 1996.

Rodgers, Lawrence. *Canaan Bound: The African-American Great Migration Novel*. Urbana: U of Illinois P, 1997.

Rosenberg, Ruth. "'You Took a Name That Made You Amiable to the Music': Toni Cade Bambara's *The Salt Eaters*." *Literary Onomastic Studies* 12 (1985): 165–94.

Rowell, Charles. "The Quarters: Ernest Gaines and the Sense of Place." *Southern Review* n.s. 21 (1985): 733–50.

————. "This Louisiana Thing That Drives Me: An Interview with Ernest J. Gaines." *Conversations with Ernest Gaines*. Ed. John Lowe. Jackson: UP of Mississippi, 1995. 86–98.

Rushdy, Ashraf H. A. "Fraternal Blues: John Edgar Wideman's Homewood Trilogy." *Contemporary Literature* 23 (1991): 312–45.

Scott, Daniel M., III. "Interrogating Identity: Appropriation and Transformation in *Middle Passage*." *African American Review* 29 (1995): 645–55.

Scruggs, Charles. *Sweet Home: Invisible Cities in the Afro-American Novel*. Baltimore: Johns Hopkins UP, 1993.

Shange, Ntozange. *Sassafras, Cypress, and Indigo*. New York: St. Martin's, 1992.

Shannon, Sandra G. "Strong Men Getting Stronger: Gaines's Defense of the Elderly Black Male in *A Gathering of Old Men*." *Critical Reflections on the Fiction of Ernest J. Gaines*. Ed. David C. Estes. Athens: U of Georgia P, 1994. 195–214.

Shelton, Frank W. "*In My Father's House*: Ernest Gaines after Jane Pittman." *Southern Review* 17 (1981): 340–45.

Shipley, W. Maurice. Rev. of *The Salt Eaters*, by Toni Cade Bambara. *College Language Association Journal* 26 (1982): 125–27.

Singh, Amritjit, Joseph T. Skerrett, Jr., and Robert E. Hogan. Introduction. *Memory, Narrative, and Identity: New Essays in Ethnic American Literatures*. Ed. Amritjit Singh, Joseph T. Skerrett, Jr., and Robert E. Hogan. Boston: Northeastern UP, 1994. 3–25.

Smith, Virginia Whatley. "Sorcery, Double-Consciousness, and Warring Souls: An Intertextual Reading of *Middle Passage* and *Captain Blackman*." *African American Review* 30 (1996): 659–74.

Smitherman, Geneva. *Talkin and Testifyin: The Language of Black America*. Detroit: Wayne State UP, 1986.

Sobel, Mechal. *Trabelin' On: The Slave Journey to an Afro-Baptist Faith*. Westport, CT: Greenwood, 1979.

Sollors, Werner, and Maria Diedrich. Introduction. *The Black Columbiad: Defining Moments in African American Literature and Culture*.

Ed. Werner Sollors and Maria Diedrich. Cambridge: Harvard UP, 1994. 1–8.

Spillers, Hortense. "Martin Luther King and the Style of the Black Sermon." *The Black Experience in Religion*. Ed. C. Eric Lincoln. Garden City, NY: Anchor, 1974. 76–98.

Stepto, Robert B. *From Behind the Veil: A Study of Afro-American Narrative*. Urbana: U of Illinois P, 1979.

Stokes, Karah. "Ripe Plums and Pine Trees: Using Metaphor to Tell Stories of Violence in the Works of Gloria Naylor and Charles Chesnutt." *The Critical Response to Gloria Naylor*. Ed. Sharon Felton and Michelle C. Loris. Westport, CT: Greenwood, 1997. 199–210.

Storhoff, Gary. " 'The Only Voice Is Your Own': Gloria Naylor's Revision of *The Tempest*." *African American Review* 29 (1995): 35–45.

Stuckey, Sterling. *Slave Culture: Nationalist Theory and the Foundations of Black America*. New York: Oxford UP, 1987.

Sundquist, Eric J. *Faulkner: The House Divided*. Baltimore: Johns Hopkins UP, 1983.

———. *To Wake the Nations: Race in the Making of American Literature*. Cambridge: Harvard UP, 1993.

Tanner, Laura. "Reading Rape." *Gloria Naylor: Critical Perspectives Past and Present*. Ed. Henry Louis Gates, Jr., and K. A. Appiah. New York: Amistad, 1993. 71–89.

Traylor, Eleanor W. "Music as Theme: The Jazz Mode in the Works of Toni Cade Bambara." *Black Women Writers (1950–1980): A Critical Evaluation*. Ed. Mari Evans. Garden City, NY: Anchor, 1984. 58–70.

Tucker, Lindsey. "Recovering the Conjure Woman: Texts and Contexts in Gloria Naylor's *Mama Day*." *African American Review* 28 (1994): 173–88.

Turner, Victor. *The Anthropology of Performance*. New York: PAJ, 1986.

Waite, Arthur Edward. *The Pictorial Key to the Tarot*. New Hyde Park, NY: University Books, 1959.

Walby, Celestin. "The African Sacrificial Kingship Ritual and Johnson's *Middle Passage*." *African American Review* 29 (1995): 657–69.

Walker, Alice. *The Color Purple*. New York: Harcourt Brace, 1982.

———. *Possessing the Secret of Joy*. New York: Pocket, 1993.

Walker, Melissa. *Down from the Mountaintop: Black Women's Novels in the Wake of the Civil Rights Movement, 1966–1989*. New Haven: Yale UP, 1991.

Ward, Catherine C. "*Linden Hills*: A Modern *Inferno*." *Gloria Naylor: Critical Perspectives Past and Present*. Ed. Henry Louis Gates, Jr., and K. A. Appiah. New York: Amistad, 1993. 182–94.

Werner, Craig. "Minstrel Nightmares and Black Dreams of Faulkner's

Dreams of Blacks." *Faulkner and Race: Faulkner and Yoknapataw-pha, 1986.* Ed. Doreen Fowler and Ann J. Abadie. Jackson: UP of Mississippi, 1987. 35–57.

West, Cornel. *Prophesy Deliverance! An Afro-American Revolutionary Christianity.* Philadelphia: Westminster, 1982.

White, Daniel. " 'Haunted by the Idea': Fathers and Sons in *In My Father's House* and *A Gathering of Old Men.*" *Critical Reflections on the Fiction of Ernest J. Gaines.* Ed. David C. Estes. Athens: U of Georgia P, 1994. 158–79.

Wideman, John Edgar. *All Stories Are True.* New York: Vintage, 1993.

————. *Brothers and Keepers.* New York: Vintage, 1984.

————. *The Cattle Killing.* Boston: Houghton Mifflin, 1996.

————. *Damballah.* New York: Vintage, 1981.

————. *Fatheralong: A Meditation on Fathers and Sons, Race and Society.* New York: Pantheon, 1994.

————. *Fever: Twelve Stories.* New York: Penguin, 1989.

————. *A Glance Away.* New York: Harcourt, Brace, and World, 1967.

————. *Hiding Place.* New York: Vintage, 1988.

————. *Hurry Home.* New York: Harcourt Brace Jovanovich, 1970.

————. *The Lynchers.* New York: Harcourt Brace Jovanovich, 1973.

————. *Philadelphia Fire.* New York: Vintage, 1991.

————. Preface. *The Homewood Trilogy.* New York: Avon, 1985. v–vii.

————. *Reuben.* New York: Henry Holt, 1987.

————. *Sent for You Yesterday.* New York: Vintage, 1988.

Wilde, Alan. *Middle Grounds: Studies in Contemporary American Fiction.* Philadelphia: U of Pennsylvania P, 1987.

Williams, Sherley Anne. *Dessa Rose.* New York: William Morrow, 1986.

Willis, Susan. *Specifying: Black Women Writing the American Experience.* Madison: U of Wisconsin P, 1987.

Wilson, Matthew. "The Circles of History in John Edgar Wideman's *The Homewood Trilogy.*" *College Language Association Journal* 33 (1990): 239–59.

INDEX

Note: the following abbreviations have been used: